Heart of the Redeemer

TIMOTHY TERRANCE O'DONNELL, S.T.D.

Heart of the Redeemer

An Apologia for the Contemporary
and Perennial Value of the Devotion
to the Sacred Heart of Jesus

IGNATIUS PRESS   SAN FRANCISCO

HOR.TPV

First edition printed by
Trinity Communications, Manassas, Virginia
© 1989 Trinity Communications

Cover by Marcia Ryan

Cover art:

The Merciful One

Berlin-Dahlem
Staatliche Museum

Reprinted, Ignatius Press 1992
ISBN 0–89870–396–4
Library of Congress catalogue number 91–76070
Printed in the United States of America

DEDICATION

This work is dedicated to a man who comes
from a land deeply committed to the Heart of Christ.
He is most certainly a "man of the heart"
who radiates the love of Christ Jesus to all men.
In him the Lord has truly blessed us all
with a "shepherd after his own heart."
With deep respect and thanksgiving
I humbly dedicate this work to our Holy Father,
Pope John Paul II.

ACKNOWLEDGMENTS

I am clearly indebted to a number of fine works on the devotion, particularly those of Fr. Larkin, Fr. Stierli, Fr. Hugo Rahner, Fr. Kern and the Apostleship of Prayer. I truly feel as a "dwarf standing on the shoulders of giants" to use the expression of St. Bernard of Chartres. I have built upon this common foundation by organizing, expanding and developing this material in a single volume. It is my earnest hope that this will meet the needs of priests and laity in their efforts to foster the devotion as a source of renewal for the Church.

I would like to thank Fr. Jordan Aumann, OP my mentor at the Angelicum in Rome.

I would also like to thank my parents for their generous love and support in nurturing me in the Faith.

Lastly, I wish to thank my dearest wife Catherine for her patient assistance in typing and proofing the manuscript. Without her loving support this book would not exist.

> "So we know and believe the love God has for
> us. God is love, and he who abides in love abides
> in him . . . . We love because he first loved us."
>   (I Jn. 4:16,19)

PUBLISHER'S ACKNOWLEDGEMENTS

The publisher gratefully acknowledges the following persons whose financial support made publication of *Heart of the Redeemer* possible:

Mrs. Ingrid D. Climis
Mr. Philip T. Crotty
Mr. David J. Duffy
Mr. & Mrs. Dave Jaszkowiak
Dr. & Mrs. Christopher Lee
Mrs. Nancy E. Lenihan
Mr. Gerald J. Lopriore
Miss Jeanette M. Maschmann
Mr. & Mrs. W. H. Power
Mr. & Mrs. Glenn Ruffner
Mr. Cornelius J. P. Sullivan

Contents

Preface

Christianity is an intensely personal religion. In saying this we do not mean that it is "private" or "individualistic". Rather, it is one way of referring to the Church's constant concern for the dignity and the rights of the human person from the time of his or her conception until the hour when one passes from earthly existence to that which is everlasting. So true is this that, when speaking of the Church's social doctrine, Pope John XXIII could write: "The cardinal point of this teaching is that individual men and women are necessarily the foundation, cause, and end of all social institutions."[1] And his successor, Paul VI, would restate that truth by observing that the "perfecting of the human person is to be considered a summary so to speak of our obligations."[2]

It should not surprise us that the Church is so intent on the dignity and rights of the person, since Christianity is an intensely personal religion in yet a more profound sense. It worships and draws its very life and meaning from the personal God who has become a human being, Jesus Christ, our brother and savior. In Him the Church knows the value that the Creator has placed on the human person. Indeed "only in the mystery of the incarnate Word does the mystery of man take on light. Christ, the final Adam, by the revelation of the mystery of the Father and His love, fully reveals man to man himself and makes his supreme calling clear."[3] In Jesus Who is "God from God and light from light" we are able to discern the loving esteem which God has for us and which we, in imitation of Him, should have for one another. To know Christ and His life is to know the deepest meaning of love, a love that is capable of

---

[1] *Mater et Magistra*, 218. This statement is repeated by the Second Vatican Council in its *Pastoral Constitution on the Church in the Modern World*, 63.

[2] Paul VI, *Populorum Progressio*, 16

[3] *Pastoral Constitution on the Church in the Modern World*, 22

giving and receiving.

Over the centuries the innumerable lessons to be learned and benefits to be drawn from the love of God for us in Christ have found concrete expression in devotion to the Sacred Heart of Jesus. By means of this devotion we are able to meditate on and draw close to the love of Christ which, as St. John Eudes wrote, is "humanly divine and divinely human."[4]

If in our own day, as many think, devotion to the Sacred Heart of Jesus is not what it once was, then the present book by Timothy O'Donnell will hopefully serve as a stimulus for a renewal. *Heart of the Redeemer* is a comprehensive and profound study not only of the origins and theology of devotion to the Sacred Heart, but of its contemporary importance as well. I find his work particularly valuable for its examination of the writings of Pope Paul VI and of our Holy Father John Paul II as they set forth the doctrine and principles which illustrate the relevance of this devotion in light of the teachings of Vatican Council II.

The present work also illuminates with abundant documentation the natural and necessary link between devotion to the Sacred Heart and devotion to the Blessed Sacrament where Christ, in full divinity and humanity, offers Himself in love to the Father and to us. *Heart of the Redeemer* quotes John Paul II as saying:

> We are called not only to meditate on, and contemplate, this mystery of Christ's love; we are called to take part in it. It is the mystery of the Holy Eucharist, the center of our faith, the center of our worship of Christ's merciful love manifested in his Sacred Heart.

So personally convinced of this truth am I that I have recently inaugurated the practice of nocturnal adoration of the Blessed Sacrament in St. Patrick's Cathedral on the First Friday of each month. For it is in this Sacrament of His love that the whole spiritual wealth of the Church is contained, as Vatican II teaches us. I am sure that such devotion to the Heart of Jesus in the Eucharist, far from being a "pietistic" and outdated form of spirituality, will in fact give new life to the Church's social apostolate. It will move us, by grace, to express our love for the person of Christ not only in prayer but in committed effort to effect and defend the dignity and rights of all that family of which He is the firstborn. For all the good that it will do to foster a love for Christ which is personal and social I warmly welcome *Heart of the Redeemer*, recommending it to clergy and laity alike.

John Cardinal O'Connor

---

[4]St. John Eudes, *Meditations on Various Subjects*, P. J. Kenedy and Sons, 1947, p. 282.

Foreword

Heart of the Redeemer is an indispensable source book on the history of the devotion to the Sacred Heart of Jesus. I say "indispensable" because it is the only book of its kind. It is not too much to call it a treasury of Catholic wisdom on the Sacred Heart.

Years of careful research have produced a one volume synthesis of how the devotion to the Heart of Jesus has developed over the centuries. The result is a breath-taking overview of how the love for Jesus Christ has grown in the hearts of the faithful from Calvary to the present day.

Development of Doctrine

In order to appreciate the valuable contribution of *Heart of the Redeemer*, we should first see something of what the Church means by development of doctrine.

By development of doctrine we mean that a revealed truth becomes more deeply understood by the faithful. The objective truth of Revelation remains essentially unchanged, but the subjective grasp of what God has revealed becomes more clearly appropriated by individual believers and even by the Church as the Mystical Body of Christ.

One of the glories of the Second Vatican Council has been to explain what true development of doctrine means and especially how it is achieved. First the basic premise that there is a growth in insight into the realities revealed by God.

> This comes about in various ways. It comes through the contemplation and study of believers, who ponder these things in their hearts. It comes from the intimate sense of spiritual realities which they experience. And it comes from the preaching of those who have received, along with the right of succession in the episcopate, the sure

charism of the truth (*Dogmatic Constitution on Divine Revelation,* 8).

We might, therefore, say that prayer and study, experience and the Church's magisterium are the four pillars on which all authentic doctrinal development is built.

The author of *Heart of the Redeemer* has given us a masterful explanation of how the revealed truth underlying the devotion to the Sacred Heart has grown in the two millennia of the Church's history.

Growth in Understanding of the Sacred Heart

What is the revealed truth which underlies the devotion to the Sacred Heart? It is the fact that God, who is love, so loved the world that He sent His only-begotten Son

- to become man and dwell among us,
- to teach us by word and example how we are to attain eternal life,
- to suffer and die for us on the Cross in order to redeem us from sin and eternal death,
- to rise from the dead and ascend into heaven,
- to send us from heaven the gift of His Holy Spirit, and to remain actively in our midst on earth, in the sacrifice and sacrament of the Eucharist.

These six elements, taken together, correspond to what we mean by the "Sacred Heart." As we honor and worship Jesus Christ under these aspects, we are practicing devotion to the Sacred Heart.

What the author of *Heart of the Redeemer* has done is to show how each of these essentials of Catholic doctrine has become more clear over the centuries. As a result, the worship of Jesus Christ under the symbolism of His Heart becomes more and more meaningful with the passage of time.

Devotion depends upon doctrine, as the will depends on the mind, for its resources of faith. Without sound doctrine, devotion becomes sentimentalism or even fanaticism. That is why a book like the present one is so necessary.

It is necessary for those who would dismiss the Sacred Heart devotion as just another, optional form of personal piety. These people must see the devotion for what it really is: the synthesis of our worship of Jesus Christ, founded on the irreversible dogmas of Catholic Christianity.

It is necessary for those who may practice the devotion but without spiritual depth. They must be awakened to the facts of their faith. Like the Samaritan woman at the well, they need to realize who it is who is speaking with them. When they recite the Litany of the Sacred Heart, the invocations are addressed to the living Jesus Christ. They speak to Him, and He speaks to them. When they make the nine First Fridays, they are receiving the Son of God who became the Son of Mary to make Holy Communion possible. When they worship before the Blessed Sacrament, they are in the presence of the same Jesus Christ who walked the streets of Palestine, worked His miracles of mercy, and preached the Sermon on the Mount.

Heart of the Redeemer was written by a layman, but an extraordinary person. His years of study and teaching of theology have equipped him to produce what I honestly believe is an extraordinary book. It should be in the hands of all the faithful, including priests and religious who wish to better understand, in our day, what St. Paul meant when he prayed for the Christians of the first century,

> to have Christ dwelling through faith in your hearts; so that being rooted and grounded in love, you may be able to comprehend with all the saints who is the breadth and length and height and depth, and to know Christ's love which surpasses all knowledge in order that you may be filled unto all the fullness of God (Ephesians 3:17-19).

Not only is devotion to the Sacred Heart not optional, it is absolutely necessary. For the same reason that the love of Christ for us is a necessary premise of our faith, and our love for Christ is a necessary principle of Christian spirituality.

This is both the beauty and the awesome conclusion of *Heart of the Redeemer*. We believers have no choice. Either we restore devotion to the Heart of Christ as the bedrock of the Christian way of life, or the world will become more and more Christless—and correspondingly godless—and we shall be held responsible by default, for the secularization that is destroying the materially over-developed society in which we live.

Fr. John A. Hardon, S.J.

Introduction

I have attempted not so much to speak with authority
of things that I know, as to seek to know them
by speaking about them with reverence.
St. Augustine, *De Trinitate*, I v. 8

In our inquiry into the devotion to the Sacred Heart and its perennial value, it is best to begin with a proper understanding of what is meant by devotion. St. Thomas Aquinas defines devotion as a willingness "to give oneself readily to what concerns the service of God" (*Summa*, II-II, q. 82 a. 1). Accordingly, the devotion to the Sacred Heart of Jesus appears essentially as a worship of and a response to the Person of Christ as viewed from the perspective of His divine and human love which is manifested through His sacred humanity and is symbolized by His wounded physical Heart. In his masterful encyclical, *Haurietis Aquas*, Pope Pius XII gives the following definition of this devotion:

> Devotion to the Sacred Heart of Jesus, by its very nature is a worship of the love with which God, through Jesus, loved us, and at the same time, an exercise of our love by which we are related to God and to other men.

From this definition it can be seen that authentic devotion to the Sacred Heart is not merely an optional set of pious practices (which may be very helpful) but an essential element of the Christian way of life. All Christians are called to the comprehension of certain truths concerning God and to a response in love to them. In living a life in imitation of Christ, as found in the Gospels and taught by the Church, the Christian should use all the spiritual

17

aids offered to him by God. He should fill his life with an ever growing and deepening love for God and his fellow man. Every Christian will build his own unique spirituality upon this common foundation, which should include a response to the Heart of Christ that gives honor to the divine love and is offered for the sake of that love.

It would be accurate to say that by the middle of the twentieth century the devotion to the Sacred Heart of Jesus had universally triumphed throughout the Church. Everywhere in the world, churches, monasteries and congregations were to be found dedicated to the Sacred Heart. In virtually every Catholic church one would find a statue of our Lord revealing his Heart. Large numbers of the faithful gathered on every continent for First Friday devotions, the Holy Hour and other pious practices associated with the devotion. This triumphal procession, however, was not welcomed in all quarters and the devotion began to draw criticism from some Catholic theologians who began to question certain aspects of these devotional exercises. Some outside, and even within, the Church questioned the theological foundation of the devotion.

Pope Pius XII was well aware of the objections which some were making to the devotion. It is because of these objections that the Holy Father wrote his encyclical on devotion to the Sacred Heart of Jesus, and in it he exhorted the faithful to "a more earnest consideration of those principles which take their origin from Scripture and the teaching of the Fathers and theologians," which form the solid foundation for the worship of the Sacred Heart of Jesus. The Pope went on to call for and stress the importance of "a profound study of the primary and loftier nature of the devotion with the aid of the light of the divinely revealed truth" so that we may "rightly and fully appreciate its incomparable excellence and the inexhaustible abundance of its heavenly favors." The Holy Father ended his appeal by requesting a "devout meditation and contemplation" upon the benefits of the devotion.

After the publication of *Haurietis Aquas*, many books were written on the devotion. These works varied tremendously in size and quality. They included pious or devotional works, popular pamphlets, and mystical writings which described extraordinary supernatural experiences.

There is still a need for a systematic theological exposition and defense of the devotion which will lead to a deeper penetration and understanding of it, as was requested by Pius XII and subsequent pontiffs. It is my most earnest hope and prayer that this book will help in some way to answer the call of the Holy Father and will contribute to a greater understanding of our Lord's Heart, which is "so full of infinite majesty and compassion."

The encyclical and devotion both, unfortunately, seem to have been down-played or overshadowed, if you will, in the wake of the Second Vatican Council. Many today object to the devotion for a variety of reasons, some manifestly superficial and others quite serious. Despite the objections, there are presently strong signs of a widespread reawakening of interest in the devotion and the contributions which it can make toward the renewal of the Church.

Some have criticized the devotion for the language used in many of the prayers addressed to the Sacred Heart. Phrases such as "prostrate before thy altar" seem to many a bit archaic and not in keeping with our modern idiom. Often times prayers and the lyrics of hymns to the Sacred Heart are considered excessively sweet and sentimental. Artistic representations of the devotion are criticized for being too saccharine and effeminate.

None of these criticisms touch what is essential to the devotion as it has been taught by the Church. They deal with external aspects; and yet we must remember that man derives his knowledge through the senses, and therefore poor art and unsuitable language may form obstacles to a deeper understanding and love of the devotion. We shall discuss some of these problems in the final section of this study, where we deal with questions of renewal and adaptation.

The more serious objections which have been raised against the devotion cannot be brushed aside but must be dealt with clearly and honestly. Critical questioning is a good thing, since it may open both the mind and heart to a deeper reflection and understanding of this "priceless gift which our Savior has given to his Church." I have formulated here what I believe to be the four major objections which have been raised to the devotion to the Sacred Heart of Jesus.

1) The devotion to the Sacred Heart rests upon a weak doctrinal base and threatens to overemphasize the humanity of Christ. This position is espoused by theologians such as Karl Barth, who places the devotion on the same level as modern Protestant biographies of the historical Jesus that have abandoned belief in the reality of the Incarnation of the Word. In his book, *Church Dogmatics*, he characterizes both forms as attempts to "find an approach to Jesus Christ which circumvents his divinity," offering an "approach to a revelation which is generally understandable and possible in the form of human judgments and human experiences. In the Heart of Jesus cult...it is blatantly a matter of finding a generally illuminating access to Jesus Christ which evades the divinity of the Word. Therefore both Neo-Protestant faith in the religious hero Jesus and the Catholic devotion to the Heart of Jesus, are to be rejected as the deification of a creature."[1]

2) There is no scriptural reference to the devotion. This criticism is frequently heard from our separated brethren and even some Catholics, who demand proof of scriptural authenticity. This is especially important since the Second Vatican Council emphasized Sacred Scripture as the foundation of theology and spirituality.

3) The devotion sprang from a mere private revelation given to a cloistered nun in 17th century France. It is therefore a new devotion and is not sanctioned by Christian tradition.

4) The devotion may have been beneficial for a particular age and cultural outlook but it is no longer suited to modern times and has become obsolete.

Although some objections are of greater importance than others, all must be answered. If any of these objections should prove true, the validity and perennial value of the devotion would be seriously shaken, if not shattered.

This work shall be divided into four sections in which we hope to achieve four goals.

First, we shall examine the dogmatic foundations for the devotion as found in Sacred Scripture and the Church's teachings concerning Christ as it took shape in the great Christological controversies in the 4th and 5th centuries. This is absolutely essential to demonstrating the perennial validity and value of the devotion.

Second, we shall then proceed to trace the historical development of the devotion which culminated in the great revelation given to St. Margaret Mary Alacoque. Here we shall glimpse the Holy Spirit at work in the dynamic living tradition of the Church. It will be a thought-provoking study which will reveal the theological richness of the devotion, its evolution and the multiple forms which it has taken throughout two Christian millennia. This investigation will probe into the patristic roots of the devotion, its flowering in the era of medieval mysticism, and developments up to the present day.

Third, we shall then examine the contemporary importance of the devotion in the life of the Church in the light of magisterial teaching. In the 19th and 20th century there is a large amount of papal teaching on the devotion. The See of Peter has given the devotion a unique position in the Church. This wealth of papal magisterial teaching will have much to say regarding the timeliness and timeless value of the devotion.

Last, we shall discuss questions of renewal and adaptation of the devotion according to the guidelines of Vatican II.

It was only after a great deal of serious reflection that I decided to write

---

[1]Karl Barth, *Church Dogmatics* Vol. I p. 2 (Edinburgh: T & T Clark, 1970) pp. 137-138.

this book which is an outgrowth of studies begun at the Angelicum in Rome in 1978. I chose to write on the loving Heart of our Lord because I believe the devotion to be of *vital* importance today. I offer here to the reader, for his prayerful reflection, three quotations from three popes of the 20th century concerning the importance of devotion to the Sacred Heart in our age:

> [Devotion to the Heart of Jesus] is the extraordinary remedy for the extraordinary needs of our times. (Pius XI, *Caritate Christi Compulsi*, May 3, 1932)

> Devotion to the Most Sacred Heart of Jesus is so important that it may be considered, so far as practice is concerned, the perfect profession of the Christian religion.... It is no ordinary form of piety which anyone at his own whim may treat as of little consequence or set aside as inferior to others. (Pius XII, *Haurietis Aquas*, May 15, 1956)

> The cult rendered to the Sacred Heart is the most efficacious means to contribute to that spiritual and moral renewal of the world called for by the Second Vatican Council. (Paul VI, *Address to the Thirty-First General Congregation of the Society of Jesus,* Nov. 17, 1966)

These three statements are well worth pondering for all those who would *sentire cum Ecclesia.*

The veneration of our Lord's Heart, insofar as it honors Christ as the source and substance of our redemption, is no ordinary devotion. It is truly *latreutical*—a devotion which is rendered to God alone. For the Heart of Christ occupies a central position, as the focal point through which everything passes to the ultimate center in the Father—*per Christum ad Patrem*. It is a devotion of tremendous theological richness, containing a complete synthesis of faith, or, as Pius XI put it *"summa totius religionis."* The devotion is at once theocentric and anthropocentric, Trinitarian and Christocentric; it emphasizes love of God and calls eloquently to the fraternal apostolate. It may also lead to that sound eucharistic piety so greatly desired by the Second Vatican Council. This is especially true since the Eucharist, as Pope Paul VI observed, is the "outstanding gift" of the Sacred Heart of Jesus.

I firmly believe that the spirituality fostered by this devotion can best meet the spiritual needs of our age. It is a practical form of spirituality which emphasizes *familiaritas cum Christo* and therefore is marvelously suited to aid priest, religious and laity alike in their journey of growth in holiness. If practiced in the family, devotion to the Heart of Jesus may greatly help to counter those pagan elements of culture which all too often work their way into the sanctuary of the home.

The devotion should be made available to *all*. Unfortunately, the widespread ignorance throughout the Church of the devotion's rich theological foundations has greatly hindered its full appreciation and practice. It is only by returning to these sources as found in Sacred Scripture, tradition and the teaching of the Church's magisterium that we can hope to renew the devotion and thereby allow it to play a central role in the larger effort to renew the Church.

Our Lord, in his apparition to St. Margaret Mary Alacoque, communicated to her that the revelation of his Heart was "a final effort" to enkindle the fire of love in a world in which "charity had grown cold." Such is the age in which we live. William Butler Yeats foresaw the crisis of our era in a prophetic poem written at the turn of the century:

> Things fall apart; the centre cannot hold;
> Mere anarchy is loosed upon the world,
> The blood-dimmed tide is loosed and everywhere
> The ceremony of innocence is drowned;
> The best lack all conviction, while the worst
> Are full of passionate intensity.

Coldness and hatred can be melted and overcome only by the fire of love. Certainly, in an age which is characterized by an increasingly hostile secularization, a spirituality which centers on love and aims at setting the world on fire is precisely what is needed to *instaurare omnia in Christo*.

> I have come to cast fire upon the earth,
> and what will I but that it be kindled?
> *Luke 13:49*

> *Timothy T. O'Donnell, S.T.D.*
> *October 16, 1989*
> *Feast of St. Margaret Mary*

I.

Dogmatic Foundations

Redeamus ad cor ut inveniamus Eum.
(Let us return to the heart so that we may find Him.)
St. Augustine

The Mystery of the Heart in Sacred Scripture:
The Old Testament

In our examination of the dogmatic foundations of the devotion to the Sacred Heart of Jesus it is most fitting that we begin by asking the question "What is meant by the heart?" Dietrich von Hildebrand, the great moral philosopher, saw the importance of this question in his book *The Sacred Heart*, where he states:

> We cannot understand the devotion to the Sacred Heart in its true meaning, or in its specific mission to melt our hearts, unless we first discover the true nature of the heart and the grandeur and glory of true affectivity.... The role that the Church grants to the devotion to the Sacred Heart and the increasing emphasis laid on this aspect of the mystery of the Incarnation, carries with it a great challenge— namely, that we deepen our understanding of the heart as one of the fundamental centers of man's soul.[1]

The word *heart* is frequently used in everyday parlance in a symbolic sense to describe emotions or attitudes (e.g., "he's big hearted," "he has a warm heart," etc.). A symbol is defined by Webster's Dictionary as "that which

---

[1]Dietrich von Hildebrand, *The Sacred Heart: An Analysis of Human and Divine Affectivity* (Baltimore: The Helicon Press, 1965) p. 18

suggests something else by reason of relationship, association, convention; especially a visible sign of something invisible." *Heart*, as a symbol, is often used to designate the person. Karl Rahner describes *heart* as a "primal word" which falls into the category of words used to designate the whole man, such as "head" or "hand".

> In the original (and not the subsequent, derived or metaphorical) sense, "heart" is a primal word. It is not susceptible of a proper definition by the joining of better known concepts. Since it has this primal character in so many cultures (Semitic, Graeco-Roman, Western, Mexican, etc.) it is clearly such a word as could be easily employed in the vocabulary of a world religion. It falls into the category of words for the whole man; that is, it signifies a human reality predicable of the whole man as a person of body and spirit.[2]

The human heart is a natural symbol for what is most intimate, most personal in man. Ladislaus Boros, S.J., in his book *God Is With Us* also stresses the universality of the physical heart of man as a symbol of his intimate personality or center:

> Heart is an image common to all mankind for the central point of a personality, the basis on which flows everything that he is and does. The "heart," therefore, signifies both the essence of the person as he actually is, and also the origin of his actions, his fundamental existential attitude. It signifies a person's disposition: the way he looks at other people, at life, and at all that exists.[3]

Anyone familiar with the magisterium of Pope John Paul II could not fail to see the importance which the Pope gives to this essential dimension in man which is so fundamental to biblical anthropology.

Aelred Watkin, speaking of the interior dimension of the heart, states:

> We have now reached the innermost recesses of the human spirit. Really to know and really to love is the action and response of our innermost personality to the personality of another…. With this ultimate knowing and loving we reach the very core of our being. How

---

[2]Karl Rahner, "Some Theses on the Theology of the Devotion" in *Heart of the Savior*, ed. by J. Stierli, (New York: Herder Pub. Co., 1958), p. 132. An excellent study of Rahner's thought concerning the importance of "the heart" can be found in M. J. Walsh, *The Heart of Christ in the Writings of Karl Rahner* (Rome: Gregorian University Press, 1977)

[3]Ladislaus Boros, *God Is With Us* (N. Y.: Herder & Herder, 1967), pp.50-1. This work by Boros was brought to my attention by Fr. Francis Larkin in his excellent little book, *Understanding the Heart.*

easily does the word 'heart' leap to mind. The heart in the sense of being the heart and core of life; the heart in the sense of that ultimate expression and experience of personality in knowing and loving. And both senses are one.[4]

The heart is the spiritual center of man's soul, the core of all volitional and emotional and intellectual activity. It therefore represents the whole man. Despite the occasional abuse of this word by sentimentalists and its rejection by rationalists, it continues to possess this rich signification today. Every failure to understand the deeper meaning of the "heart" is a profound tragedy for the human spirit for this is how God has chosen to reveal himself in Sacred Scripture: *Cor ad cor loquitur.*

This symbolic understanding of the heart as the "center of man" has a firm foundation in Scripture. It is in fact the most important and most frequent word in Old Testament anthropology. *Leb* and *lebab* occur over 858 times in the Old Testament.[5] McKenzie's *Dictionary of the Bible* shows that the word heart means even more in Hebrew than it does in English.[6] In Semitic thought, it signifies the entire interior life of a person. The Old Testament does use the word in its literal sense as a physical organ (Ex. 28:29; I Sam. 25:27), but normally it is used in this figurative sense. Below we have selected several passages which illustrate this usage:

> Why do you harden your hearts, as Egypt and Pharaoh hardened their hearts? (I Sam. 6:6)

> Therefore, you shall love the Lord your God, with all your heart.... Take to heart these words which I enjoin on you today. (Dt. 6:5-6)

> I will write it in their heart, and I will be their God, and they shall be my people. (Jer. 31:33)

There are also many instances in which God uses "heart" as applied to himself:

> When the Lord saw that the wickedness of man on the earth was great, and that man's every thought and all the inclinations of his heart

---

[4] Aelred Watkin, *The Heart of the World* (London: Burns & Oates, 1954), p. 6.

[5] Malatesta & Solano, *The Heart of Christ and the Heart of Man* (Rome: Pontifical Gregorian University, 1978) p. 2.

[6] J. McKenzie, *Dictionary of the Bible* (Milwaukee: The Bruce Publishing Co., 1965) p. 343; cf. George A. Buttrick ed., *The Interpreter's Dictionary of the Bible* Vol. 2 (N.Y./Nashville: Abingdon Press 1965) pp. 549-550.

were only evil, He regretted that he had made man on the earth and was grieved to the heart. (Gen. 6:5-6)

The Lord hath sought him a man according to his own heart. (I Sam. 13:14)

And I will give you pastors according to my own heart and they shall feed you with knowledge and doctrine. (Jer. 3:15)

And I will rejoice over them, when I shall do them good; and I will plant them in this land in truth, with my whole heart. (Jer. 33:41)

These texts which refer to the heart of God always deal with his relationship to man and often communicate his will for them. Below is a complete list of explicit Old Testament references to the heart of God as given in *The Heart of Christ and the Heart of Man:*[7]

Yahweh to Eli: I Sam. 2:35 and to Jehu: II Kings 10:30
Samuel to Saul: I Sam. 13:11
Yahweh to the people through Jeremiah: Jer. 3:15
Idolatry is against the will of Yahweh's heart: Jer. 7:31; 19:5; 32:35
God's plan for dealing with men is in his heart
    - to punish them: Is. 6:34; Jer. 23:20; 30:24
    - to do them good: Jer. 32:41; Ps. 33:11
David's prayer: II Sam. 7:21
God's mercy towards men: Lam. 3:33
He moans for them: Jer. 48:36
He vows never to curse and destroy creation again: Gen. 8:21
His abhorrence of idolatry: Jer. 44:21
His awe-inspiring care for man: Job 7:17
His attention to man: Job 31:14
He hides things in his heart: Job 10:13
His promise to Solomon: his heart and his eyes (see Solomon's prayer
    I Kings 8:29) will also dwell with his Name in the Temple (I Kings
    9:3; par. 2 Chr. 7, 16). This means his all-seeing attention,
    participation, good will, affection.
God is characterized by his compassionate love: Hos. 11:8-9

Perhaps a word would be appropriate here to speak about the application of the biblical expression "Heart of God" to the Heart of Christ. God, of course, is pure spirit and has no heart or body. So, in these passages Scripture is speaking metaphorically to communicate a truth about God. When we

---

[7]Malatesta & Solano, *The Heart of Christ and the Heart of Man, op. cit.*, pp. 7-8.

speak of our Lord's Heart, however, this is literally true, for as Vatican II so beautifully proclaimed, Jesus loved and continues to love us with a human heart (*Gaudium et Spes* 1, 22). Accordingly, we may truly apply those biblical references of God's Heart to the Heart of Jesus. Our Lord's human thoughts and desires were in perfect harmony with God the Father. God's will did in fact become incarnate in the heart of his Son. The sentiments which Sacred Scripture attribute to God in all truth exist in the Heart of Jesus. For this reason we may appropriately apply to the heart of our Lord what the Scripture states of the Heart of God.

The word heart is also frequently used in the Psalms (113 times), for example:

> Thou hast put joy in my heart.   Ps. 4

> Take delight in the Lord and he will give you the desires of your heart.   Ps. 37 (36)

> With my whole heart I seek thee.... I have laid up thy word in my heart.   Ps. 119 (118)

Here also we may see instances of biblical expressions using the word "heart" which may be applied to the Heart of Christ. Whatever good is said of the human heart, whether referring to love, honesty or purity, it may be appropriately applied to the most perfect Heart. The Church has always taught that Christ's human virtues possessed all the perfection possible in a human nature. His Heart represents them all; accordingly, we say in the Litany of the Sacred Heart: "Heart of Jesus, abyss of all virtues."

Many of these references to "heart" in the Psalms and elsewhere are not messianic passages and of course we are using an accommodated sense. Because of this, we must not exaggerate their importance for exegetically establishing the devotion to the Sacred Heart. Nevertheless, these numerous texts may be authentically applied to Christ. They convey truths about the Heart of Jesus in a powerful and beautiful way, using biblical language to convey His love for God, his compassion for sinful man, his intense suffering for our redemption, etc. This greatly enhances our understanding of the "unfathomable riches" of the Heart of Christ and therefore can strengthen our prayer life and our union with Him.

The Church herself has always recommended this accommodated application and has done so once again in the *General Instruction on the Liturgy of the Hours*:

The person who prays the psalms in the Liturgy of the Hours prays not so much in his own person as in the name of the Church, and, in fact, in the person of Christ himself.

The person who prays the psalms in the name of the Church should be aware of their total meaning, which was the reason for the Church's introduction of the psalter into its prayer. This messianic meaning was fully revealed in the New Testament and indeed was publicly acknowledged by Christ the Lord in person when he said to the apostles: "All that is written about me in the law of Moses and the prophets and the psalms must be fulfilled" (Luke 24:44). The best known example of this messianic meaning is the dialogue in Matthew's gospel on the messiah as Son of David and David's Lord: there, Psalm 110 is interpreted as messianic.

Following this line of thought, the Fathers of the Church saw the whole psalter as a prophecy of Christ and the Church and explained it in this sense; for the same reason the psalms have been chosen for use in the sacred liturgy. Though somewhat tortuous interpretations were at times proposed, yet, in general, the Fathers, and the liturgy itself, could legitimately hear in the singing of the psalms the voice of Christ crying out to the Father, or of the Father conversing with the Son; indeed, they also recognized in the psalms the voice of the Church, the apostles and the martyrs. This method of interpretation also flourished in the middle ages; in many manuscripts of the period the Christological meaning is by no means confined to the recognized messianic psalms but is given also to many others. Some of these interpretations are doubtless Christological only in an accommodated sense, but they have the traditional approval of the Church.[8]

The Church in her common teaching and practice shows us that it is most appropriate and accurate to apply scriptural passages containing the word "heart" to the Heart of Christ. Indeed, the entire Divine Office itself springs

---

[8]*General Instruction of the Liturgy of the Hours*, n. 108, 109.

from the Heart of the Savior: "Thus in the heart of Christ the praise of God finds expression in human words of adoration, propitiation and intercession."[9]

There are some references, however, which are of even greater importance. In the Messianic Psalms, there are explicit references to the heart of the Messiah. Here there is no question of accommodation.[10] The application of the Messianic Psalms to the Messiah are authenticated by our Lord himself and his apostles. Applying the doctrine of typology,[11] these series of prophecies give profound insights into the heart of the Redeemer who was to take human form.[12] Hugo Rahner clearly saw the importance of these texts and stated:

> Here we are to discuss only those Messianic texts of the Old Testament whose reference to Jesus is guaranteed by the witness of the New. What we wish to prove is that God really intended the revelation of the Heart of the Messiah, and that this revelation belongs to the original message and meaning of inspired Scripture.[13]

There are five such texts to which Rahner makes reference. Each of these prophecies of the Old Testament are authenticated by the explicit revelation of their fulfillment in the New Testament. They speak eloquently of how the Messiah would surrender his will, suffer and immolate his heart in order that

---

[9]*Ibid.*, n. 3.

[10]The right use of the spiritual sense is found in Pius XII, *Divino Afflante Spiritu*, Densinger-Schönmetzer, *Enchiridion Symbolorum Definitionum et Declarationum* (Rome: Herder, 1976) nos. 3826-3828.

[11]The doctrine of typology states that God, as the principal author of Sacred Scripture, directed salvation history in such a way that certain historical persons, things and events in the Old Testament must be considered as "types", i.e., figures which are prophetic in that they foreshadow corresponding persons, things and events in the New Testament. Our Lord and his apostles made use of this sense of Scripture. *cf. The New World Dictionary Concordance to the New American Bible* (New York: World Publishing, 1970) pp. 710-711.

[12]Of course, the Messianic Psalms only prefigure the messiah and do so imperfectly. Accordingly, a prudential judgment must be made *in the light of tradition and the official teaching of the Church concerning the Person of Christ* as to which parts of the psalm may be attributed to our Lord.

[13]Hugo Rahner, "On the Biblical Basis of the Devotion" in *Heart of the Savior*, ed. by J. Stierli, *op. cit.*, pp. 22-24. Some have inaccurately claimed that Pius XII's encyclical *Haurietis Aquas* rejected the exegesis of Rahner but this is not the case. The Pope in his use of scripture focuses on those passages which manifested the principal object of the devotion, namely divine love. See also Alban J. Dachauer, *The Sacred Heart: A Commentary on Haurietis Aquas* (Milwaukee: The Bruce Publishing Co., 1959) pp. 50-1 and Card. Ciappi, *The Heart of Christ, the Center of the Mystery of Salvation* (Rome: CdC Pub., 1983) pp. 203-206. These passages which speak of the human heart of the messiah are listed by C.J. Moell, "Devotion to the Sacred Heart," *New Catholic Encyclopedia* 1967, Vol. XII, p. 818.

Israel might be redeemed. The first is taken from Psalm 40 (39) v. 7-9:

> Sacrifice and oblation thou didst not desire, but thou hast given
> me an ear ready to listen. Burnt offering and sin offering thou didst
> not require; then said I, Behold I come.
> That is what is laid down for me where the book lies unrolled.
> To do thy will, O my God, is all my desire.
> I carry thy law in the midst of my heart.

That this prayer is made in the name of the Messiah is confirmed by the
Epistle to the Hebrews 10:5-7. This is the prayer of Christ when he "cometh
into the world." It beautifully represents what was contained in the heart of
Jesus of Nazareth as shown in his complete, loving surrender to the will of his
Father.

In Jeremiah 30:21, the self-surrendering Messiah is seen in greater depth
as the new David who comes forth from the people he will save:

> Their leader shall be of themselves: and their prince shall come
> forth from the midst of them;
> And I will bring him near, and he shall come to me, for is not this
> the man who gives his heart in pledge and so draws near to me?

In this text Christ, as the high priest, "approaches" the altar of sacrifice
in response to God's call. He is called upon to give his heart as a pledge—to
pour out his life in order to offer the fruits of salvation to all men. Our Lord
did in fact give his heart to the Father as he approached the altar of sacrifice
at the Last Supper and on Calvary.

Next, in Psalm 22 (21) we are given an intimate glimpse into the interior
life of our Lord's heart. This psalm was upon Christ's lips during his death
agony on the cross: "Now from the sixth hour there was darkness over the
whole land until the ninth hour. But about the ninth hour Jesus cried out with
a loud voice, saying, 'Eli, Eli, lema sabacthani,' that is, 'My God, My God, why
hast thou forsaken me' " (Mt. 27:45-6).

Further New Testament references to the Psalm are found in John 19:24
and Matthew 27:35, where the evangelists speak of the Roman soldiers
dividing the garments of Jesus, "that Scripture might be fulfilled." The Psalm
is messianic and speaks movingly of the heart of our dying Savior:

> I am poured out like water; and all my bones are scattered.
> My heart is become like wax melting in the midst of my bowels. (v.
> 14-15)

The innermost being of our Lord cries out, expressing the sorrow of his breaking heart. The image of melting wax points to the immolation and spiritual death of this heart. Hugo Rahner demonstrates the profound impact this verse had on the early Christians by offering St. Justin's (c. 150 AD) reflection, taken from his Dialogue with the Jew Tryphon:

> Now the passage, "All my bones are poured out and scattered like water; my heart is become like wax melting in the midst of my belly," foretold what would happen on that night when they came to the Mount of Olives to arrest Him. For in the memoirs of the Apostles and their successors, it is written that His sweat poured out like drops of blood as He prayed and said: "If it be possible let this cup pass from Me." His heart and bones were evidently quaking, and his heart was like wax melting in his bosom, so we may understand that the Father wished His Son to endure in reality these sufferings for us and may not declare that, since He was the Son of God, He had no feeling of what was done and inflicted upon Him.[14]

This scriptural passage leads us directly to one of the primary characteristics of the devotion to the Sacred Heart—an intense compassion for the broken, human heart of our Lord.

This psalm tells us even more of the Heart of the Messiah in verse 27, where it joyfully breaks through its anguish:

> Their hearts shall live for ever and ever;
> All the ends of the earth shall remember and shall be converted to the
> Lord.

Our Lord rejoices here that through the death of his heart, living hearts shall spring forth.

The prophetic death cry of Psalm 69 (68) also contains verses which refer to Christ, according to New Testament witness (Jn. 2:17, 15:25; Rom. 15:3; Acts 1:20). Just before verse 22, which foretells the offer of gall and vinegar to the Messiah for drink, we find the following lamentation:

> Reproach has broken my heart and I am cast down
> And I looked for one that would grieve together with me, but there
> was none: and for one that would comfort me, and I found none.
> (v.21)

Here the heart of our Lord is seen as breaking in a desolation which nears

---

[14]St. Justin, *Dialogus cum Tryphone Judaeo* in J. P. Migne, ed. *Patrologiae cursus completus Graeca* Vol. 6 (Paris: Garnier Fratres, 1878) 718-719.

despair (*Opprobrium fregit cor meum et defici*). Scripture here gives us an inspired and intimate view of the anguish of a tormented human heart at the point of death (*Et exspectavi commiserantem, sed non fuit; Et consolantes, sed non inveni.*—Vulgate). It is a passage which has often aroused a deep longing in devout souls to comfort our Lord in his suffering.

As in Psalm 22 (21), here also the understanding of our Lord's suffering can help us to appreciate the intensity of joy which springs from this broken heart, which gathers heaven, earth and sea

> into the song of jubilant redemption I will praise the name of God with a canticle: and I will magnify him with praise... You who seek God, your hearts shall live again. (v. 31-33)

Once again the immolated heart of the Messiah brings life and light to the hearts of men (Hebrew *lebab*; Greek Septuagint *psyche*; Latin Vulgate *cor*).

The last text which we will examine from the Old Testament is taken from Psalm 16 (15) and refers to Christ's joy at the resurrection:

> For this reason my heart is glad and my soul rejoices, moreover my body also will rest secure, for thou wilt not leave my soul in the abode of the dead nor permit thy holy one to see corruption. (v. 9-10)

St. Peter himself used this verse as a witness to the Messiah in his first sermon:

> Since David was a prophet, he said of the Christ, foreseeing his resurrection, that he would not be left in the place of death nor would his body see corruption. (Acts 2:30-31)

St. Paul also bears witness to the same passage in Acts 13:35. This is the psalm of the heart's joy at being delivered from suffering. The great paradox is again presented: from the heart of the Lord Jesus, crushed in death, now flows the living streams of the Spirit. Hugo Rahner beautifully summarizes the view of Christ which emerges from these prophecies:

> One sublime picture of the innermost dispositions of the future Messiah; and the element that fuses them is the heart. The heart of the Lord's anointed is submissive to the God that sent Him, it is humble and self-sacrificing. It is a heart full of majestic anger, or sunk in mortal anguish, or leaping with ecstatic joy. [15]

---

[15]J. Stierli, ed., *Heart of the Savior, op. cit.,* pp. 22-24.

Although we have limited our discussion to a select number of texts which speak *explicitly* of the heart, it is important to remember that the principal object of the devotion to the Sacred Heart is God's merciful love for man. Therefore, it would be important to recall here that there are divers images of this divine love in the Old Testament. These beautiful images also manifest the devotion. Since

> these images were presented in the Sacred Writings foretelling the coming of the Son of God made man, they can be considered as a token of the noblest symbol and witness of that divine love, that is, of the most Sacred and Adorable Heart of the Divine Redeemer.[16]

The readings for the Mass of the Sacred Heart reflect this teaching. God's covenant with Israel was itself a manifestation of this divine love:

> For you are a people holy to the Lord your God; the Lord your God has chosen you to be a people for his own possession, out of all the peoples that are on the face of the earth. It was not because you were more in number than any other people that the Lord has set his heart upon you and chosen you, for you were the fewest of all peoples; but it is because the Lord loves you and is keeping the oath which he swore to your fathers, that the Lord has brought you out with a mighty hand and redeemed you from the house of bondage, from the hand of Pharaoh king of Egypt. Know therefore that the Lord your God is God, the faithful God who keeps his covenant and steadfast love with those who love him and keep his commandments to a thousand genera-tions.... (Dt. 7:6-9)

The tender image of the Lord God as shepherd found in Psalm 23 (22) is another striking passage. This image was to be used and brought to perfection by Christ himself.

> The Lord is my shepherd; I shall not want.
> In verdant pastures he gives me repose;
> Beside restful waters he leads me; he refreshes my soul.
> He guides me in right paths for his name's sake.
> Even though I walk in the dark valley
> I fear no evil; for you are at my side
> With your rod and your staff that give me courage.
> You spread the table before me in the sight of my foes;
> You anoint my head with oil; my cup overflows.
> Only goodness and kindness follow me all the days of my life;

---

[16]Pius XII, *Haurietis Aquas, AAS* 48, 1956, p. 317.

And I shall dwell in the house of the Lord for years to come.

The prophet Hosea has given us a number of beautiful images. He speaks of God's love as that of a faithful, long-suffering husband calling back an unfaithful wife:

> And I will visit upon her the days of Baalim to whom she burnt incense and decked herself out with her earrings, and with her jewels, and went after her lovers, and forgot me, saith the Lord.
>
> Therefore, behold I will allure her, and will lead her into the wilderness: and I will speak to her heart.
>
> And I will give her vinedressers out of the same place, and the valley of Achor for an opening of hope: and she shall sing there according to the days of her youth, and according to the days of her coming up out of the land of Egypt. (Hos. 2:13-15)

At other times Hosea speaks of the divine love as that of a father harking back to his tender care for his young son:

> Because Israel was a child, and I loved him: and I called my son out of Egypt. As they called them, they went away before their face.... And I was like a foster father to Ephraim, I carried them in my arms: and they knew not that I healed them. I will draw them with the cords of Adam, with the bands of love: and I will be to them as one that taketh off the yoke on their jaws: and I put his meat to him that he might eat. (Hos. 11:1-4)

Both images are united by the prophet in his final chapter where he speaks of God's merciful love:

> Return, O Israel, to the Lord thy God: for thou hast fallen down by the iniquity. Take with you words, and return to the Lord, and say to him: Take away all iniquity, and receive the good: and we will render the fruit of our lips.
>
> Assyria shall not save us, we will not ride upon horses, neither will we say any more: The works of our hands are our gods, for thou wilt have mercy on the fatherless.
>
> I will heal their breaches, I will love them freely: for my wrath is turned away from them.
>
> I will be as the dew, Israel shall spring as the lily, and his root shall shoot forth as that of Libanus. They shall be converted that sit under his shadow: they shall live upon wheat, and they shall blossom as a vine: his memorial shall be as the wine of Libanus.
>
> Ephraim shall say, What have I to do anymore with idols? I will hear him, and I will make him flourish like a green fir tree: from me is

thy fruit found. (Hos. 14:2-9)

The prophet Isaiah speaks also of this bountiful love of God culminating in the image of undying maternal love:

> Thus saith the Lord: In an acceptable time I have heard thee, and in the day of salvation I have helped thee: and I have preserved thee, and given thee to be a covenant of the people, that thou mightest raise up the earth, and possess the inheritances that were destroyed: That thou mightest say to them that are bound: Come forth; and to them that are in darkness: Show yourselves. They shall feed in the ways, and their pastures shall be in every plain. They shall not hunger, nor thirst, neither shall the heat nor the sun strike them: for he that is merciful to them, shall be their shepherd, and at the fountains of waters he shall give them drink. And I will make all my mountains a way, and my paths shall be exalted. Behold these shall come from afar, and behold these from the north and from the sea, and these from the south country. Give praise, O ye heavens, and rejoice, O earth, ye mountains, give praise with jubilation: because the Lord hath comforted his people, and will have mercy on his poor ones.
>
> And Zion said: the Lord hath forsaken me, and the Lord hath forgotten me. Can a woman forget her infant, so as not to have pity on the son of her womb? And if she should forget, yet will not I forget thee. Behold, I have graven thee in my hands: thy walls are always before my eyes. (Is. 49:8-16)

These few images taken from the Old Testament communicate the love of God in a most elevated and striking way, yet Pius XII wrote, "it was only an advance symbol of that burning charity which mankind's promised Redeemer, from His most loving Heart, was destined to open to all and which was to be the type of His love for us and the foundation of the new covenant."[17]

This new covenant would be sealed by the pierced Heart of the Savior who would write it on the hearts of the new Israel:

> The Lord hath appeared from afar to me. Yea I have loved thee with an everlasting love, therefore have I drawn thee, taking pity on thee.
>
> Behold the days shall come, saith the Lord, and I will make a new covenant with the house of Israel, and with the house of Juda: Not according to the covenant which I made with their fathers, in the day that I took them by the hand to bring them out of the land of Egypt: the covenant which they made void, and I had dominion over them,

---

[17]Pius XII, *Haurietis Aquas, op. cit.*, p. 319.

saith the Lord.

But this shall be the covenant that I will make with the house of Israel, after those days, saith the Lord: I will give my law in their bowels, and I will write it in their heart: and I will be their God, and they shall be my people. And they shall teach no more every man his neighbour, and every man his brother, saying: Know the Lord: for all shall know me from the least of them even to the greatest, saith the Lord: for I will forgive their iniquity, and I will remember their sin no more. (Jer. 31: 3, 31-34)

New Testament

These messianic prophecies lead us quite naturally into our examination of the heart (*kardia, koilia* and *splancha*)[18] as found in the New Testament. Christ himself spoke of the heart in this figurative sense many times in his preaching:

Blest are the pure in heart (Mt. 5:8)

Why do you think evil in your hearts? (Lk. 5:22)

For a man's words flow out of what fills his heart. (Mt. 12:34)

For where our treasure is, there will your heart be also. (Lk. 12:34)

O foolish and slow of heart to believe. (Lk. 24:25)

When speaking of the effect of Christ's words on the road to Emmaus, the two disciples exclaimed, "Did not our hearts burn within us while he walked with us on the way and opened to us the scriptures" (Lk. 24:32)? Such was the effect of our Lord's teaching, which provides yet another illustration of the use of the heart in the New Testament.

There are several times in the New Testament where Christ himself explicitly refers to His own heart. The two we shall offer here are taken from the Gospel of St. Matthew. The first speaks briefly yet movingly of our Lord's compassion for the suffering of the crowds who followed him:

My heart goes out to my people. (Mt. 15:32)

The other text in which Christ refers to his own heart is found in Matthew 11:28:

---

[18]The Vulgate speaks of *cor, venter* and *viscera*. The word and all these near synonyms have what Hugo Rahner calls a "primal meaning in all human language" and are therefore strict equivalents. J. Stierli, ed. *Heart of the Savior, op. cit.*, pp. 17-21.

Come to me all you who labor and are overburdened, take my yoke
upon you and learn from me, for I am meek and humble of heart.

This is indubitably one of the most beautiful scriptural references to the
heart of Jesus. For this reason the Church uses this text in one of its gospel
readings for the Solemnity of the Feast. However, exegetically speaking, we
should not overemphasize the importance of this text, since the expression
"humble of heart" may have been a common Semitic metaphor which was
meant to be contrasted with the "conceit of heart" characteristic of the
Scribes and Pharisees. Regardless of the strict exegesis, the Lord is in some
way drawing attention to his heart as a symbol of his meekness and humility.
In the practical or existential order, this text has had a profound and lasting
impact on the development of the devotion. It has inspired Christians
throughout the centuries to respond to our Lord's invitation to come and
learn of his heart. The text has highlighted that aspect of the devotion which
stresses *imitatio Christi*—as is evidenced by the common prayer: "Jesus, meek
and humble of heart, make my heart like unto thine."

St. Paul in his epistles also speaks of the heart (*kardia*) on at least 50
occasions. Below are some examples taken from his epistles.

For with the heart a man believes unto justice. (Rom. 10:10)

God has sent the Spirit of his Son into our hearts. (Gal. 4:6)

I have you in my heart, all of you. (Phil. 1:7)

St. Paul, in his letter to the Philippians, speaks explicitly of Jesus' heart when
he states: "For God is my witness how I long for you all in the heart
[*splancha*—literally the bowels, including upper intestines, heart, liver and
lungs; it is the precise equivalent of *kardia*; cf. Ez. 11:19; Jer. 31:33][19] of Christ
Jesus" (Phil. 1:8).

There are four other texts which, although they do not mention the word
heart, have been historically and theologically of far greater importance in
the growth of the devotion to the heart of our Lord than even those which
explicitly mention his heart. Each of these texts is intimately connected with
the others. All four of these texts or instances are to be found in the Gospel
of St. John. This is why the devotion is considered to be of Johannine origin

---

[19]Hugo Rahner in *Heart of the Savior, op. cit.*, pp. 20-1; see also William Barclay, "The
Letter to the Philippians" in *The Daily Study Bible Series* (Philadelphia: The Westminster
Press, 1975) pp. 17-18; Kathryn Sullivan, *New Testament Reading Guide* Vol. 9
(Collegeville: Liturgical Press, 1960) p. 13-14.

Figure 1: *Icon of Christ in the National Museum, Ohrid, 1262-1263. Christ here is directing our gaze toward his bosom, thereby leading us to contemplate his interior life.*

and why the beloved disciple is frequently referred to as the evangelist of our Lord's heart. The first passage deals with John's reclining on the bosom of Jesus during the Last Supper. The Scripture, referring to this, reads as follows:

> Now one of his disciples, he whom Jesus loved, was reclining at Jesus' bosom. Simon therefore beckoned to him, and said to him, "Who is it of whom he speaks?" He therefore, leaning back upon the bosom of Jesus, said to him, "Lord, who is it?' (Jn. 13:23-25)

John again emphasizes this incident at the end of his Gospel:

> Turning round, Peter saw following them the disciple whom Jesus loved, the one who at the supper had leaned back upon his breast and said, "Lord who is it that will betray thee?" (Jn. 21:20)

Despite the fact that this event (exegetically speaking) does not form a scriptural foundation for the devotion to the Heart of Jesus, it has greatly influenced its development regarding one of its aspects of both biblical and patristic importance: the Heart of Christ is the fountain of living water from which the faithful may draw torrents of heavenly graces, knowledge and comforts. Origen, Augustine and many other Fathers spoke of our Lord's heart when commenting upon this text, as we shall see later.

The second instance of which we must take account is that of the risen Christ showing himself to St. Thomas. The text reads as follows:

> Then he said to Thomas, "Bring here thy finger, and see my hand; and bring here thy hand and put it into my side; and be not unbelieving but believing." Thomas answered and said to him, "My Lord and my God."

St. John appears to give great importance to Jesus' appearance to Thomas as he alone mentions it. He is also the only evangelist to mention that Jesus showed them his side (Luke mentions only the hands and feet). This event he connects with the piercing of the side on Calvary. The encyclical *Haurietis Aquas* refers to this very passage to show that from the very beginning, Christians adored and loved the human nature of Christ with particular regard to the wounds which penetrated into the core of his being:

> Moreover, is there not contained in those words "My Lord and my God" which St. Thomas the Apostle uttered, and which showed he had been changed from an unbeliever into a faithful follower, a profession of faith, adoration and love, mounting up from the wounded human nature of his Lord to the majesty of the divine

Figure 2: A 19th century engraving interpretation of Christ and St. John at the Last Supper.

Person?[20]

The initial revelation of the heart of Jesus may be said to have taken place on Calvary with the opening of his side and the piercing of his Heart. This particular episode may be considered the first glorious appearance of that heart. Christ, in showing his open wound in his side to Thomas, sought to lead him to faith. And likewise, as Christians down through the ages have testified,

---

[20]Pius XII, *Haurietis Aquas*, *Acta Apostolicae Sedis* (48) 1956 pp. 337-339.

Figure 3: *Stone carving of St. Thomas and Christ (11th century).*

our Lord continues to show us his opened heart to strengthen our faith and our love and to lead us into the sanctuary of his love.

In order to understand the next text it is important to recall that water is often used in Scripture as a symbol of God's grace and blessings. Let us turn to the writings of the prophets to illustrate this point.

> The desert and parched lands will exult; the steppe will rejoice and bloom....
> Waters will burst forth in the desert and rivers in the steppe. (Is. 35:1,6)

> The afflicted and the needy seek water in vain, their tongues are parched with thirst. I the Lord will answer them; I, the God of Israel will not forsake them. I will open up rivers on the bare heights and fountains in the broad valleys. (Is. 41:17,18)

> Thus says the Lord who made you...I will pour out water upon the thirsty ground, and streams upon the dry land; I will pour out my spirit upon your offspring, and my blessing upon your descendents. (Is. 44:1,3-4)

> All you who are thirsty, come to the water! (Is. 55:1)

> I will pour clean water upon you to cleanse you from all your impurities, and from all your idols I will cleanse you. I will give you a new heart and place a new spirit within you taking from your bodies your stony hearts and giving you natural hearts. I will put my spirit within you and make you live by my statutes, careful to observe my decrees. (Ez. 36:25-27)

> But thus says the Lord...they have forsaken me the source of living waters. (Jer. 2:12-13)

The third text contains the words of Christ himself:

> On the last and great day of the festivity, Jesus stood and cried saying: "If any man thirsts, let him come to me and drink, who believes in me. As the Scripture says: 'Streams of living water shall flow from his bosom'." (Jn. 7:37-38)

The festivity referred to here by St. John is the feast of the Tabernacles.[21]

---

[21]John L. McKenzie, *Dictionary of the Bible, op. cit.*, p. 863-4. A fine exegesis of the passage is given by Barclay in "The Gospel of St. John" Vol. I in *The Daily Study Bible Series, op. cit.*, pp. 247-252.

It was the most joyous of all the Jewish feasts celebrated at that time. The festivities occurred at the end of the Jewish year in the month of Tishri (September-October) and lasted for one week. It was primarily a festival of thanksgiving. God was praised for his abundant blessings during the past year and prayers were addressed to Him in an effort to secure similar blessings in the upcoming year. During the days of celebration the people lived in tents in remembrance of their forefathers' 40 year sojourn in the desert. Prayers were offered for rain in the forthcoming year. On the final day a large procession would be formed in which all the people would carry branches. The procession, led by the high priest who carried a golden urn, would make its way to the fountain of Siloam. Here the priest would draw water and carry it to the temple where it would be solemnly poured out over the altar of sacrifices. This would be done to recall Moses' miracle of making water gush forth from a rock. This was followed again by prayers, seeking the blessings of rain from heaven.

It was here in the court of the Temple, that Christ, the true source of water from heaven, stood in their midst and proclaimed himself to be the fountain of living water spoken of by the prophets. "On the last and great day" of the feast of Tabernacles, the Jews would remember the messianic promise of living water (Is. 12:3; Ez. 47:1-12; Zech. 13:1). The Messiah was expected to be a second Moses. He was to work the two Mosaic miracles: the multiplication of bread and the striking of water from the rock. Appropriately, when our Lord revealed himself on these two occasions, the people openly proclaimed him the Messiah (Jn. 6:14, 7:41). As St. Paul later testified, Christ himself was the rock from which the living waters of the Holy Spirit were to pour forth when he was on Calvary:

> And all ate the same spiritual food, and all drank the same spiritual drink, for they drank from the spiritual rock which followed them, and the rock was Christ. (I Cor. 10:4)

John clearly connects these words of our Lord with the piercing of Jesus' side on Calvary, as we shall see later.

Much has been said of the Alexandrian and Ephesian readings of this passage. The question here involves the punctuation given the verse, which can alter the sense of the text. The Alexandrian punctuation, which is found in Origen, tends to see the waters as flowing from the believer:

> If any man thirsts, let him come to me and drink. He that believes in me as the Scripture says, "Streams of water shall flow from his bosom."

The Ephesian reading (which is traced back to the followers of St. John at Ephesus and the Apostle himself), however, sees the waters as flowing *directly* from Christ:

> If any man thirst, let him come to me; And let him drink, who believes in me. As the Scripture says: Streams of living water shall flow from his bosom.

Too much should not be made of the differences between the two readings of this verse since, of course, even the Alexandrian reading would acknowledge Christ as the *ultimate* source of the heavenly water. That this water finds its source in Jesus (in the Ephesian sense) is confirmed by modern exegesis[22] and other passages of Scripture. When speaking to the Samaritan woman, Jesus said,

> Every one who drinks this water will thirst again. He however who drinks the water I will give him shall never thirst; but the water I shall give him shall become in him a fountain of water springing up into life everlasting. (Jn. 4:13-14)

Again, the last promise of God in the Bible is that of living water, "I am the Alpha and the Omega, the beginning and the end. To him who thirsts I will give the fountain of the water of life freely" (Rev. 21:6). In addition to this scriptural evidence, the Ephesian reading also has the overwhelming support of the Fathers of the Church as being the most ancient and apostolic.

Early Christian art also bears eloquent testimony to the apostolic origin of the Ephesian punctuation. In the Roman catacombs, for instance, many paintings of Moses striking the rock may be found. This signified to the early Christian the crucifixion of Christ and the opening of his side. One may also see many drawings and early mosaics depicting the Lamb described in Revelation 22:1-2, from whom "the river of the water of life" flows. In the catacomb of Priscilla an anonymous Christian scratched on the wall of the baptisterium, "If any man thirsts let him come to me." In the church of St. John Lateran there are pillars which were decorated with inscriptions in the year 430 AD. These decorations were undertaken by the then deacon and future Pope Leo the Great. One such inscription dealing with baptism reads, "This is the fountain of life which takes its rise from the wound of Christ and washes over

---

[22]National Office—Apostleship of Prayer, ed., *In The Bible, The Mystery of the Heart of Jesus* (Tamil Nadu, India: The National Office—Apostleship of Prayer), pp. 68-78. This source book provides an excellent outline and insightful analysis of all the major Biblical passages we have presented here.

the whole earth."[23] Finally, Pope Pius XII himself, in his encyclical *Haurietis Aquas*, used the Ephesian reading as the correct one. Thus we may conclude that the Ephesian reading is universally acknowledged as the most accurate by Scripture itself, tradition and modern exegesis.

It is also important to note here before leaving this passage that the word for bosom (*koilia*) in John 7:35 is a synonym for, and may be translated *heart* or *heart's core*, with the same extended spiritual sense which we have seen in the Old Testament. Accordingly, Hugo Rahner states that we may translate this passage as follows:

> If any man is thirsty and believes in me, let him come and drink of me. For it is written in Scripture: "Streams of living water shall flow from my heart."[24]

This is in fact the translation given in the Revised Standard Version: "Out of his heart shall flow rivers of living water."[25] Just as the water libation was being poured out in the sanctuary of the temple by the priest in anticipation of the coming Messiah, so Jesus here calls men to the royal sanctuary of his heart and bids them to drink the waters of eternal life. His heart is indeed the innermost sanctuary of that temple which is his Body.

From the prophecy concerning the living water which flows from the interior of Christ, St. John leads us finally to the piercing of the side and heart. Immediately after our Lord reveals his heart as the source of living waters in John 7:37-38, the Evangelist promptly adds, "He said this of the Spirit whom they who believed in him were to receive; for the Spirit had not yet been given, since Jesus had not yet been glorified" (Jn. 7:39). When was our Lord glorified? St. John tells us that after Judas left the Last Supper and the "hour" of our Lord's passion had begun, this is the time of Christ's glorification. Thus, paradoxically, the cross—the nefarious symbol of death—is to become the glorious sign of Christ's triumph. "When he had gone out, Jesus said, 'Now is the Son of Man glorified, and God is glorified in him. If God is glorified in him, God will also glorify him in himself and will glorify him at once' " (Jn. 13:31-32). The Lord is glorified and the spirit is given with the completion of the passion and death of Jesus.[26] The opening of our Lord's side and heart on the cross had the most profound impact upon St. John. Here is the event as

[23]*Ibid.*, pp. 75-76.

[24]J. Stierli, ed., *op. cit.*, p. 31.

[25]RSV, Catholic Edition, (London: Catholic Truth Society). The Philips Modern English Bible renders it "inmost heart".

[26]Raymond Brown, "The Gospel of St. John" Vol. 13 of *New Testament Reading Guide*, *op. cit.*, pp. 91-2.

narrated by the evangelist:

> But when they came to Jesus, and saw that he was already dead they
> did not break his legs; but one of the soldiers opened his side with a
> lance, and immediately there came out blood and water. And he who
> saw it has borne witness, and his witness is true, and he knows that he
> tells the truth, that you also may believe. For these things came to pass
> that the Scripture might be fulfilled, "Not a bone of him shall you
> break." And again, another Scripture says "They shall look upon him
> whom they have pierced." (Jn. 19:33-37)

Let us take note of the exceptional insistence of St. John. Our Lord was
already dead and it should have made little difference whether his legs were
broken or his side pierced with a lance. After clearly stating the fact, he insists
on it: "He who saw it has borne witness, and his witness is true." This
reiteration was not sufficient! He goes on to say: "He knows that he tells the
truth." This is almost as if the evangelist is making an oath of declaration or
a profound protestation. St. John, however, does not even stop there. He
continues and refers to a prophecy: "For these things came to pass that the
Scripture might be fulfilled, 'Not a bone of him shall you break'." This still
will not suffice and the evangelist quotes yet another prophecy: "And again
another Scripture says, 'They shall look upon him whom they have pierced'."

Here we have an extraordinary affirmation which is not to be found
anywhere else in St. John's Gospel, even regarding the Lord's death or
resurrection. He proclaims the fact and twice reaffirms its truth with a kind
of oath and twice more with prophecy taken from the Old Testament.

The prophecies quoted by John show that the piercing of our Lord's side
was no mere accident but a vital part of the divine plan. This may be seen with
even greater clarity when we realize that the wounding of Christ's side was a
violation of both Jewish and Roman law.

The first prophecy, "Not a bone of his shall you break," is taken from
Exodus 12:46, which deals with the Jewish preparation of the Paschal lamb
before their flight out of Egypt. It is repeated in the book of Numbers 9:12
("You must not break any of its bones.") where the Jews are given instructions
and told to celebrate the Passover every year. In both passages it is the Lord
who speaks. St. John applies this image of the Paschal Lamb to Christ as the
true lamb whom the others merely prefigured.

Many texts in Scripture refer to Christ as a lamb:

The suffering servant in Isaiah:

> He was spurned and avoided by men, a man of suffering, accus-

tomed to infirmity, one of those from whom men hide their faces, spurned and we held him in no esteem. Yet it was our infirmities that he bore, our sufferings he endured, while we thought of him as stricken, as one smitten by God and afflicted.

But he was pierced for our offences, crushed for our sins: upon him was the chastisement that makes us whole, by his stripes we were healed.

We had all gone astray like sheep, each following his own way; but the Lord laid upon him the guilt of us all. Though he was harshly treated, he submitted and opened not his mouth; like a lamb led to the slaughter. (Isaiah 53:3-7)

St. John the Baptist, upon seeing Jesus approaching him,
proclaimed to the people:

Behold the lamb of God who takes away the sin of the world! (John 1:29)

St. Peter makes a similar reference:

You know that you were redeemed from the vain manner of life handed down from your fathers, not with perishable things, with silver or gold, but with the precious blood of Christ, as of a lamb without blemish and without spot. (I Peter 1:18-19)

In the Book of Revelation there are over 30 references to Christ as "the Lamb" who was sacrificed and immolated for all men but now reigns in heavenly glory.

It is manifestly the intention of St. John to acknowledge Christ as the perfect Paschal Lamb who won redemption for his people on the cross. The piercing of our Lord's side was the final act which sealed his perfect sacrifice.

The second prophecy, "They shall look upon him whom they have pierced" is taken from the prophet Zechariah.

I will pour out on the house of David and on the inhabitants of Jerusalem a spirit of grace and prayer; and they shall look upon him whom they have pierced, and they shall mourn for him as one mourns for an only son, and they shall grieve over him as one grieves over a first born. (Zech. 12:10)

This passage parallels the description of the Lord's suffering servant in chapter 53 of Isaiah. St. John applies this passage in Zechariah to the crucified Christ on two occasions. The first is the passage we are studying (Jn. 19:37) and the second occasion is found in the book of Revelation where St. John speaks of the coming of Christ:

> Behold he comes with the clouds, and every eye shall see him, and they
> also who pierced him. And all the tribes of the earth shall wail over
> him. (Rev. 1:7)

The seeing of the Pierced One in the book of Revelation is a source of
lamentation which leads to faith, love and conversion. He is the fount of
"grace and prayer" which will be poured upon the people. This looking up
suggests the image of Christ upon the Cross. Our Lord himself proclaimed:
"And I, when I am lifted up from the earth, will draw all men to myself" (Jn.
12:32). This was already foreshadowed in our Lord's conversation with
Nicodemus:

> And as Moses lifted up the serpent in the wilderness so must the Son
> of Man be lifted up, that whoever believes in him may have eternal
> life. (Jn. 3:14-15)

So it is by seeing the Pierced One whose side is opened on the cross that
men are drawn to faith and love. John, having personally witnessed this
wounding on the cross was profoundly moved by it. This is why he speaks of
our Lord's revealing the wound in his side to Thomas, urging the doubting
apostle to put his hand there: "...bring here thy hand, and put it into my side
and be not unbelieving but believing" (Jn. 20:27).

We should now like to turn our attention to the flow of the blood and
water which issued from the wound after the violent thrust of the spear. St.
John states: "One of the soldiers opened his side and immediately there came
out blood and water" (Jn. 19:34). St. John also reconfirms this in his first
epistle: "This is he who came in water and blood, Jesus Christ; not in the water
only, but in the water and the blood" (I Jn. 5:6). It is in the blood of Christ
that we have our redemption and the new and everlasting covenant (Eph. 1:7;
Col. 1:20; Heb. 9:12-18; I Jn. 1:7; Mt. 2:24-28). With the piercing of his side,
Christ shed the last drops of his most precious blood which completed the
sacrifice of our redemption. The flow of water is a messianic sign that our
redemption is completed. As we have observed, this event is the fulfillment
of our Lord's promise of living water to the Samaritan woman (Jn. 4:13-14)
and to the people when he revealed his heart as the source of this living water
in John 7:37-38.

In addition to the prophetic parallel between Moses miraculously drawing water from the rock (Ex. 1:1-7; Num. 2:7-13) and St. Paul's reference to
Christ as the rock (I Cor. 10:4) struck by the lance from whom spiritual waters
flow, there are several other Old Testament prophecies which we must
examine. Many of these prophecies were used by Pius XII in his encyclical

Haurietis Aquas. The first, from which the encyclical derives its name, is taken from the prophet Isaiah: "You shall draw waters with joy out of the Savior's fountain" (Is. 12:3). This passage, the Pope observes, with "highly significant imagery" foretold the wondrous graces which would spring forth in the Christian era from the wounded side of Christ where the faithful would drink from the fount of salvation.

Another deeply significant prophecy is taken from the prophet Ezechiel, who speaks of a healing water which will "flow from the sanctuary of the temple" (Ez. 47:1-12). Our Lord himself referred to his body as a temple (Jn. 2:17-19) and spoke of streams that would flow from his body (Jn. 7:37-38). Therefore, it is quite appropriate that we apply this prophetic text here.

The most important prophecy, however, is taken from the prophet Zechariah:

> On that day there shall be opened to the house of David and to the inhabitants of Jerusalem a fountain to purify from sin and uncleanliness. (Zech. 13:1)

In the foregoing chapter, Zechariah had prophesied that men would look upon the one whom "they had pierced" and would mourn over him "as the death of an only son" (Zech. 12:10). He then recalls how "*on that day*" all the families shall mourn for him (Zech. 12:13-14) and immediately adds in the next verse, "On that day a fountain will be opened," (Zech. 13:1) and men cleansed of their sin.

The day that men shall be cleansed *is* the day they shall see the Pierced One. Accordingly, it was when Christ's side was opened up and his heart pierced that the cleansing waters of forgiveness and redemption poured forth.

As we shall see later, the early Christians and the Fathers of the Church saw the tremendous significance of the flow of blood and water from our Lord's side. From this wound, out of which both blood and water flowed, we are shown that the Heart of Jesus is the source and fountain of the living water which gives us the life of grace, the sacraments, the Church and the Holy Spirit (Jn. 7:38)[27].

Although the text speaks only of the side, Pius XII, in *Haurietis Aquas*, reminds us that

> What is here written of the side of Christ, opened by the wound from

---

[27] An excellent exegesis of John 19:26f and its significance for ecclesiology can be found in Msgr. Jorge Mejia "Born From the Side of Christ: An Orientation for the One Church" in *Civilization of Love* (San Francisco: Ignatius Press, 1985) pp. 101-143.

the soldier, should also be said of the Heart which was certainly reached by the stab of the lance, since the soldier pierced it precisely to make certain that Jesus Christ crucified was really dead.[28]

This would be expected since the thrust of the lance did not just break the surface skin but was a violent thrust which pierced his heart in order to insure death. Roman soldiers at that time were trained to use this very thrust which was to pierce the heart of their foe.[29]

From this brief overview of the meaning of the heart in Sacred Scripture, several things emerge as clear: 1) The Bible in general sees the heart of man as the central point within him where he is most himself. It is to this point that God addresses himself; 2) The *leb* or *lebab* of the Old Testament and the *kardia*, *koilia* or *splancha* of the New Testament have the same meaning: the true directive center of the person from which arises all his thoughts and feelings. The term heart in its figurative sense as the center of being or consciousness has a solid foundation in both the Old and New Testament. (In the Church's liturgy down through the ages the use of heart in its spiritual sense has been maintained. It is in this sense that the devotion to the Sacred Heart of Jesus is to be understood.) 3) The word "heart" in its extended sense is applied to both God and man. 4) God truly intended the revelation of the Heart of the Messiah. This revelation of the Heart of the Savior belongs to the "original message and meaning" of Sacred Scripture. 5) Although there is no *specific* mention of the veneration of the physical heart of Christ (this being a later development in mystical theology) it is possible to find, within the limits of sound exegesis, all the central ideas which suggest and foster devotion to the Heart of our Lord. It was this conviction which led Pius XII to write:

> We are absolutely convinced that not until we have made a profound study of the primary and loftier nature of this devotion with the aid of the light of the divinely revealed truth, can we rightly and fully appreciate its incomparable excellence and the inexhaustible abundance of its heavenly favors.[30]

The importance of this biblical anthropology and theology of the heart has been clearly seen and forcefully stressed by Cardinal Ratzinger:

---

[28]Pius XII, *Haurietis Aquas, op. cit.*, p. 334.

[29]Pierre Barbet, *A Doctor at Calvary* (Garden City, New York: Image Books, 1963) p. 138.

[30]Pius XII, *op. cit.*, p. 315.

All of this comes to show that Christian piety must involve the senses, which receive their order and unity from the heart, and also the feelings, which have their seat in the heart. It is clear that such piety, centered in the heart, corresponds to the image of the Christian God, who has a heart. It is also clear that all of this is, in the end, an expression and an application of the *mysterium paschale*, which is where we find the recapitulation of the story of God's love for man.... The pierced Heart of the Crucified is the literal fulfillment of the prophecy concerning the Heart of God, which overturns his justice with compassion and precisely in this way remains just. Only in this concordance between Old and New Testament can we behold the full extent of the biblical message concerning the Heart of God, the Heart of the Divine Redeemer.[31]

Since the devotion focuses in a special way upon God's love, we should also make reference here to the numerous passages in Sacred Scripture which reveal in a particular way the love of God. In the Old Testament we saw how the writings of the prophets contain many beautiful images of God's love for his people. More importantly, throughout the New Testament we find numerous instances in which the sentiments of the Heart of Christ are revealed. These may help us to understand more fully the depth of our Lord's love and the mystery of his Heart, understood as the deepest personal center and source of all affectivity.

One would certainly think of his parables of the Good Shepherd (Jn. 10:1-18), the Prodigal Son (Lk. 15:1-31), and the Good Samaritan (Lk. 10:30-37) which powerfully convey a sense of his merciful love. The countless miracles of healing also show Christ's great compassion for human suffering. The beatitudes (Mt. 5:1-12) given in the Sermon on the Mount most beautifully reveal the great love of our Lord's Heart. Other examples would be his love for the young man seeking discipleship (Mk. 10:17-22); the widow and her son (Lk. 7:11-15); the woman caught in adultery (Jn. 8:1-11); the penitent woman who was forgiven her sins "because she has loved much" (Lk. 7:47); the little children he blessed (Mk. 10:13-16); and the multitudes he fed who "were like sheep without a shepherd" (Mk. 6:34).

Several passages especially stand out as beautiful manifestations of the deep emotion and love of our Lord's Heart. They reveal instances of Christ's holy affectivity and through that the qualities of his Sacred Heart:

---

[31] Joseph Cardinal Ratzinger, "The Paschal Mystery as Core and Foundation of Devotion to the Sacred Heart" in *Towards a Civilization of Love* (San Francisco: Ignatius Press, 1985), pp. 156, 159.

The raising of Lazarus

When, therefore, Mary came where Jesus was, and saw him, she fell at his feet, and said to him, "Lord if thou hadst been here, my brother would not have died." When, therefore, Jesus saw her weeping, and the Jews who had come with her weeping, he groaned in spirit and was troubled, and said, "Where have you laid him?" They said to him, "Lord, come and see." And Jesus wept. The Jews therefore said, "See how he loved him." (Jn. 11:32-36)

The lamentation for the people of Jerusalem

"Jerusalem, Jerusalem, thou who killest the prophets, and stonest those who are sent to thee! How often would I have gathered thy children together as a hen gathers her young under her wings, but thou wouldst not...." And when he drew near and saw the city, he wept over it, saying, "If thou hadst known, in this thy day, even thou, the things that are for thy peace." (Lk. 13:34, 19:41-2)

The institution of the Eucharist

And when the hour had come, he reclined at table, and the twelve apostles with him. And he said to them, "I have greatly desired to eat this passover with you before I suffer...." (Lk. 22:14-15)

The promise of the Spirit

"Let not your heart be troubled.... If you love me, keep my commandments. And I will ask the Father and he will give you another Advocate to dwell with you forever, the Spirit of truth.... I will not leave you orphans; I will come to you. Yet a little while longer and the world no longer sees me. But you see me, for I live and you shall live. In that day you shall know that I am in my Father, and you in me, and I in you. He who has my commandments and keeps them, he it is who loves me. But he who loves me will be loved by my Father, and I will love him and manifest myself to him." (Jn. 14:1, 15-21)

The agony in the garden

And he began to be saddened and exceedingly troubled. Then he said to them, "My soul is sad even unto death. Wait here and watch with me".... And he himself withdrew from them about a stone's throw, and kneeling down he began to pray, saying, "Father, if thou art willing remove this cup from me; yet not my will but thine be done." And there appeared to him an angel from heaven to strengthen him. And falling into an agony he prayed the more earnestly. And his sweat became as drops of blood running down upon the ground. (Mt. 26:37-38; Lk. 22:41-44)

Forgiveness for his executioners

And when they came to the place called the Skull, they crucified him there, and the robbers, one on his right hand and the other on his left. And Jesus said, "Father, forgive them, for they do not know what they are doing." (Lk. 23:33-34)

Promise of salvation to the good thief

Now one of those robbers who were hanged was abusing him, saying, "If thou art the Christ, save thyself and us!" But the other in answer rebuked him and said, "Dost not even thou fear God, seeing that thou art under the same sentence? And we indeed justly, for we are receiving what our deeds deserved; but this man has done nothing wrong." And he said to Jesus, "Lord, remember me when thou comest into thy kingdom." And Jesus said to him, "Amen I say to thee, this day thou shalt be with me in paradise." (Lk. 23:39-43)

The gift of Mary as Mother of the Church

When Jesus, therefore, saw his mother and the disciple standing by, whom he loved, he said to his mother, "Woman, behold thy son." Then he said to the disciple, "Behold thy mother." (Jn. 19:26-27)

It is by returning to the Word of God that we may see clearly the perennially valid elements of the devotion to the Heart of Jesus: the Father's merciful love for sinful men, the wondrous grandeur of the human and divine love in our Lord's heart; reparation, sacrifice, and more. These scriptural themes of the devotion are constantly surging forth anew and remain ever fresh as they grow and flourish within the bosom of Mother Church.

Christological Heresies & the Early Councils of the Church

As Cardinal Newman observed in his masterful *Essay on the Development of Christian Doctrine*, "Christianity is a historical fact which impresses itself upon the mind and is reflected upon by human reason."[32] Through this reflection Christianity will expand in numerous directions with all its parts congruent, definitive and immutable. Such developments in the Christian faith are to be expected as natural since all other human ideas develop in time. Christianity differs from other mere human philosophies or religions not in kind but in origin. Although Christianity is of a divine origin and is

---

[32]Newman, Card. J. H., *Essay on the Development of Christian Doctrine*, (Westminster, Md.: Christian Classics, Inc., 1968)pp. 33-54.

guided by a divine spirit, it is also an "earthen vessel", being the religion of men.

Christianity's profession of truth necessarily involves the refutation and condemnation of errors. It is often, however, errors or corruptions which arise and call for attention first. These can, strangely enough, in a certain positive sense assist the Church in so far as they lead to true developments and hence to a greater comprehension of Christian truth. This truth, having developed and grown in clarity through exposition, shines forth in all its beauty.

Whenever the truth has been disputed, Christian tradition has always argued from Scripture; but argument implies deduction, which is development. The Scripture itself must allow development if it is to convey a true and living idea and not remain mere words. Newman, in his *Essay*, gives the following example from St. John's gospel to illustrate this point: "The Word became flesh" (Jn. 1:14).

Three vast questions immediately spring into the mind: What is meant by "the Word"? What is meant by "flesh"? What is meant by "become"? The answers to these three questions require a process of investigation which is a development. The answers to these questions will also suggest a series of secondary questions and propositions which gather around this one phrase in Scripture. These take the form of a doctrine which imbeds the idea more deeply in the mind. Many questions concerning the Scripture itself, such as its canon, its inspiration, whether it is self-interpretive or needs an authoritative comment—all these vital questions find no answer on the surface of Scripture. In actuality, God in his providence has left these answers to time, with its controversies and vicissitudes which make up the slow process of thought.

Since the devotion to the heart of Jesus is Christocentric in its orientation, it is necessary in the establishment of the devotion's dogmatic foundation that we turn to the early controversies which dealt with the person of our Lord. The devotion, though centering upon the Person of Christ, also understandably incorporates profound Trinitarian insights and reveals the grandeur of Christ's mediatorship.[33]

Who Is Christ?

The dogmatic foundation for the veneration of the physical heart of Christ is based upon the Church's answer to this question. This important question was answered by the Church with great clarity as a result of the Christological heresies which plagued her in the early centuries.

Who is Christ? The Council of Chalcedon (451) is normative of Christianity's central understanding of the mystery of Christ Jesus. The Council's teaching may be summarized in the following four points:

    a) Jesus is truly God
    b) Jesus is truly man
    c) Jesus is one person
    d) Jesus has two distinct natures

We shall discuss each of these truths separately, following the path of doctrinal development in the Church, which led to the teaching of Chalcedon.

a) Jesus is truly God. It was the Council of Nicea which dealt with this question in response to the teaching of Arius. It is Paul of Samosata, the Bishop of Antioch, not Arius, to whom we must first look as the true father of those heresies which separated Christ from God. Paul stated that Jesus the man was distinct from the Logos. God for Paul, was one not only in essence but in Person as well. The Church was not slow in dealing with his errors. At Antioch, three provincial councils were held between 264 and 269 which solemnly excommunicated Paul and condemned his fallacious views. The Fathers at these councils, thinking that the term *homoousian* (one substance) might mistakenly be interpreted in pagan philosophical fashion, refused to accept it in fear of denying the true personhood of the Trinity.

Closely affiliated with Paul was Lucian, who edited the Septuagint and

---

[33]Such a study of the basic foundations of our faith is sadly necessary given the secularized habits and widespread religious ignorance of so many Christians. The decline in orthodox religious education in many countries in the West (along with certain cultural factors) is responsible for this to a large extent. This lack of an orthodox religious formation has made it difficult for many well-meaning Christians to understand many key theological doctrines associated with the devotion (e.g., reparation). Many in the Church, including priests and religious, have been taught certain reductionistic christologies which have been based on a truncated "scientific exegesis". A number of these have seriously distorted the teachings of the Church. This has prevented many from understanding how the devotion to the Heart of Christ draws together all the great Christological truths of the Faith.

died a martyr's death. Lucian had a profound influence on the school of Antioch. Among those to fall under his influence were Eusebius, the future bishop of Nicomedia, and a young cleric by the name of Arius.

Arius was born in Libya but was raised in Antioch where he attended school with Eusebius. In 318 he was made presbyter and presided over the church named Bucalis in Alexandria, and was on very good terms with the bishop of the city, Alexander.

Alexandria was a wealthy commercial city steeped in intellectual tradition. Here, in this cosmopolitan city of the Empire, Roman, Jew, African, native Egyptian and Greek met and carried on a fruitful exchange of ideas. In this setting, the Alexandrian church became the center of a great apologetic movement establishing a school of catechetics which grew quite famous. It was in the year 319, when the Patriarch Alexander was presiding over some of the scholastic exercises, that one of the clerics, Arius, put forth a question concerning the true meaning of the words "Son of God".

Since all human language is derived from those things which surround us in this world, no words can fully express the supernatural mystery of God and the Eternal Son who became incarnate. Christ called himself *the Son of God* and, inspired by the Holy Spirit, St. John the Evangelist calls our Savior the "Word"—"In the beginning was the Word and the Word was with God and the Word was God," (Jn. 1:1). Arius, putting aside the orthodox interpretation of St. John, stepped forward and asked: "If God the Son was begotten of the Father, does that not imply that the Father existed before Him?"[34] The bishop after patiently exhorting and arguing with Arius, was forced to excommunicate him. At first he brought forth this heresy in the form of a complex question but when offered the orthodox answer he was defiant and denied the divine sonship in everything but name. Socrates, in his *Historia Ecclesiae*, writes concerning Arius:

> He opposed it [the orthodox answer] vehemently, and asserted that if the Father had begotten the Son, he who was begotten had a beginning of his being, and consequently there was a time when he could not have been; and that it also followed that the Son had his beginning from nothing.[35]

Thinking in human terms, a son must of necessity be younger than he who begets; Arius applied this human concept to God who is in essence eternity,

[34]M. L. Cozens, *Handbook of Heresies* (London: Sheed & Ward, 1974) p. 31.
[35]Charles J. Hefele, *A History of the Christian Councils*, Vol. I (Edinburgh: T. T. Clark, 1894), p. 243.

where words such as *before* and *after* are of no significance. This destructive over-simplification of the Triune mystery vitiated the traditional Christian understanding of the eternal Son.

> Had not their understanding been entirely withdrawn from them, what has been urged before upon the plain authority of Holy Scripture, must have effectually convinced them that there is not the least affinity between Him and any created being whatsoever. Since He is God He cannot possibly be a creature, and it is the height of blasphemy to say that He is one. It is only of beings who are made and created that we can say rightly they were made out of nothing, and they did not exist before they were born.[36]

Failing to realize that the essence of sonship is receiving from the begetter his own nature, Arius failed to grasp that because God's nature is unalterable and eternal, Christ the Son must be both eternal and unalterable as the Father. Arius argued thus:

> He is Son, therefore posterior to the Father; therefore not eternal; since the Father is eternal and the Son not, He is unlike the Father.[37]

When Arius and his followers were presented with the scriptural verses that bore witness to the divinity of our Lord, they would acknowledge that he was Lord and God but not necessarily and essentially. This divine honor was ascribed to him only because the Father willed Christ to be. Christ now resembled a gnostic emanation, a super angelic being directly created by God. Arius held that Christ was only allowed by God to share in the divine honors as a result of his fidelity to the Father. The problem this raises is that if Christ's nature could change here, could it not also allow for the possibility of sin? Arius thought this highly improbable, but possible, to the shock of all Christian believers. According to Arian thinking, God is absolutely one, in every sense of the word. As in the teaching of Islam, he is in no sense generated and in no sense does he generate as one communicates His essence. God may communicate outside himself, as can be seen from creation, but not within himself. Thus, when Sacred Scripture speaks of God as Father, it always speaks in the sense of a created communication, whether it be the Word of St. John or the rest of rational creation. For all these reasons Arius denied that God could be the Father of a true natural Son. Christ was the Son of God

---

[36]W. C. L. trans., *The Orations of St. Athanasius Against the Arians* (London: Griffith, Farran, Ikeden & Welsh), p. 82.

[37]M. L. Cozens, *Handbook of Heresies, op. cit.*, p. 31.

only as a unique creature. To settle this question, the Council of Nicea was called in 325.

In the course of the discussions it became increasingly obvious to the Arian party that their belief was opposed to tradition and would find little favor with the majority of the bishops. The church historian Rufinus describes the Council's deliberation, stating:

> ...that they then held daily sessions, and that they would not decide lightly or prematurely upon so grave a subject; that Arius was often called into the midst of the assembly; that they seriously discussed his opinions; that they attentively considered what there was to oppose to them; that the majority reflected the impious system of Arius; and that the confessors especially declared themselves energetically against the heresy.[38]

In an effort to save Arianism, a group was formed consisting of twelve bishops of the original Arian party and led by Eusebius of Nicomedia. Athanasius christened them "the Eusebians". This group submitted to the Council a profession of faith so ambiguous that both Catholics and Arians could sign, in the hope of allowing for an Arian interpretation. Although we no longer possess a copy of this document we are told by Theodoret that it aroused such indignation that it was torn to pieces.

The term *homoousion* which means "of the same substance" or "consubstantial" was adopted by the orthodox party as a sure test for orthodoxy. Many bishops, if not a majority, viewed the term suspiciously. It was a semi-philosophic, non-biblical term, and many bishops questioned whether it should be used at all. In the past, it had been used by the Gnostics to explain their numerous emanations; the Sabellians used it to defend the identity of Father and Son, and therefore it had been rejected by the Fathers in a synod at Antioch some sixty years earlier.

Socrates and Theodoret mention that Eusebius of Caesarea,[39] who was a strong Arian sympathizer, fought against its adoption. In its place, Eusebius submitted before the Council the baptismal creed of his church in which the term *homoousion*, which means "similar substance" was used. He hoped that this might be accepted as an adequate expression of the Church's teaching on the point of dispute. Certainly, from a scriptural and traditional point of view, the creed of Eusebius was unassailable. It was orthodox as far as it went but the question was whether or not it went far enough. Had this problem

---

[38]Charles J. Hefele, *A History of the Christian Councils*, Vol. I, *op. cit.*, p. 283.

[39]H. J. Schroeder, *Disciplinary Decrees of the General Councils* (New York Vail Ballou Press, 1937), p. 15.

never been brought up it would have been more than adequate. It predicated of the Son every honor and dignity save a oneness of substance. To remedy the situation, Constantine, at the suggestion of Hosius and the orthodox party proposed that the creed be accepted with the insertion of *homoousian* as the term of orthodoxy to avoid any vagueness or ambiguity. The orthodox group accepted the term as expressing the traditional understanding of the Church's teaching that Christ is the Son of God.

As a further guard against allowing an Arian interpretation, the phrase "of one substance of the Father" was added through the efforts of Athanasius. Along with the creed the Council added an anathema against all who would teach to the contrary. Led by Alexander and Athanasius, the Fathers of Nicea, in condemning this heresy, stated the traditional Catholic teaching with greater precision and clarity:

> We believe in one God, the Father Almighty, Maker of all things visible and invisible, and in one Lord Jesus Christ, the Son of God, the only-begotten of the Father, that is of the substance of the Father, God from God, light from light, true God from true God, begotten not made, of the same substance with the Father, through whom all things were made both in heaven and on earth; who for us men and for our salvation descended, became incarnate, and was made man, suffered and rose again the third day, ascended into heaven and will come to judge the living and the dead. And in the Holy Ghost.
>
> Those who say: there was a time when He was not, and He was not before He was begotten, and that He was made out of nothing; or who say that He is of another hypostasis or another substance [than the Father], or that the Son of God is created or is susceptible of change or alteration, [them] the Catholic and Apostolic Church anathematizes.[40]

It was the purpose of this profession of faith drawn up by the Council Fathers to make the Church's belief in the divinity of Christ *absolutely clear.* This is precisely why the Creed is repetitive. The Church's faith must be unequivocal on such a vital point. Christ is called the "only-begotten of the Father" (*unigenitum Dei*) to distinguish his origin of Father from all other possible types of origin found in creation. Accordingly, Christ is totally unique in his procession from the Father, in contrast to angelic and human beings, who are also called sons of God in Sacred Scripture.

He is "of the substance of the Father" (literally "out of the being" (*ousia*)

---

[40]Denzinger-Schönmetzer, *Enchridion Symbolorum* (Rome: Herder Publishing Co., 1976), (125) p. 52-55.

of the Father) which states that unlike creatures who come from God's free act (contingent being), his existence is not dependent upon the will of the Creator.

He is "God from God" (*Deum de Deo*), showing that he shares perfectly in the one and same divine nature and yet the two persons are really distinct as one eternally generates and the other is eternally generated.

He is "light from light" (*lumen de lumine*) to show the identity and absolute oneness of divine essence as the radiance from a light is identical with the light from which it shines. He is "true God from true God" (*Deum verum de Deo vero*) to clearly show what is meant by profession the divinity of Christ. Since the truth signifies agreement, the Father and Son are equally and fully divine. They differ only in their relation—the Father begets and the Son is begotten.

"Begotten not made" (*genitum non factum*) illustrates the great mystery that within God himself a generation goes on from all eternity. The generation is absolutely different from all other generation in the created order, since there is no cause or effect, no change, no new being.

"Of the same substance with the Father" (*consubstantialem Patri*) (*homoousious*) shows the plurality of persons in God but that there is only one God, only one divine nature.

The anathemas further stress with the greatest clarity the eternity of the Son, for there "never was a time when he was not." Furthermore, he is neither a creature "made out of nothing" nor is he "of another substance of the Father."

This Son of God who, along with the Father and Holy Spirit, created *ex nihil* and continues to sustain this universe, was not made himself. Since the Son is creator he is not a creature. It was this Son who in the fullness of time became a man for the salvation of man, suffered the ignominious death of the cross, rose, and ascended into the glory of heaven. Jesus Christ is truly God.

b) Jesus is truly man. This truth was stressed in the Gospels, the Epistles of St. John and the writings of St. Ignatius of Antioch. After the passing of the first and second generations of Christians this truth was attacked by some who believed that the body or material reality was evil. Accordingly, it was utterly blasphemous to say that the Deity had truly become man. This heretical type of thinking has emerged throughout history and has assumed a great variety of names such as Gnosticism, Docetism, Manichaeism, Albigensianism, Jansenism, and Puritanism. (It is of interest to note here that contrary to what one often hears, the Church, in her constant defense of the central mystery of Christianity—the Incarnation—has always taught the goodness of material creation and the holiness of human sexuality.)

As Arianism had attacked the divinity of Christ, so Apollinarianism attacked the humanity of Christ. Apollinaris, the Bishop of Laodicea, force-fully taught the true divinity of Christ and that the Son possessed the fullness of Deity. Unfortunately however, in his valiant effort to defend the oneness of Christ's Person, he denied that our Lord possessed a human soul as the principle of all human activity. He adhered to the Platonic teaching that man was made up of three elements: body, soul and spirit. Although Christ had human flesh and the lower animal soul which is the principle of the body's sensitive movements, he lacked a rational soul with its intellect by which we know and its will by which we choose. This rational soul was replaced by the Word; thus, according to this teaching, in Christ we have the Word in a human body. When St. John speaks in his Gospel of the Word becoming flesh, he uses flesh not as signifying merely a body but as the *totus homo*. The heresy of Apollinaris, while appearing to simplify the doctrine of the Incarnation, in fact stripped it of its reality and true value. The Divinity and Manhood of Christ were both debased: his humanity was not a nature but merely flesh, and his divinity was subjected to the successive acts proper to a created intelligence, which made it mutable.

Apollinaris was attacked by many Fathers of the Church (most notably St. Basil) and his heresy was condemned at the Council of Rome (382) in the Tome of Pope Damasus I:

> We anathematize those who say that in the human body [of Christ] the Word of God dwelt in place of the rational and intellective human soul; because the very Son and Word of God did not take the place of the rational and intellective soul in his body, but he assumed and preserved a soul like ours [that is, a rational and intellective soul] but without sin.[41]

The Christ of Apollinaris was consubstantial with the Father and was therefore truly God. He was not however consubstantial with us in his humanity. This heresy led to a greater development of the Church's under-standing of the relationship between the Incarnation and the Redemption, which led to the soteriological principle of the Fathers, that "nothing is healed unless it is assumed." In the sin of Adam, man's entire nature was wounded. This original sin not only affected the body and the sensitive powers but also (and more importantly) that in us which is spiritual and rational, the intellect and will. If our Savior assumed only a human body then only the body is healed

---

[41]*Ibid.*, (159), p. 68.

by him. As St. Paul observed, the deep wound caused by Adam's misuse of his free-will could only be healed by the free act of the new Adam. Unless Christ possessed a fully human soul he was not capable of a free and fully human act. Jesus Christ is truly man.

c) Jesus is one Person. This truth was defended by the Council of Ephesus against Nestorianism. Nestorius, the Patriarch of Constantinople, began by denying Mary's dignity as the Mother of God:

> They ask...whether Mary may be called Theotokos. Has God then a mother? In that case we must excuse pagans, who spoke of mothers of the gods. Paul is not a liar when he affirms that the Godhead in Christ is without father or mother or genealogy of any kind. Mary did not give birth to God. A creature cannot deliver her Creator, but only a man who is the instrument of the divinity. I honor this garment which he uses, for the sake of him who is hidden within and that cannot be separated from the vesture it wears. I separate the two natures, even while I unite my respect. See what it means. The one who was formed in the womb of Mary was not God himself, but God assumed him, and because of him who assumes, the one assumed is also called God.[42]

By taking this position, Nestorius attacked the unity of person in Christ. He held that in Christ there were not two natures but two persons. This novel teaching caused a storm of controversy and greatly offended the people of the East who had a strong devotion to the Mother of God. They instinctively knew that if Mary was denied the dignity of divine motherhood their faith would be weakened and all that they held concerning her Son would be placed in jeopardy.

St. Cyril of Alexandria rejected this teaching and issued his famous *Twelve Condemnations of Nestorian Errors Concerning Christ.*[43] He also sent letters to Nestorius and to Pope Celestine who condemned the heresy. Nestorius refused to yield and called for a general Council. The Emperor Theodosius, with the acquiescence of the Pope, did just that and a great Council gathered at Ephesus in 431. Nestorius was summoned three times to appear at the Council but refused and sent back contemptuous replies. The Council called forth witnesses and proceeded to condemn and depose Nestorius. His false teachings were repudiated and the traditional Catholic teaching was restated with greater clarity:

[42]Charles J. Hefele, *op. cit.*, Vol. III, p., 12.
[43]Denzinger-Schönmetzer, *Enchiridion Symbolorum, op. cit.*, (252-263), p. 93-96.

For we do not say that the nature of the Word became man by undergoing change; nor that is was transformed into a complete man consisting of soul and body. What we say, rather, is that by uniting to himself in his own person a body animated by a rational soul, the Word has become man in an inexpressible and incomprehensible way and has been called the Son of Man; not merely according to will or complacency, but not by merely assuming a person either. And we say that the natures that are brought together into true unity are different; still, from both there is one Christ and Son; not as though the difference between the natures were taken away by their union, but rather both divinity and humanity produce the perfection of our one Lord, Christ and Son, by their inexpressible and mysterious joining into unity.... It was not that first an ordinary human being was born of the holy Virgin, and then the Word descended upon that man; but in virtue of the union he is said to have undergone birth according to the flesh from his mother's womb, since he claims as his own birth, the generation of his own flesh.... Thus [the holy Fathers] have not hesitated to call the holy Virgin *Mother of God*.[44]

St. Cyril and the Council began by affirming that "Emmanuel is truly God, and the holy Virgin is, therefore, Mother of the Word of God." This statement implicitly maintains that since the child born of Mary was a divine person, Mary was mother of the one she bore in her womb. Mothers give birth not to natures but to children, that is, to persons: therefore to call Mary "Mother of God" is clearly to affirm the true doctrine of the Incarnation. Mary is literally the Mother of God in two ways: first, in her maternity she contributed everything to the formation of Christ's human nature, as every mother contributes to the unborn child in her womb; and second, she conceived and bore the Second Person of the Blessed Trinity according to the human nature that the Eternal Son assumed. To affirm the *Theotokos* is to believe in God the Son made man. This title given by the Church to Mary implicitly reveals that her entire life was enfolded in the mystery of Triune love: She is daughter of the Father, mother of the Son, and spouse of the Holy Spirit. This Marian doctrine protects the central truth of the Christian religion.

The Council taught that the Son was not united to a being which already existed but that Christ's human nature, when first created by God, was not given a solely human existence for even a single moment. From the very beginning it existed, not as an independent nature or essence but as the human nature of the Son. Christ's human nature was united to his divinity in a union so intimate that even the analogy of our own union of soul and body

---

[44]*Ibid.*, (250-251) pp. 92-93.

as man is inadequate. Using the more precise terminology of the Church, we see that "the Word of God the Father was hypostatically united to flesh and that Christ is one having his own flesh, that is, one person who is both God and man." The word hypostatic means that the two natures of Christ are united *personally*. This was done in such a wondrous fashion that, although the source from which the union was effected was two distinct natures (these remaining essentially unchanged), the being in which the union was accomplished was one person or individual (*hypostasis*) and that individual was divine.

This doctrinal teaching is of vital importance if we are to understand the dogmatic foundation for the devotion to the Sacred Heart, which focuses upon the human heart of the divine Savior as a proper object of adoration. This is because, as we shall see later, the heart is part of Christ's sacred humanity. The Council Fathers issued the following condemnation of Nestorius which was received with universal rejoicing by the people of Ephesus:

> As, in addition to other things, the impious Nestorius has not obeyed our citation, and did not receive the holy bishops who were sent by us to him, we were compelled to examine his ungodly doctrines. We discovered that he had held and published impious doctrines in his letters and treatises, as well as in discourses which he delivered in this city, and which have been testified to. Urged by the canons, and in accordance with the letter of our most holy father and fellow-servant Coelestine, the Roman bishop, we have come, with many tears, to this sorrowful sentence against him, namely, that our Lord Jesus Christ, whom he has blasphemed, decrees by the holy Synod that Nestorius be excluded from the episcopal dignity, and from all priestly communion.[45]

Nestorius weakened the redeeming work of Christ through his denial that our Lord's humanity was the vehicle of our redemption. In his anathemas directed against St. Cyril, he condemns those who maintain "that the flesh which is united with God the Word is by the power of its own nature life-giving."[46] This is because the heresiarch denied that this flesh truly belonged to the Word. It was predicated to someone (a human person) other than God. This "someone" is linked to God by dignity and by the Godhead's divine indwelling. The Fathers of Ephesus repudiated such thinking and

---

[45]Hefele, *op. cit.*, Vol. III, p. 51.

[46]*Ibid.*, p. 37. We attribute these anathemas to Nestorius by convention; they are probably spurious, but they nonetheless reflect the views held by Nestorius at that time.

divine indwelling. The Fathers of Ephesus repudiated such thinking and agreed with St. Cyril who anathematized those who do not profess "that the flesh of the Lord is life-giving and that it belongs to the very Word of God."[47]

Nestorius, quite logically, also condemned those who "in confessing the sufferings of the flesh ascribed these also to the Logos of God."[48] Since the man Jesus was only the temple or vesture of the Word, only a man died. The Council of Ephesus again sided with Cyril who said,

> The Word of God suffered in the flesh, and was crucified in the flesh, and experienced death in the flesh, and became first born from the dead, inasmuch as he is, as God, both life and giver of life.[49]

Jesus Christ is one person.

d) Jesus has two distinct natures. It was Eutyches (378-454), the Archimandrite of a monastery at Constantinople, who attacked this teaching. The heresiarch's strong opposition to Nestorianism led him into the opposite heresy which taught that when the divine nature had been united to the human nature in the person of Christ, his human nature was merged into the divine in such a way that from the first moment of the Incarnation the human nature was absorbed and only the divine nature remained. This heresy later came to be known as Monophysitism (*monos* - one; *physis* - nature).

Flavian, the Patriarch of Constantinople, accused Eutyches of Apollinarist tendencies and called him to defend himself before a local synod. After delaying for some time he finally arrived at the synod. When asked, "Do you confess the existence of two natures in Christ even after the Incarnation, and that Christ is consubstantial with us?" he responded, "I confess that before the union Christ was of two natures, but after the union I confess only one nature."[50] Eutyches was deposed and excommunicated by the synod; but through the influence of his friend, the eunuch Chrysaphius, he received the protection of the Emperor. Both Eutyches and Flavian appealed to Rome for the support of Pope Leo I. The Pope, after carefully studying the matter, condemned Eutyches and confirmed the action of Flavian and the bishops. He issued his decision in a Dogmatic Letter to Flavius, otherwise known as "The Tome of Leo". This Tome was subsequently accepted at the Council of Chalcedon and was incorporated in its totality into the Council's teaching.

---

[47]Denzinger-Schönmetzer, *op. cit.*, (262), p. 95.
[48]Hefele, *op. cit.*, p. 37.
[49]Denzinger-Schönmetzer, *op. cit.*, (263), p. 96.
[50]Hefele, *op. cit.*, p. 202.

This fifth-century text bears eloquent testimony to the Church's clear understanding of our Lord's person and mission. The following quotation, taken from the Tome, refers to the heart of the matter:

> Therefore, the proper character of each nature was kept inviolate, and together they were united in one person. Thus was lowliness assumed by majesty, weakness by power, mortality by eternity; and a nature that could not be defiled was united to one that could suffer in order to repay the debt attaching to our state. Hence, as was suitable for the alleviation of our distress, one and the same mediator between God and men, himself man, Christ Jesus, was both mortal and immortal under different aspects. In the full and perfect nature of true man, therefore, the true God was born—perfect in every characteristic proper to us as well as in every one proper to himself.
>
> And so the Son of God, descending from his heavenly throne, yet not leaving the glory of the Father, enters into this world's weakness and is generated in a new manner: because, though invisible in his divine nature, he has become visible in ours; and, though surpassing comprehension, he has wished to be comprehended; though remaining prior to all time, he has taken on existence in time; and, though Lord of the universe, he has hidden his limitless majesty and assumed the form of a servant. God though he is, subject neither to suffering nor death, he has not disdained to become man, subject to both suffering and the law of death. With a new birth too he has been born: for a virgin undefiled, though experiencing no carnal pleasure, furnished the substance for his human flesh. From his mother, our Lord received his nature, but no guilt. Yet the miraculous manner of our Lord Jesus Christ's birth, born as he was from the womb of a virgin, does not make his nature any different from ours. For the same person is true God and true man; and there is no deception in this unity in which the lowliness of man and the dignity of God are joined. For, as God, he suffers no change because of his condescension, nor as man, is he absorbed by the divine dignity; for each nature performs the functions proper to itself, yet in conjunction with the other nature: The Word does what is proper to the Word, and the humanity what is proper to the humanity. The one shines forth in miracles; the other is the subject of mistreatment. And as the Word does not leave aside the glory that he has, equal to the Father's, neither does the humanity relinquish the nature of our race.[51]

The Council of Chalcedon, which soon followed (451), was indisputably the work of Pope Leo I. The Council was attended by over 600 bishops and was to remain the largest council of the Church until Vatican II. When the

---

[51]Denzinger-Schönmetzer, *op. cit.*, (293-294), pp. 103-104.

Nicene Creed and Leo's Tome were read in the Council hall, the jubilant Fathers cried out: "This is the faith of the Fathers. This is the faith of the apostles. This is the faith of all of us.... Peter has spoken through Leo!"[52]

In addition to fully endorsing this teaching, the Council also wished to proclaim a shorter summary of this doctrine. The Fathers wished to affirm the awful mystery of the hypostatic union in which two natures remained truly distinct yet were bound together by a single divine personality. The Council declared:

> Following the holy Fathers, therefore, we all with one accord teach the profession of faith in the one identical Son, our Lord Jesus Christ. We declare that he is perfect both in his divinity and in his humanity, truly God and truly man composed of body and rational soul; that he is consubstantial with the Father in his divinity, consubstantial with us in his humanity, like us in every respect except for sin. We declare that in his divinity he was begotten of the Father before time, and in his humanity he was begotten in this last age of Mary the Virgin, the Mother of God, for us and for our salvation. We declare that the one selfsame Christ, only-begotten Son and Lord, must be acknowledged in two natures without any commingling or change or division or separation; that the distinction between the natures is in no way removed by their union but rather that the specific character of each nature is preserved and they are united in one person and one hypostasis. We declare that he is not split or divided into two persons, but that there is one self-same only-begotten Son, God the Word, the Lord Jesus Christ. This the prophets have taught about him from the beginning; this Jesus Christ himself taught us; this the creed of the Fathers has handed down to us.
>
> As these truths, therefore, have been formulated with all possible accuracy and care, the holy, ecumenical council has ordained that no one may bring forward or put into writing or devise or entertain or teach to others any other faith.[53]

Jesus Christ has two distinct natures.

Conclusion

In commenting on the definition of Chalcedon, Pius XII, in his encyclical *Sempiternus Rex*, states:

> This profound doctrine, derived from the Gospels, does not differ from the decree of the Council of Ephesus and while it rejects

---

[52]Pius XII, *Sempiternus Rex*, AAS 43 (1951), p. 633.
[53]Denzinger-Schönmetzer, *op. cit.*, (301-303), pp. 108-109.

Eutyches, it does not spare Nestorius; and with it the dogmatic definition of the Council of Chalcedon is in perfect harmony when it affirms
clearly and precisely in the following words that in Christ there are two
distinct natures but one person....

If it is asked how it happens that the Council of Chalcedon used
such clear and efficacious language in refuting error, we think it is
because it avoided ambiguity and used the most apt terms. In the
definitions of Chalcedon the same meaning is given to the two words
"person" and "hypostasis" (*prosopon-hypostasis*), while the word "nature" (*physis*) has another sense and its meaning is never attributed to
the other two.

Hence it is wrong to say that the Council of Chalcedon corrected
what the Council of Ephesus had defined, as the Nestorians and
Eutychians once stated and as some modern historians hold. On the
contrary, one Council completes the other in such a way that the
harmonious synthesis of the fundamental doctrine about Christ became more apparent in the second and third Ecumenical Councils
held in Constantinople.[54]

This doctrinal achievement of Chalcedon, which is the summit of the
dogmatic edifice built by Nicea, Constantinople and Ephesus, gives us the
Church's final classic and definitive outlines of the mystery of the Incarnation.
From this time onward the Church prayed and meditated upon this mystery.
Her theologians, saints, mystics and faithful brought to light different aspects
of this awesome mystery by their prayerful reflection. Papal and conciliar
teachings have only refined and clarified these most fundamentally essential
dogmatic statements of truth proclaimed by these early councils.

In its totality, we may see the clarity of the truth which the Church
proclaims to the world concerning the person of Christ. The essentials of this
truth may be summarized in the following manner:

- that Christ assumed a real and not just an apparent body;
  He was born of a woman, from whom he received a truly
  human nature.
- that in becoming man, he assumed not only a body but also
  a rational soul, with intellect and will. Christ therefore had
  a divine and human mind, a divine and human will.
- that the two natures in Christ are united to form one individual. Christ is one person, the second person of the
  Trinity.

---

[54]Pius XII, *Sempiternus Rex*, AAS 43 (1951) p. 635-636.

- that in Christ each of the two natures remains unimpaired, they are not confused or changed in their respective properties; nor are they divided or separated, as though merely co-existing side by side.
- that in becoming man, Christ was and remains true God, one in nature with the Father. When St. Paul speaks of God "emptying himself" to become man, this does not mean that God somehow ceased to be God.
- that even as man, Christ is absolutely sinless; He not only did not sin, but he could not sin because he was God; only in the spurious supposition that Christ has two persons is sin conceivable, since the human person might then commit sin, while the divine person would be perfectly holy. Since Christ was utterly sinless, he was also free from concupiscence or unruly passions, and also free from such effects of concupiscence as positive ignorance or error.
- that the reason for the Incarnation was redemptive; Christ was born into the world "for our salvation," to undergo the meritorious death that, except for this mortality, would have been impossible.
- that Mary is consequently not only Mother of Christ but Mother of God, since He was "born of Mary" in time who is begotten of the Father in eternity.
- that, since the Savior was one person, whatever he did (or does) was (and is) done simultaneously by both natures, although in different ways. When Christ talked and walked and ate and slept and died, it was the God-man who did all these things. When he worked the miracles of healing disease, calming the storm at sea, and raising the dead, it too was the God-man who did all these things. Now at the right hand of his Father, it is the same God-man who is our heavenly high priest and who on the last day will come to judge the living and the dead.[55]

As we can see, such truths will have an effect upon the manner in which we speak about Christ. For example, eternity will be related to his divinity and temporality to his humanity. Both however are related to a concrete subject, i.e., an individual person. This is why, as we have briefly seen, the title

---

[55]J. Hardon, *The Catholic Catechism* (Garden City, NY: Doubleday & Co., Inc., 1975), pp. 140-141.

of *Theotokos* is most fittingly applied to Mary:

"Mary is the <u>Mother</u> of God"
/
one who exercises maternal function to <u>Him</u>
/
(Person of Divine nature who is God)

This truth is further illustrated by the fact that we may say: "God died for our sins." Now of course it is impossible to kill divinity or God but Jesus did die for our sins and he is an individual subject. Divinity did not watch from the cross as the Gnostics and Docetists claimed, but each part of our Lord's being intensely experienced that which was proper to it. The qualities of divinity and humanity are of the same person. Jesus loves us with a human love of such wondrous depth that we cannot begin to imagine it and an eternal love so infinite and magnanimous that it transcends the understanding.

It is here, in the mystery of His love, in the *mystery* of the Incarnation, that the devotion to the Sacred Heart of Jesus has its dogmatic foundations. Here, in the core of the mystery of the God-man, the human mind is dumbfounded. Jesus is the only one who became the God-man and he tells us little of what it is like. We must avoid the ever-present temptation to which people so frequently succumb: that when confronted with a mystery, we latch on to only part of it rather than accept the mystery in its totality. These great truths of the Incarnation clearly set forth the reasons why we must honor the heart of Jesus—our Lord's heart is hypostatically united to his divine Person.

When we speak of honor or veneration of the Sacred Heart it is important to know with precision what we are saying. There is a distinction between the one to whom the honor is given and the reason why honor is given. There is, however, a unity of subject—only one honor is given. In Catholic theology there exist two basic types of honor: 1) *latria*, which is adoration proper to the uncreated (God) and 2) *dulia*, which is honor or veneration proper to created excellence (man and angel). To Christ, the Incarnate Word, *latria* is due to his person, for he is divine. In classical times, if a man was to have won a race, he was given a wreath or garland: this wreath honors the head but it is the *person* who is honored by this. In like manner, when we speak of Christ's Precious Blood or his Sacred Heart, *latria* is called for because we always honor the person. Here a further distinction must be made for the sake of clarity, that within the cult of honor itself there are two types: 1) proper, which is given to the person, and 2) relative, which is given to a thing associated to a person (as one would honor a picture of the pope, a loved one, an image or a relic). Accordingly, we relatively adore the cross, not properly, but as it is associated to the person of Christ and his total gift of self. Here we turn to the Angelic Doctor or *Doctor communis Ecclesiae*, St. Thomas Aquinas. St. Thomas beautifully synthesizes Catholic teaching in the third part of the *Summa Theologica* where he brilliantly sets forth the fittingness of the adoration of Christ's humanity:

> If therefore in one man there are several causes of honor, for instance, rank, knowledge, and virtue, the honor given to him will be one in respect of the person honored but several in respect of the causes of honor; for it is the man that is honored, both on account of knowledge and by reason of his virtue.
>
> Since, therefore, in Christ there is but one Person of the divine and human natures, and one hypostasis, and one suppositum, He is given one adoration and one honor on the part of the Person adored; but on the part of the cause for which He is honored we can say that there are several adorations, for instance that He receives one honor on account of His uncreated knowledge, and another on account of His created knowledge. But if it be said that there are several persons or hypostases in Christ, it would follow that there would be, absolutely speaking, several adorations. And this is what is condemned in the Councils. For it is written in the chapters of Cyril: "If anyone dare to say that the man assumed should be adored besides the Divine Word, as though these were distinct persons, and does not rather honor the Emmanuel with one single adoration, according as the Word was made flesh, let him be anathema."

St. Thomas continues pointing out the two ways in which we may comprehend the adoration due to Christ's sacred humanity.

> As stated above (A. I.) adoration is properly due to the subsisting hypostasis: yet the reason for honoring may be something non-subsistent, on account of which the person, in whom it is, is honored. And so the adoration of Christ's humanity may be understood in two ways. First, so that the humanity is the thing adored, and thus to adore the flesh of Christ is nothing else than to adore the incarnate Word of God, just as to adore a King's robe is nothing else than to adore a robed King. And in this sense the adoration of Christ's humanity is the adoration of *latria*. Secondly, the adoration of Christ's humanity may be taken as given by reason of its being perfected with every gift of grace. And so in this sense the adoration of Christ's humanity is the adoration not of *latria* but of *dulia*. So that one and the same Person of Christ is adored with *latria* on account of His Divinity, and with *dulia* on account of His perfect humanity. Nor is this unfitting. For the honor of *latria* is due to God the Father Himself on account of his Godhead; and the honor of *dulia* on account of the dominion by which He rules

over creatures. Therefore on Ps. 7:1, O Lord my God, in Thee have I hoped, a gloss says: "Lord of all by power, to Whom 'dulia' is due: God of all creation, to whom 'latria' is due."[56]

Applying the principles set forth by the Angelic Doctor, we can see that the Devotion to the Sacred Heart calls for proper *latria* insofar as the Heart is united to the very Person of our Lord, who is God. The Church and her greatest theologians have always taught this concerning the adoration due to the Sacred Humanity of Christ. St. Thomas bases his teaching upon the Second Council of Constantinople, the Chapters of St. Cyril of Alexandria preserved in the great Council of Ephesus and St. John Damascene's *De Fide Orthodoxa*.

Our Lord's physical heart is venerated not for itself but because it belongs to the Divine Person of the Redeemer. The Savior's divine and human love as *symbolized* by his wounded heart are not the proper objects of honor but the *ratio honoris* or reason for it. From this we can see that our Lord's heart is the object of a two-fold cult of *latria*: one proper, because of the uncreated excellence of the divine person of the Word with whom it is united; and the other relative, when considered as the *symbol* of the divine love. We should also mention that according to the teaching of St. Thomas, the Heart of the Savior is also the object of a cult of relative *dulia* when considered as a symbol of the created charity which informs his human will.

The Heart of the Incarnate Word has been universally acknowledged by popes, theologians, saints and the faithful as the most fitting symbol of the love with which the divine Redeemer loves his Eternal Father and all mankind. The adoration of the Sacred Heart of Christ, as we have seen, is soundly based upon Catholic doctrine concerning the Person of Christ. Pius VI, in his constitution *Auctorem Fidei*, which dealt with the Jansenist crisis (which we shall study in greater detail in the historical section), clearly defended the adoration of Christ's sacred humanity:

> Those who adore the heart of Christ adore it as it is. They are worshiping the heart of the person of the Word, to whom it is inseparably united—even as the bloodless body of Christ in the three days of death was adorable in the sepulchre without separation from the divinity.[57]

This same teaching was again to be proclaimed by Pius XII:

---

[56] St. Thomas Aquinas, *Summa Theologica*, P. III, Q. 25, a. 1 & 2.
[57] Denzinger-Schönmetzer, *op. cit.*, (2663), p. 535.

Nothing therefore prevents our adoring the Sacred Heart of Jesus Christ as having a part in and being the natural and expressive symbol of the abiding love with which the divine Redeemer is still on fire for mankind. Though it is no longer subject to varying emotions of this mortal life, yet it lives and beats and is united inseparably with the Person of the divine Word and, in Him and through Him, with the divine Will. Since then the Heart of Christ is overflowing with love both human and divine and rich with the treasure of all graces which our Redeemer acquired by His life, sufferings and death, it is therefore the enduring source of that charity which His Spirit pours forth on all the members of His Mystical Body.[58]

So solid is the dogmatic foundation for this devotion that Pope Pius XII goes on to state:

In truth, if the arguments brought forward which form the foundation for the devotion to the pierced Heart of Jesus are duly pondered, it is surely clear that there is no question here of some ordinary form of piety which anyone at his own whim may treat as of little consequence or set aside as inferior to others....[59]

Pope Pius bases the latreutic worship of the Heart of Christ upon two points: 1) the truth of the hypostatic union and 2) the heart as the natural sign and symbol of Christ's love for mankind. Here the Holy Father clearly demonstrates the strength of the devotion's doctrinal foundation which rests upon an article of faith.

That all may understand more exactly the teachings which the selected texts of the Old and New Testament furnish concerning this devotion, they must clearly understand the reasons why the Church gives the highest form of worship to the Heart of the divine Redeemer. As you well know, venerable brethren, the reasons are two in number. The first, which applies also to the other sacred members of the Body of Jesus Christ, rests on that principle whereby we recognize that His Heart, the noblest part of human nature, is hypostatically united to the Person of the divine Word. Consequently, there must be paid to it that worship of adoration with which the Church honors the Person of the Incarnate Son of God Himself. We are dealing here with an article of faith, for it has been solemnly defined in the general Council of Ephesus and the second Council of Constantinople.

The other reason which refers in a particular manner to the Heart

---

[58] Pius XII, *Haurietis Aquas*, AAS 48 (1956), p. 336.

[59] *Ibid.*, p. 346. (We shall discuss this point further in the final section which deals with the devotion and the magisterium.)

of the divine Redeemer, and likewise demands in a special way that the highest form of worship be paid to it, arises from the fact that His Heart, more than all the other members of His body, is the natural sign and symbol of His boundless love for the human race. "There is in the Sacred Heart," as our predecessor of immortal memory, Leo XIII, pointed out,"the symbol and express image of the infinite love of Jesus Christ which moves us to love in return.[60]

In scholastic terminology we may speak of our Lord's physical Heart as the *signum* (sign) or *symbolum* (symbol). The *res signata* (the thing signified) is the whole Person of Christ in his three-fold love (sensible, infused, divine) and the *ratio significatus* is the relation between the two.

The wounded Heart of Christ and the three-fold love it signifies are necessary elements of the devotion. The Heart, as we have seen, is the *symbolum* and the three-fold love is the *ratio* or motive for the cult offered to the Heart of Jesus. In fact, the *ratio* for the relative cult of *latria* is the Word's divine uncreated love.

Although our Lord's Heart and three-fold love are part of the essential object of the devotion, its ultimate or final object is the divine Person of the Word since both truly belong to Him. Simply stated it is our divine Lord and Savior Jesus Christ who is adored in his glorious Heart!

As we said at the beginning of our Christological study, the devotion to the Sacred Heart also leads one into the center of the mystery of the Holy Trinity. Since the devotion has as its object the divine uncreated love of the Word, the love of the most Blessed Trinity is also an integral part of the total object of the devotion to the Sacred Heart. This divine uncreated love is common to all Three Persons and is the *ratio* for all the glorious gifts given to humanity. Therefore since the Word made flesh reveals to us the unseen love of the Father and the Holy Spirit, we must conclude that the Triune love is to be included as a proper and immediate object of the devotion.[61]

Here in the great unchanging Catholic truths concerning the mystery of the Incarnation we may see clearly the solid doctrinal foundation of the devotion to the wounded Heart of Christ—the Heart of the God-Man.

---

[60]*Ibid.*, p. 316.

[61] An excellent study of the relationship between the most Holy Trinity and the Sacred Heart in Pius XII's *Haurietis Aquas* can be found in Card. Luigi Ciappi OP, *The Heart of Christ the Center of the Mystery of Salvation* (Rome: CdC Publ., 1983) pp. 125-161.

II.

The History of the Devotion

With the Incarnation of our Lord, history has taken on a new significance. Christ's direct intervention has elevated and transformed human history to a higher plane where it takes on a supernatural significance. Because of this divine entrance, the importance of history and the historical argument cannot be overlooked.

We are turning to history here to examine the dynamic living tradition of the Church, ever receptive to the inspiration of the Holy Spirit which "will blow where it will" (Jn. 3:9). It is important in this study to understand the concept of development or expansion of Christian teaching. Here we again turn to Cardinal Newman's *Essay on the Development of Christian Doctrine*:

> ...the increased expansion of the Christian creed and ritual, and the variations which have attended the process in the case of individual writers and churches, are the necessary attendants on any philosophy or polity which takes possession of the intellect and heart, and has had any wide or extended dominion ... from the nature of the human mind; time is necessary for the full comprehension and perfection of great ideas; and ... the highest and most wonderful truths, though communicated to the world once and for all by inspired teachers could not be comprehended all at once by the recipients, but, as being received and transmitted by minds not inspired and through media which were human have required only the longer time and deeper thought for their full elucidation.[1]

---

[1]Newman, *Essay on the Development of Christian Doctrine, op. cit.*, pp. 29-30.

These profound truths concerning development in Christianity and the dynamic nature of the living tradition of the Church are of vital importance in our study of the historical origins of the devotion to the Heart of Jesus.

This understanding of the vital importance of history in the Church's tradition finds clear expression in the teachings of Vatican Council II.

> This tradition which comes from the Apostles develops in the Church with the help of the Holy Spirit. For there is a growth in the understanding of the realities and the words which have been handed down. This happens through the contemplation and study made by believers, who treasure these things in their hearts (see Luke, 2:19, 51) through a penetrating understanding of the spiritual realities which they experience and through the preaching of those who have received through episcopal succession the sure gift of truth. For as the centuries succeed one another, the Church constantly moves forward toward the fullness of divine truth until the words of God reach their complete fulfillment in her. (*Dei Verbum*, n. 8)[2]

The Problem of the Origin of the Devotion

Devotion to the Sacred Heart of Jesus was often viewed in the past as a 17th-century phenomenon based solely upon the private revelations of St. Margaret Mary Alacoque. This viewpoint is found in both the *Dictionnaire de Spiritualité*[3] and the *Dictionnaire de Théologie Catholique*.[4] However, a more careful study reveals that the earliest Christians contemplated the crucified Savior with deep veneration and love. They meditated upon his wounds, with a special emphasis upon the wound in his side. At a later date, under the inspiration of the Holy Spirit (long before our Lord revealed his heart in apparitions), men came to see in the opened side the wounded Heart of the Lamb. These Christians were understandably drawn to venerate that heart and applied to it what the early Christians had taught of the open wound of the side. But before we begin tracing the lengthy history of the devotion, it would be best first to establish a general framework for this investigation.

Devotion to the Sacred Heart of Jesus is intimately associated with the most fundamental teachings of the Gospel: a) Jesus is the personified revela-

---

[2]Walter M. Abbott, ed. *The Documents of Vatican II* (NY: American Press, 1966) p. 116; cf. *Sacrosantum Oecumenicum Concilium Vaticanum II* (Typis Polyglottis Vaticani, 1966), 429-430."

[3]Auguste Hamon, "Devotion au Sacré Coeur," *Dictionnaire de Spiritualité* vol. II, par. 5 (Paris: Benuchesnenet Ses Fils, 1948) p. 1023.

[4]J. Bainvel "La Devotion au Sacré Coeur," *Dictionnaire de Théologie Catholique* Vol. III, par. 1 (Paris: Librairie Letouzey Et Aré, 1938), p. 303.

tion of the Father's infinite love; b) as true God and true man, he has a personal interest in every human being ("But as for you the very hairs of your head are numbered" Mt. 11:30); c) this caring love was seen from the very outset to be symbolized in Christ's human heart. These truths have had profound effects on the Church throughout its earthly pilgrimage, especially evident in numerous saints and theologians, but also in the faithful. In the words of Pius XII:

> We are convinced, then, that the devotion which We are fostering to the love of God and Jesus Christ for the human race by means of the revered symbol of the pierced Heart of the crucified Redeemer *has never been altogether unknown* to the piety of the faithful, although it has become more clearly known and has spread in a remarkable manner throughout the Church in quite recent times. Particularly was this so after our Lord Himself had privately revealed this divine secret to some of His children to whom He had granted an abundance of heavenly gifts, and whom He had chosen as His special messengers and heralds of this devotion.[5] [Emphasis mine]

By exhorting scholars to study the historical roots of the devotion, Pius XII emphasizes the great importance of history in understanding the development of the Church's teachings.

Since the veneration of the Sacred Heart is an outgrowth of devotion to Christ's sacred humanity, its history is to be found in a deliberate return to the fundamental conceptions drawn out of and elaborated by theology in the first millennium of the Christian era. Although it must be admitted that it was only after the year 1000 that the devotion took on definitively recognizable forms, its roots lie deep in Scripture (as we have seen) and patristic theology. The Fathers fostered those vital elements which implicitly led to the external manifestations of the devotion. This viewpoint is clearly contained in the writings of Pius XII:

> In fact, there have *always been* men specially dedicated to God who, following the example of the beloved Mother of God, of the Apostles and the great Fathers of the Church, have practiced the devotion of thanksgiving, adoration and love towards the most sacred human nature of Christ, and especially towards the wounds by which His body was torn when He was enduring suffering for our salvation. [emphasis mine]
>
> Moreover, is there not contained in those words "My Lord and My God" which St. Thomas the Apostle uttered, and which showed

---

[5]Pius XII, *Haurietis Aquas*, AAS 48 (1956), p. 338.

he had been changed from an unbeliever into a faithful follower, a profession of faith, adoration and love, mounting up from the wounded nature of his Lord to the majesty of the divine Person?

It must not be said that this devotion has taken its origin from some private revelation of God and has suddenly appeared in the Church; rather, it has blossomed forth of its own accord as a result of that lively faith and burning devotion of men who were drawn towards the adorable Redeemer and His glorious wounds which they saw as irresistible proofs of that unbounded love.[6]

The central point of the devotion is the symbol of our Lord's human heart from which all graces flow to redeem and sanctify mankind. This is seen in the prayers for the Solemnity:

Jesus has loved us with a human heart and His Heart is still burning with love for us: To show us the greatness of His love, He wished His Heart to be pierced with a lance and He showed it to us as a striking image of His love.... Almighty and Eternal God, You willed that Your only begotten Son should be pierced by the soldier's lance as he hung upon the cross so that from His open Heart might be poured out upon us streams of mercy and grace. Grant that the Heart of Your Son ever burning with love for us may inflame our hearts with love for Him and enkindle in us a true love for others. Thus the hearts of all men united amongst themselves by their mutual love will be united within the Heart of Your Son by their love for Him.[7]

Pius XII, quoting Leo XIII in *Haurietis Aquas*, points out that "there is in the Sacred Heart the symbol and express image of the infinite love of Jesus Christ which moves us to love him in return."[8]

Hugo Rahner states that the Fathers and theologians from St. Augustine and St. Cyril of Alexandria down to St. Peter Canisius speak of the fountain of living waters (of charity) as taking their source in the side of Christ.[9] By this the Fathers meant that the Spirit was poured forth on mankind because he who possessed the Spirit in all its fullness had immolated his Heart. As a direct result, the Church and all that it effects (i.e., the sacraments and the life of grace) flow out from the Heart of Christ as the work of the Holy Spirit.

---

[6]*Ibid.*, pp. 338-340.

[7]National Office Apostleship of Prayer Eucharistic Crusade, *Liturgy of the Mystery of the Heart of Christ* (Orlando, Fla.: S. H. Pub. Center, 1976), p. 102-103.

[8]Pius XII, *Haurietis Aquas, op. cit.*, p. 316; cf. *Annum Sacrum, Acta Leonis* Vol XIX, 1900, p. 76.

[9]Hugo Rahner, "The Beginnings of the Devotion in Patristic Times," in *Heart of the Savior*, ed. by J. Stierli, (New York: Herder Publishing Co., 1958), p. 38.

Because of this truth, asceticism and mysticism in the Church have been constantly nurtured by the reference given to us by St. John of the water flowing from the side of Christ. The early history of the devotion may be truly said to be a history of the interpretation of the following phrase of St. John: "From His heart [*koilia*] shall flow rivers of living water." (Jn. 7:38).

In this section we shall trace the history of the Devotion as it is implicitly found in the writings of the Fathers, down through its various stages of development, culminating in the revelations given to St. Margaret Mary Alacoque.

The Fathers of the Church
The Golden Age: The Second to the Sixth Century

The age of the Fathers of the Church generally coincides with the first Christian millennium. We shall divide this period into two sections: The Golden Age, from the second to the sixth centuries; and the Silver Age, from the seventh to the eleventh century. This era saw the development of the basic elements which became the constant recurring themes of devotion to the Sacred Heart.

The basis of the Fathers' teaching, as we have mentioned, is their statements concerning the Biblical notion of the fountain of living waters which flow from the wounded side of Christ (Jn. 7:37-39, 13:23, 19:33-38). The Spirit is given to man through the death of that Man who possessed the fullness of the Spirit. The Spirit brings forth the Church, the sacraments and the life of grace. It is with a special emphasis that the Fathers see the Church as having been formed from the side of Christ as he died on the cross, just as Eve was formed from the side of Adam as he slept.

The Fathers do not dwell upon an "intellectual" discussion of this event but pass immediately to its implications for the spiritual life: the Christian must drink the waters from this heavenly fountain, and approach through the gate of his side.

Several questions arise here: Did the Fathers connect the objective reality of the redemption in the blood and water which flowed from our Lord's side or heart with the subjective reality of his love as the cause of that Redemption? And did the Fathers view Christ's pierced side or heart as the symbol of the love with which He redeemed us?

For the most part, I have found the answers to these questions to be in the negative but there are some very important texts which do serve as a basis for such thinking.[10] It certainly must be granted (since the Fathers were writing not only on a theoretical but also on a spiritual level) that these rich and ponderous ideas concerning the fountain of grace flowing from our Lord's side or pierced heart, rose up in the heart of the believing Christian in the form of prayer.

We should also remember that the early attacks of the Christological heresies gave a tremendous impetus to the exaltation of Christ's human nature. This in turn led to the development of loving devotions to the blood and wounds of Christ—especially the wound in the side. Also, by the third century in Rome (according to a regulation of Hippolytus), Christians there were directed to meditate upon the pierced side of the Christ at the ninth hour (3:00 p.m.).

Pilgrimages to the Holy Land openly began in 325, due in part to the favorable climate created by the catechumen emperor Constantine. Journeys to the holy places associated with the earthly life of Jesus served, in a special way, to foster devotions to Christ's sacred humanity.

Thanks to the efforts of St. Helen, who worked closely with St. Macarius, the bishop of Jerusalem (313-334), relics of the cross were being venerated throughout the Christian world by the fourth century. Many Christians were to suffer martyrdom by the eighth century at the hands of the Iconoclasts for their devotion to images, especially those of crosses and crucifixes.[11] That these devotions to the cross have a long tradition in the Church can be seen from the fact that the Persians had put the early Christians to death for refusing to trample on the image of the cross. This shows clearly that from a very early date crosses were a part of Christian devotion and were venerated.[12]

Also the early Irish, Gallican, Spanish and Syrian liturgies were filled with reference to the blood, wounds and pierced side of Christ.

Let us now turn our attention to the specific writings of the Fathers which fostered devotion to the Sacred Heart of Jesus. It is important to recall here, regarding the "conflicting" interpretations of the Alexandrian and Ephesian punctuation of John 7:36-39, that the overwhelming majority of Fathers have favored the Ephesian punctuation which *directly* refers to Christ as the source

---

[10]The text from St. Justin already given which was presented in the scriptural section is a fine example of a patristic text with a medieval ring.

[11]The Apostleship of Prayer Directors Service, "Devotion to the Sacred Heart at the Present Time," *The Apostleship of Prayer*, I (January, 1971), p. 19.

[12]*Ibid.*, p. 19. There is also some evidence from the excavations at Herculaeum in Italy that crosses may have been used by the Christians in the first century.

of the living waters. As we have mentioned in the Scripture section, modern exegesis has also confirmed this interpretation.

This interpretation, which sees Christ as the source of the living waters, can be traced back to the followers of St. John the Apostle at Ephesus and probably back to the Beloved Apostle himself. This is the more ancient and authoritative interpretation of the passage. Our first writer, Hippolytus of Rome (130-235), was a pupil of Irenaeus, who had been a disciple of Polycarp of Smyrna, who was a disciple of St. John the Apostle. He was a priest of some importance in the Church of Rome. He was exiled to Sardinia with Pope St. Pontian and died a martyr for the faith. He wrote a commentary on the prophet Daniel. This is the oldest (c. 204 AD) existing exegetical writing of the early Church prior to the writings of Origen. In it he writes:

> This stream of the four waters flowing from Christ we see in the Church. He is the stream of living waters, and he is preached by the four evangelists. Flowing over the whole earth, he sanctifies all who believe in him. This is what the prophet heralded with the words: "Streams flow from his heart [*koilia*]."[13]

It is commonly held that the allusion to a "prophet" is an expression of an ancient tradition which goes back to Ephesus. This tradition sees St. John the Evangelist as "the prophet."

St. Irenaeus (c. 130-202) gives the same doctrine as Hippolytus. He was born in Smyrna and after studying under St. Polycarp (the disciple of St. John) he became the bishop of Lyons in France. After writing several books against the errors of Gnosticism, he died a martyr for the faith. He gives us the earliest reference to the mystery of Christ's heart. For Irenaeus, the water (the Holy Spirit) flows directly to us from Christ. The Church is the channel of living water which flows to us from the heart of Christ:

> Where the Church is, there is the Spirit of God; and where the Spirit of God is, there is the Church and all grace. But the Spirit is truth. Therefore whoever does not partake of this Spirit is not fed at the breast of Mother Church, and cannot drink from the crystal clear spring which flows from the body of Christ.[14]

This teaching preached by St. Irenaeus of Lyons finds a continuing expression in part of the *Acts of the Martyrs of Lyons and Vienna*. In this

---

[13]Hippolytus, *Daniel* I, 1 in G. N. Bonwetsch ed., *Berlin Corpus* (GCS), vol. I p. 1, pg. 29, 1. 11-16.

[14]Irenaeus, *Adversus Haereses* III, 24 1 in J. P. Migne ed., *Patrologiae cursus completus Graeca* Vol. 7 (Paris: Garnier Fratres, 1878), c 966.

fragmentary writing, preserved by Eusebius of Caesarea, it is reported of a deacon named Sanctus that

> ...he himself remained unbending and unyielding, strong in his confession of faith, refreshed and strengthened by the heavenly spring of living water which comes forth from the Heart of Christ.[15]

The martyr Sanctus here beholds a vision of the glorified Christ, the celestial rock from whose interior the fountain of grace flows.

In yet another text, Irenaeus states:

> As the rock gave forth water to drink to the thirsty Jews in the desert, the Rock which was Christ Jesus now gives to believers to drink the spiritual waters which lead to eternal life.[16]

And again:

> Christ suffers and gives life. He is fastened with nails and yet is the source of the living waters. This water is the Spirit.[17]

St. Justin the Martyr (c 100-163) was born a pagan but converted to Christianity at Ephesus. He became a great apologist for the Christian faith and died a martyr in the Flavian Amphitheatre in Rome. For St. Justin also, Christ is the spiritual source of the living waters. He speaks frequently of Christ as "the pierced one" from whom the new Israel is born. In his *Dialogues with the Jew Tryphon* (c. 150) he refers to the human body of Christ (true man) as a source of grace:

> We Christians are the true Israel which springs from Christ, for we are drawn out of his heart [*koilia*] as out of a rock.[18]

Further on he speaks of the glorious witness of Christian martyrdom:

---

[15]Eusebius, *Historia Eccles*, V. 1, 22 in J. P. Migne ed., *Patrologiae cursus completus Graeca* Vol. 20, *op. cit.*, c. 418. We are here following Hugo Rahner who sees in the phrase "ek tes nedyos Christou" a clear reference to John 7:37 and therefore justifies rendering the Greek "from the Heart of Christ." G. A. Williamson in the Penguin edition of Eusebius' *History of the Church* also sees a definite reference to John 7:37 and translates the phrase "from the depths of Christ's being."

[16]Irenaeus, *Adversus Haereses* V, 1, 1 in *Sancti Irenaei*, tr. and ed. W. Wigam Harvey (Cambridge, 1857) vol. 2, p. 315.

[17]*Ibid.*, IV, 18, 2, 1173.

[18]Justin, *Dialogues* 135, 5 *Patrologia cursus completus Graeca* Vol.. 6, *op. cit.*, 787 St. Justin gives us the oldest *explicit* extrabiblical reference to the heart (*kardia*) of Christ in this work.

It is a joy for us to go to death for the name of the glorious rock. He makes living water overflow into the hearts of those who through him love the Father of the universe, and he satiates those who wish to drink of the water of life.[19]

In St. Justin's Biblical and messianic Christology, it is in Christ, "the great Pierced One," that the words of the prophet Zechariah are fulfilled:

And I will pour out upon the house of David and upon the inhabitants of Jerusalem, the Spirit of grace and of prayers. And they shall look upon me whom they have pierced.... In that day there shall be a fountain open to the house of David and to the inhabitants of Jerusalem; for the washing of the sinner.... (Zech. 12:10, 13:1).

Hugo Rahner believes that St. Justin here is "surely" following the tradition of preaching begun by St. John himself.[20]

This same doctrine is also to be found in the writings of St. Cyprian (210-258). He was born in Carthage and became a convert to Christianity. He eventually became bishop of that city and for him is claimed the honor of having died a martyr for the faith. In one of his letters he writes:

Can he who is not inside the Church water from the fountains of the Church? ... The Lord cries out that whoever thirsts should come and drink the rivers of living water which have flowed from his bosom.[21]

St. Ambrose, the great bishop of Milan (339-397), who was to baptize St. Augustine, continued this tradition in the canticle which he wrote in commenting on Psalm 33:

Drink of Christ, for he is the fountain of life. Drink of Christ, for he is the stream whose torrents brought joy to the City of God. Drink of Christ, for he is peace. Drink of Christ, for the streams of living water flow from his bosom.[22]

Apollinaris, the bishop of Hierapolis in Phrygia (160-207), speaks of that unity of the divine and human which was in the redeeming blood of Christ and also of the gift of the Spirit:

---

[19]*Ibid.*, IV, 18, 2, 787.

[20]J. Stierli, ed., *Heart of Savior, op. cit.*, p. 45.

[21]Cyprian, *Epistola*, 73, 10-11.

[22]Ambrose *Enarrationes in 12 Psalmos* I, 33 in J. P. Migne, *Patrologia cursus completus Latina* Vol. 14 (Paris: Garnier Fratres, 1878), 983-984.

> It is Christ who has let his side be pierced, it is he who let flow from
> his wounded side the two streams which make all things new again:
> water and blood, that is, logos and pneuma, word and spirit.[23]

Hugo Rahner states that this text represents the same vision that St. John had
in the Apocalypse which reveals the slaughtered lamb as the source of living
water (Apoc. 7:17, 22:17).[24]

Another theme found in the writings of the Fathers which contributed to
the rise of the devotion is that of the Church being born from the wounded
side of Christ. This sprang from St. Paul's teaching concerning Christ as the
second spiritual Adam (I Cor. 15:45). There are numerous instances of this
teaching in patristic works. The brilliant Latin theologian Tertullian (c.
160-235) states:

> If Adam is a type of Christ then Adam's sleep is a symbol of the death
> of Christ and by the wound in the side of Christ was formed the Church,
> the true Mother of all the living. [25]

St. Augustine, in his commentary on St. John's Gospel, writes:

> The first woman was called Life and Mother of the living. The second
> Adam with bowed head slept on the cross, in order that a spouse might
> be formed for him from that which flowed from his side as he slept.
> Death, by which the dead come to life again! What could be more
> cleansing than this blood? What more healing than this wound?[26]

This teaching of Augustine which is found throughout his writings worked its
way into the popular catechesis of the early Church. The bishop of Carthage,
Quodvultdeus (d. 453), was a friend and disciple of Augustine. In his instruction to the catechumens in his see he writes:

> Now let our Bridegroom climb onto the cross and sleep there in death,
> and let his side be opened and the virgin bride come forth. As once
> from the side of Adam Eve was formed, so let the Church be formed
> now from the side of the dying Christ, as he hangs on the cross. Oh
> wonderful mystery! The bride is born from the bridegroom![27]

---

[23]Apollinaris, *Corpus Apologetarum*, IX, 487.

[24]J. Stierli, ed., *op. cit.*, p. 46.

[25]Tertullian, *De Anima*, 43 in Migne, *Patrologia cursus completus Latina* Vol. 2, *op. cit.*,
1463.

[26]Augustine, *Tractatus in Joannem* IX, 10 in Migne, *Patrologia cursus completus Latina*
Vol. 35, *op. cit.*, 1463.

[27]Quodvultdeus, *De Symbolo ad Catechumenos* in Migne, *Patrologia cursus completus
Latina* Vol. 40, *op. cit.*, 645.

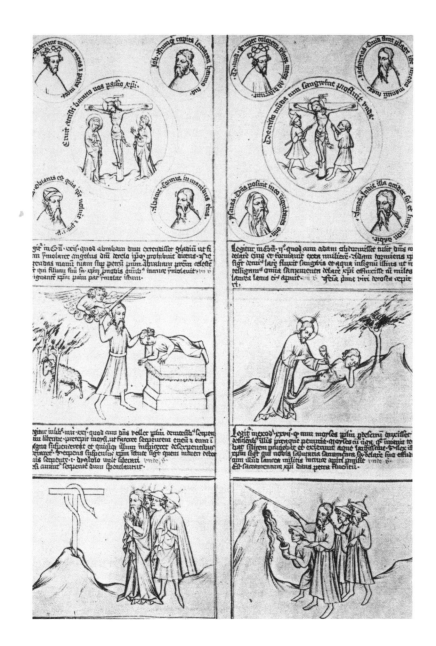

Figure 4: Typological scenes. Biblia Pauperum. Bavaria, 1414.

Figure 5: John upon the bosom of Christ. The Last Supper, Floreffe Bible, c. 1156.

Another theme which is found in the writing of the Fathers, which is intimately connected with the Church being born of the wounded side, is that of the blood and water symbolizing the two chief sacraments of the Church: Baptism and Eucharist. The early Christians were deeply aware of this profound symbolism.

St. John Chrysostom, the eloquent bishop of Constantinople, was born in the year 347 in Antioch (the town in which our Lord's disciples were first called Christians). He writes:

> Nay in addition to this, a wonderful mystery was then effected. "Blood and water at once flowed out of the wound." It is not by mere chance or unwittingly that these two fountains sprang up at this juncture. It is because blood and water are two constitutive elements of the Church. Those already admitted to the sacred rites know this well; those, I mean, who have been regenerated in the waters of Baptism and who in the Eucharist feed on Christ's flesh and blood. It is to this one source that all the Christian mysteries trace back their origin. And so when you apply your lips to this awesome cup, do it as though you drank that

Figure 6: The Gospel Book of Francis II: The crucifixion. Bibliothèque Nationale, Paris.

precious blood from the open side of Christ Himself.[28]

An even more explicit reference to this truth is found in Chrysostom's *Instruction to Catechumens*:

> Do you wish to learn from another source the power of this blood? See where it began to flow, from what spring it flowed down from the cross: it issued from the Master's side. The Gospel relates that when Christ had died and was still hanging on the cross, the soldier approached him and pierced his side with the spear, and at once there came out water and blood. The one was a symbol of Baptism, the other of the mysteries. That soldier, then, pierced his side: he breached the wall of the holy temple, and I found the treasure and acquired the wealth.[29]

We find the same teaching in Chrysostom's counterpart in the West, St. Augustine. The Doctor of Grace states:

> Adam sleeps, that Eve may be born; Christ dies, that the Church may be born. When Adam sleeps, Eve is formed from his side; when Christ is dead, the spear pierces his side that the sacraments may flow forth whereby the Church is formed.[30]

Yet another theme important for the development of the devotion is that of St. John drawing living waters from the Heart of Jesus. Numerous Fathers have written on this theme which was taken from the Gospel of St. John (13:23) where the Beloved Disciple is seen reclining on the bosom of our Lord at the Last Supper.[31]

Paulinus, the bishop of Nola (353-431) was the foremost Christian Latin poet of the Patristic Age. He knew St. Ambrose, St. Martin and St. Augustine and is an excellent example of this patristic theme. He writes in one of his letters:

---

[28]John Chyrsostom, *In Joannem Homil.* 85, J. P. Migne, *Patrologia cursus completus Graeca* Vol. 59, 463.

[29]From St. John's use of such highly significant imagery, we can clearly see how devotion to the wounded heart of the Savior would develop out of the riches of such a text.

[30]Augustine, *Tractate in Joannem* IX,10 in Migne, *Patrologia Latina*, Vol. 35, *op. cit.*, 1463.

[31]In reference to the same scriptural text, St. Ambrose states that there "he became acquainted with the mysteries of the divine wisdom" and likewise Chrysostom writes, "He who was the Son of thunder here drank at the divine fountain." Augustine also states: "John who rested on the bosom of our Lord as he lay at the last supper, drew loftier mysteries from his inmost heart."

So the blessed John who reclined on the Lord's breast, and who drank in a perception deeper than that of all other creatures from the very heart of Wisdom who created all things, became drunk with the Holy Spirit who searcheth even the deep things of God.[32]

Pope St. Gregory the Great (540-604) also speaks of this doctrine. He states:

At the table of the Paschal Mystery, he rested at the eternal fount of life, on the bosom of the Savior. Drawing in the uninterrupted streams of heavenly doctrine, he was filled with divine and mysterious revelations so that his spirit, raised up, contemplated, and his evangelical voice proclaimed "In the beginning was the Word."[33]

Referring to the unity of the divine and human natures in Christ, many of the Fathers often speak of the *manifestations of human love* in Christ in their scriptural commentaries and homilies.[34] Our Lord, being truly man, loved us with a human heart and therefore with a complete and fully human love. From the many instances of this, I have selected two passages for illustration. The first is taken from Eusebius of Caesarea (265-339), the Father of Church History. He writes:

Christ was never severe with the weak nor showed harshness, even to the arrogant and the proud. His heart always showed itself full of sweetness towards all men without exception. To all he showed with authority the things of God.[35]

The second text is taken from St. Augustine:

Are not all the treasures of wisdom and knowledge hidden in Thee reduced to this, that we learn from Thee as something great that Thou are meek and humble of heart?[36]

Another very important patristic theme which gave rise to the devotion is that of *Jesus accepting suffering through his merciful love.* This is mentioned

---

[32]Paulinus, *Epistola* 21, 4 in Migne, *Patrologia Latina*, Vol. 61, *op. cit.*, 251.

[33]Gregory the Great, *Liber Sacramentorum, In Nativ. S. Joannem* in Migne, *Patrologia Latina*, Vol. 78, *op. cit.*, 34.

[34]See Basil, *Epist.* 261, 3 in Migne, *Patrologia Graeca*, Vol. 32, p. 972; Ambrose, *De fide ad Gratianum*, in Migne, *Patrologia Latina*, Vol. 16, 594; Augustine, *Enarr in Ps. LXXXVII*, 3 in Migne, *Patrologia Latina*, Vol. 37, 1111.

[35]Eusebius of Caesarea, *In Isaiam XLII*, v. 2-3 in Migne, *Patrologia Graeca*, Vol. 24, *op. cit.*, 386-387.

[36]Augustine, *De Sancta Virginitate* in *Patrologia Latina*, Vol. 140, *op. cit.*, 416.

constantly throughout the patristic writings. St. Augustine, in commenting upon Psalm 56, puts on the Savior's lips the words: "My heart is ready, O Lord, my heart is ready." And then these thoughts:

> What am I to do? They have dug a ditch for me. While they have set a trap for my feet, I must prepare my heart for resignation. My heart must be ready to suffer.[37]

Hesychius of Jerusalem (c.450), the exegete of the allegorical Alexandrian school, writes: "He has felt great grief strike his heart through love for us. This is why he could say 'My heart is sorrowful unto death'."[38] A Syrian manuscript of the fourth century expresses similar sentiments:

> His heart has been filled with sorrow because of our sins, an effect of love for his creatures who are exposing themselves to doom. He grieves as well for those who are putting him to death. In praying for them with tears, he shows how to deal with those who treat us badly. He shows us how to offer supplication for them.[39]

St. Hilary of Poitiers (c. 315-367), who was called "the Athanasius of the West", was the first great dogmatist and exegete in the West. He introduces in this text an additional theme of *consolation for the suffering Christ*. This is a theme which has always been a part of Christian piety:

> Ready to die for us, he was assailed by another wish reflected to us in the Psalms "I looked for someone to be with me in my suffering and I found no one." He had come to save the lost sheep of Israel, but he found no one to console him and show him compassion in the midst of his anguish.[40]

Lastly, Theodoret of Cyr (393-466) speaks of Christ's redemptive suffering and death as a source of joy to him:

> His crown of thorns was the diadem of his charity, the charity which led him spontaneously to accept the ignominies and torments which would bring him to his death. He calls the day of his death the day of "joy to his heart".[41]

Another patristic theme which emerges is that the heart of the Christian

---

[37] Augustine, *In Psalmo LVI* in Migne, *Patrologia Latina*, Vol. 36, *op. cit.*, 671.

[38] Hesychius, *In Psalmos* 58, v. 17 in Migne, *Patrologia Graeca*, Vol. 93, *op. cit.*, 1318.

[39] *Patrologia Syriaca*, Vol. I ed. by R. Graffin (Paris: Firmin-Didat et Socii, 1894), 562.

[40] Hilary, *In Psalmo 69, 21* in Migne, *Patrologia Latina* Vol. 9, *op. cit.*, 127.

[41] Theodoret, *In Cant.*, III v. 11 in Migne, *Patrologia Graeca*, Vol. 8, *op. cit.*, 127.

who follows in the footsteps of Christ should be like that of his Savior. ("It is now no longer I that live, but Christ lives in me" Gal. 2:20). I have selected two such instances of this theme. The first is from St. John Chrysostom who had such a deep devotion to the Apostle of the Gentiles:

> This heart is higher than the heavens, greater than the earth, more splendid than pure light, more burning than fire...we can affirm with safety that the heart of Paul was as the heart of Christ.[42]

The second quote is taken from St. Gregory the Great, commonly considered by historians as the "Father of the Middle Ages". Much of medieval piety finds its source in his writings. This is especially true of the unity which St. Gregory established among the heart, love and fire. According to Hugo Rahner, this unity worked its way into and contributed to the devotion to the Sacred Heart in the latter Middle Ages. St. Gregory writes:

> Our heart is to be the altar of God. Fire should burn there constantly. There we should constantly feed the flame of our love for God. He who strokes within himself this fire of charity offers himself as a holocaust in the midst of this flame which consumes him. He puts himself as a victim on the altar of his own heart, burning with the ardor of charity.[43]

An additional source of patristic theological reflection which nurtured the devotion is the Fathers' commentaries on the Canticle of Canticles. Although there is no direct link between the two, it cannot be doubted that the imagery contained in this book would arouse Christian love and lead to the devotion. The following select verses point to this connection:

> The king brought me into his storerooms (1:3)
> I languish with love (2:5)
> My dove in the clefts of the rock, in the hollow of the wall, show me
>   thy face (2:14)
> I will seek him whom my soul loveth (3:2)
> [day of Espousals] ...the day of the joy of his heart (3:11)
> Thou hast wounded my heart (4:8)
> Put me as a seal upon thy heart...for love is as strong as death (8:6)

Pope St. Gregory the Great furnishes us with a fine example of how the Fathers interpreted these texts. In his commentary on the Canticle of Can-

---

[42]Chrysostom, *Ad Rom.*, 32, in Migne, *Patrologia Graeca*, Vol. 60, *op. cit.*, 679-680.
[43]Gregory the Great, *Moralia in Job*, in Migne, *Patrologia Latina*, Vol. 76, *op. cit.*, 328.

ticles, he writes:

> Arise, my love, my sister, and come, my dove, in the clefts of the rock, in the hollow places in the wall. By the clefts of the rock I mean the wounds in the hands and feet of Christ hanging freely on the cross. By the hollow places in the wall I mean the wound in his side made by the lance. Like the dove in the rock the simple soul finds in these wounds the food that will strengthen her.[44]

All the commentaries of the Fathers state that the Canticle reflects the relationship of the soul with Christ. Eventually this was to work its way into the devotion to the Heart of Jesus and become a major theme.

The Silver Age: The Seventh to the Eleventh Century

This period is known in Western history as "the Dark Ages." It was a period of social chaos which resulted from the collapse of the Roman Empire and the subsequent barbarian invasions. During this period, many classical works were lost, including the writings of the Fathers. It was also an age in which Christian writers seemed to lack the creative originality which characterized much of the early patristic literature. Fortunately for Christian civilization, both the patristic tradition and learning were preserved in the monasteries. St. Benedict (480-553), seeking refuge from the chaotic distractions of Rome, established his famous monastery at Monte Cassino on a great cliff in a remote region in central Italy. The great "father of western monasticism" composed his famous rule which enables "the heart to become broadened, and with the unutterable sweetness of love we move down the ways of the commandments of the Lord."[45] It was from these bastions of light and learning that the medieval form of the devotion to the Sacred Heart was to spring. During this age, the two great patristic devotional themes were maintained: 1) the apostle John receiving the waters of saving truth while reclining on the bosom of our Lord at the Last Supper; and 2) the living waters of divine grace flowing from the pierced side of Jesus.

Several writers from this period bear testimony to this fact. The first for our consideration is St. Bede (637-735), who writes: "Due to a privilege, his because of his special purity, St. John was able to drink at that fountain, the bosom of Jesus."[46] St. Bede, in commenting on the verse *"Vulnerasti cor*

---

[44]Gregory the Great, *In Cant.* in Migne, *Patrologia Latina*, Vol. 79, 499.

[45]St. Benedict, *Reg.* in Migne, *Patrologia Latina* vol. 66, 218.

[46]Bedae, *Opera Quae supersunt Omnia*, ed. J. A. Giles (Londinii: Veneunt apud Whittaker et Socios, 1843), Vol. V & VI, Homilia XXXV, p. 258-266.

meum" in the Canticle of Canticles, speaks of the wounded heart as the great love of Christ for his Church which springs from the love of our Lord's human heart and as the effect of his divine love. "'Thou hast wounded my heart, my sister my spouse.' This word is to be taken simply, for by mentioning the wounded heart, it expresses the greatness of Christ's love for his Church." This commentary is important as an early and direct reference to the heart itself as an expression of love.[47]

Alcuin (735-804), a key figure in the Carolingian renaissance, related St. John's privilege of resting on the bosom of Christ to St. Paul's expression: "...Christ in whom every treasure of wisdom and knowledge is hidden" (Col. 2:3). He also wrote of Christ in his Commentary on the Canticle of Canticles, stating that "the day of his espousals was the day of joy for his Heart, the day of redemption of the human race."[48]

St. Peter Damian (d. 1072) speaks of a "fountain of eternal life" in reference to the bosom of Christ. St. Anselm, the "Father of Scholasticism", also harks back to this theme: "What sweetness in this pierced side. That wound has revealed to us the treasures of his goodness, that is to say, the love of His Heart for us."[49]

During this period of transition, there are a few texts which point to the existence of some devotion to the Sacred Heart in the monasteries. These were not separate devotions with their own liturgy, but were part of the general monastic focus upon the person of Jesus. These texts show this period as a vital bridge which allowed patristic concepts to influence medieval theologians. There are numerous illustrations and illuminations taken from manuscripts of monastic devotional books. Here one can find specific references to all the great patristic themes which touched upon the devotion. This is especially true of the streams of living water flowing from the pierced side of Christ.

All the graces which flow from the bosom of Christ come to be seen more and more during this period as personal gifts which our Lord gives to those who draw near. In the writings of the 11th century we begin to see more explicit references to the heart as the source within the wounded side from which all the treasures of wisdom and grace flow.

A prime example of this shift can be seen in the writings of St. Anselm of Canterbury:

---

[47]*Ibid., In Cantica Canticorum*, Vol. IX & X, p. 279.

[48]Comment. in Canticum, *Patrologia Latina*, vol. 100, 649.

[49]Anselm, *Liber Meditationum et Oratium 10* in Migne, *Patrologia Latina,* Vol. 158, *op. cit.,* 762.

Jesus, dear as he inclines his head in death; dear, in the extending of his arms; dear in the opening of his side. Opened so that there is revealed to us the riches of his goodness, the charity, that is, of his heart towards us.[50]

In summarizing this section on the history of the devotion in the Patristic era, we see that these great and holy men touched upon all the essential elements which were developed in the later Middle Ages. These developments grew directly and organically out of the scriptural and patristic roots of the devotion.

The Early Medieval Period (1100 - 1250)

One thing emerges as certain: there was no *sudden* discovery of the Sacred Heart in the Middle Ages as many accounts have implied. What we have, as we have said, is a gradual, unconscious development. There are many patristic texts which have a "medieval" sound to them and many medieval teachings on the Sacred Heart which appear to echo the wealth of patristic theology.

The organic transition was accomplished through a contemplation of three basic patristic themes: 1) the wounded side of Christ, 2) the veneration of St. John the Apostle, and 3) the love theme in the Canticle of Canticles. This led to an open veneration of the Sacred Heart during this period. It is also important to remember that it was during this period that the crucifix was accepted as an image of Christ, popular enough to be used on the altar.

It is to St. Bernard, the Abbot of Clairvaux (1070-1153), that much credit is due for the rise of the devotion to the Sacred Heart of Jesus. In his writings and sermons he made constant and explicit references to the Heart of the Savior. This devotion sprang from his mystical love for Christ, especially in the mysteries of his birth and his passion. He writes in his *Vitis Mystica*:

I will say with David, "I have found my heart to pray to my God" (2 Kings 7:27); yes, I have found there the heart of my Lord, of my Friend, of my Brother, that is to say, the Heart of my amiable Redeemer. [51]

In his "Sermon on the Canticle of Canticles," he proclaims:

The secret of His Heart is laid bare in the wounds of his body. One can easily read in them the mystery of God's infinite goodness and merciful tenderness which came down to us like a dawning from on

---

[50]*Ibid.*, p. 761.
[51]Bernard, *Vitis Mystica* in Migne, *Patrologia Latina*, Vol. 184, *op. cit.* 642.

wounds. How could you indeed, Lord, show us more clearly than by your wounds that You are indeed "full of goodness and mercy abounding in love."[52]

These texts are indicative of much of St. Bernard's writings. Of perhaps even greater importance is the impact which he had on the subsequent writings of the Cistercians. In the 12th century there were an enormous number of Benedictine and Cistercian writers (especially in Germany) who wrote devotional literature on the Sacred Heart. Among those most illustrious for the spreading of the devotion during this period, we have St. Bernard, whom we have mentioned, his close friend Abbot William of St. Thierry (d. 1148), and Gilbert of Hoyland (d. 1160), the Abbot of Swenshed on the Scottish border.[53]

A fine example of the devotion at this time may be seen in a prayer to the Sacred Heart taken from a German prayerbook of the 12th century. This prayer shows how a profound theological understanding of the Sacred Heart could be united with a fervent veneration:

> Lord Christ, Son of God, for the dread with which your Sacred Heart was seized when you, Lord Christ, surrendered your holy limbs to suffering, and for your love and loyalty towards men, I beg you to comfort the pain of my heart, as you comforted the pain of your disciples in the days of your resurrection.[54]

It is also from this period that we receive the first great hymn to the Sacred Heart, "*Summi Regis Cor*". This hymn is yet another early example of this fine union of the rich theological doctrine of the Devotion with the personal piety of the time. This hymn was written in the Premonstratensian monastery of Steinfeld in the Eifel and is attributed to Blessed Hermann Joseph (1150-1241). It speaks movingly of "the man of sorrows" whose Heart, pierced by the lance, is overwhelmed with suffering and love. This wounded heart *seeks a response of love and sympathy*. The physical wounded heart is united to the spiritual heart which was also wounded by suffering and love. At the end of the hymn this bleeding and glorified heart becomes the sanctuary into which the faithful long to enter.

---

[52]Bernard, *In Cant.* 61 in Migne, *Patrologia Latina*, Vol. 183, *op. cit.*, 1072.

[53]The devotion in this period is also to be found in the writings of Abbot Guarricus of Igny, Richard of St. Victor (d. 1153), Abbot Willeram of Ebersberg (d. 1085), Abbot Rupert of Deutz (d. 1135), Abbot Wolbero of St. Pantalcon in Cologne (d. 1167), and many others.

[54]J. Stierli, *op. cit.* p. 66.

All hail to the Heart of our most high King!
With joyful heart I salute thee.
I delight to embrace thee.
It is my heart's desire.
Give me courage to speak to thee.

Oh how bitter was thy death;
How strong, how ardent that last breath.
How it pierced the sacred cell
Where the life of the world willed to dwell,
Tearing through thee, most sweet Heart.

By the death that thou didst bear,
When thou for me hung suffering there,
Heart, my own heart's dear delight,
Keep my love within thy sight.

O sweet Heart, chosen over all,
Cleanse my heart, so prone to fall,
So hardened in its vanity.

Through the marrow of my heart,
Guilty, sinful, set apart,
May the love flow swift and strong
Till my heart, thus borne along,
Lies wounded in that loving flame.
Open, open wide and fair,
As a rose of fragrance rare;
Join my heart to thine anew.
Heal, then, once more pierce it through.
Can a heart that loves feel pain?

Gentle Heart, I love thee dear;
To my own heart bend, incline,
Till my heart can cling to thine
Devoutly, pressing close to thee.

Open, open rose of the Heart,
Whose perfume is so sweet.

Let us live so, Heart to heart,
Wounded, Jesus, as thou art.
If through my heart thou wilt but strike
With shame's arrow, sharp and dire.
Put my heart within thine own,
Hold me, leave me not alone.

Here my heart shall live and die,
To thee ever drawing nigh;
Strongly would it thirst for thee,
Jesus, say not no to me,
That it may rest in thee, content.[55]

Lastly, it was during this period that we have the first *recorded* apparition of our Lord revealing his Sacred Heart as a symbol of his love for mankind. St. Lutgard of St. Trond (d. 1246) was the recipient of this blessing. She is also the first among the mystics to report an exchange of hearts. This mystical experience was later to be found in the lives of such saints as Catherine of Siena and Rose of Lima. At the age of 17, St. Lutgard had decided to devote herself entirely to Christ, but was constantly pursued by the amorous promptings of a young man. Our Lord appeared to her and showed her the wound in his side and said, "From now on seek not the flatteries of a foolish man. This must be the constant object in your contemplation and love."[56]

After this vision Lutgard became a Benedictine and eventually a Cistercian. Our Lord gave to her a special grace which enabled her to understand the Latin Psalms. So ardent was her love for Christ that she found even this gift insufficient and said to Christ: "What use to me, an uneducated peasant girl, is the knowledge of the mysteries of Holy Scripture?" "What then do you want?" asked our Lord. "I want your Heart!" "And still more do I want yours!" "Yes, Lord, but in such a way that you temper the love of your heart to that of mine, and that I may possess my heart under the sure protection of yours." And our Lord exchanged the two hearts.[57]

The Flowering of the Middle Ages
Up to the Time of Margaret Mary

By the middle of the 13th century the devotion to the Sacred Heart of Jesus had literally burst forth in so many areas, and in the writings of so many Christians, that all we can hope to accomplish here is a sketch or main outline of this phenomenal growth.

During this period (1200-1400) the devotion was spread to the laity

---

[55]Quoted in *Devotion to the Heart of Jesus* (Rome: Institute of Spirituality, Pontifical Univ. of St. Thomas Aquinas, 1982) pp. 57-58. Other versions can be found in *Devotions for Holy Communion from the Roman Missal and Breviary*, published by Burns, Oates and Washburn in London. CF. also M. Williams, *The Sacred Heart in the Life of the Church*, (New York, 1957), pp. 41-43.

[56]Karl Richstaetter, *Illustrious Friends of the Sacred Heart of Jesus* (London: Herder, 1930) p. 44.

[57]*Ibid.*, p. 44.

Figure 7: St. Lutgard by Caspar de Crayer, 1652.

through their contact with monasteries and convents. This is evident from the fact that reference to Christ's Heart began to be found in the secular writings of the time. The major contributions in this period flowed from a union of theological reflection and mystical piety. Along with the traditional patristic themes, the return of the Crusaders from the Holy Land added renewed devotional fervor to the Sacred Humanity of Christ, especially in terms of his passion, death and resurrection. This is also the period during which we see the rise of Gothic art with its predominate image of Christ suffering on the cross. It is most common to find in this popular image of Christ crucified a stream of blood pouring out of the open side and falling into a cup held by an angel or a saint. Once again, here before us is the patristic understanding which sees all graces and blessings as flowing from the wounded side and heart within.

During this era, we also witness great advances in theology and the rise of the Dominicans and Franciscans who gave a tremendous impetus to the devotion to the Sacred Heart of Jesus. Theology found its greatest teachers in the mendicant communities and these, along with those they influenced, greatly contributed to the building of the devotion into the life of the Church.

St. Margaret Mary, in her vision of October 4, 1673, acknowledges St. Francis of Assisi (whose feast it was) as a great friend of the Sacred Heart. [58] The *Legenda S. Francisci* seems to testify to this truth. It relates how the crucifix of St. Damian entrusted to Francis the task of restoring the house of God and goes on to say: "Then his heart was wounded and melted at the thought of the Passion of the Lord" (*"Ab illa hora vulneratum et liquefactum est cor eius ad memoriam dominicae passionis"*). [59]

What had moved the heart of Francis so deeply was not only the external sufferings of our Lord but the internal sufferings of his heart. This spirit was communicated by Francis to his brethren. Our Lord, by bestowing the gift of the stigmata on St. Francis on Mount Alverno, demonstrated his special love for this man. The visible wounds of Christ which he carried in his own body and heart led to his deep understanding of the wounded heart of Christ. This is the great truth captured by Murillo in his famous painting where the dying Jesus, with right arm free of the restraining nail, reaches down to embrace St. Francis and draw him to his heart.

---

[58] J. Stirli, *op. cit.*, p. 45.

[59] See M. A. Habig, ed. St. Francis of Assisi: *Omnibus of Sources*, (Chicago, Ill.: the Franciscan Herald Press, 1976). Bonaventure's *Legenda Major* (pp. 627-787) is filled with references to the heart of Francis and the wounded side and heart of Christ. Francis' love for the crucified is particularly emphasized in the section which deals with the stigmata. See also the *Legenda Minor* and note the Fourth Lesson (p. 795).

Figure 8:

Giotto:

St. Francis of Assisi

receiving the Stigmata,

c. 1267.

The Louvre.

This truth finds a magnificent and lucid expression in the writings of St. Bonaventure (d.1274) who stood out among the Franciscans as their chief exponent of the Sacred Heart. St. Bonaventure had a deep devotion to the passion of our Lord. In his work *Itinerarium Mentis in Deum* he speaks of the goal of a perfect union of hearts between the Christian and God. He states that this can be attained only through a passionate love of Christ crucified (*via autem non est nisi per ardentissimum amorem Crucifixi*).[60] There are many references to the Heart of Jesus throughout his writings but the classic expression of his own heart's love of the Sacred Heart is found in his little book on the preaching of the mystery of our Lord's heart:

> The heart I have found is the heart of my King and Lord, of my Brother and Friend, the most loving Jesus.... I say without hesitation that His heart is also mine. Since Christ is my head, how could that which belongs to my head not also belong to me? As the eyes of my bodily head are truly my own, so also is the heart of my spiritual Head. Oh, what a blessed lot is mine to have one heart with Jesus! ...Having found this heart, both Yours and mine, O most sweet Jesus, I will pray to you my God.[61]

The devotion to the Heart of Jesus, as expressed by St. Angela of Foligno and St. Margaret of Cortona, seems to be imbued with the Franciscan spirit of the devotion. There was also a large number among the southern German Franciscans who gave similar expressions of devotion to the Sacred Heart. David of Augsburg was filled with the fiery, mystical love of his founder, St. Francis, and his disciple, St. Bonaventure. He speaks of the pierced Heart of Jesus as the symbol of his love:

> From the burning Heart of Jesus flows his blood, hot with love.
> Jesus showed us from the Cross his faithful heart, glowing with love, since the death of our souls touched him more nearly than the death of his body. Ah, dearest Lord Jesus Christ, what great love and faithfulness wilt thou show to the soul when thou displayest thy riches and openest thy Heart to thy beloved friends![62]

He also has left us prayers to the Sacred Heart which combine a rich theology with mystical fervor. The following is an excellent example:

> Beloved Lord Jesus Christ, warm, burn through my heart, which longs

---

[60]Bonaventure, *"Itinerarium Mentis in Deum"*, *Opera Omnia*, Vol. V, pp. 295-313.

[61]Bonaventure, "The Mystical Vine, Chp. 3", *Opera Omnia*, Vol. VIII, p. 53.

[62]K. Richstaetter, *Illustrious Friends of the Sacred Heart, op. cit.*, p. 59.

for thee, with the love-warm blood which flowed from thy burning Heart on the Holy Cross. That it flowed from a hot heart, it was itself a living witness. Thy body was dead and cold, and thy blood of itself could not have flowed, nor even have been moved. It should naturally have ceased to circulate, as we see in dead bodies. But not so with thee! By this it is given us to understand that it was still so hot with the glow of thy Heart's love that it ran down like a sweet fountain from thy wounded side.[63]

One of the greatest contributions to the devotion to the Heart of Jesus in the Middle Ages, however, was made by the Dominicans. Germany was the chief area of their work. In that province the Order had 46 monasteries and over 70 convents of Dominican nuns. The sons of St. Dominic, as preachers, writers and spiritual directors, influenced all they came in contact with in their zealous apostolic labors. This was especially true of nuns and devout laymen. The Friars spoke of our Lord's heart in reference to their mystical devotion to the suffering and death of Christ. Through a contemplation of the wounds inflicted upon Christ, the devout Christian was led to a contemplation of his Heart, which was suffering and wounded with love. The Dominicans united this meditation on the Passion with a deep reverence for the Blessed Sacrament and thereby formed a complete and profound spirituality which centered around the Sacred Heart of Jesus.

St. Albert the Great (1206-1280) is an early leader and influential spokesman for this spirituality. He speaks of the devotion to the Sacred Heart in his sermons and theological treatises. St. Albert built upon the inheritance of the preceding centuries and gave a strong theological impetus to the Devotion. He had a major influence in Germany during the 13th century and a lasting impact on the subsequent development of the devotion. In his writings we clearly see the flow and continuity of doctrine from patristic theology into medieval theology. From the Fathers, St. Albert took his special emphasis on the pierced side of Jesus as the source of all grace:

> The water from his side and that which he poured from his Heart are witnesses of his boundless love. (*Sermo 27 de Eucharistia*)[64]
> ...His side in which rest all the riches of God's knowledge and wisdom; he showed his Heart, which had already been wounded by his love for us before it was struck by the point of the lance. (*In Joanem* 20, 20)[65]

---

[63]*Ibid.*, p. 60.

[64]Albertus Magnus, *Opera Omnia* Vol. 13, ed. August Bornet, (Paris: Ludovicum Vives, 1899), p. 777.

[65]Albertus Magnus, *Opera Omnia* Vol. 24, ed. August Bornet, *op. cit.*, p. 684.

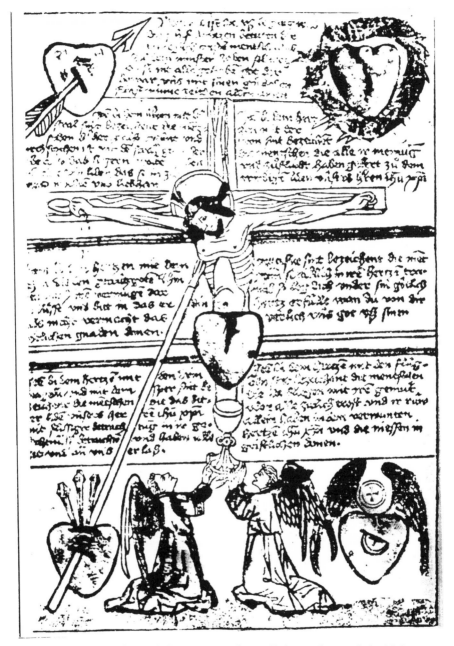

Figure 9: The Heart of Jesus is here presented as suffering and wounded with love, with Eucharistic overtones. Fifteenth century German engraving.

St. Albert also made use of the patristic veneration of the Apostle John who drank the treasures of divine wisdom at our Lord's heart. Even more importantly, he speaks of the patristic doctrine of the Church being born with the opening of his heart. At that moment on the Cross our Lord sanctified his spotless Bride with his redeeming blood:

> In three ways did he espouse himself to the Church on the Cross: through his blood; through the stretching out of his arms to embrace his bride in intimate love; and after his death, through the opening of his side, from which the Church proceeded with the principal mysteries, the blood of redemption and the water of atonement. (*In IV Sententiarium.* 1, a. 2)[66]

From these key ideas, which may be traced back to the second century, St. Albert related the devotion to the Heart of Jesus to the Precious Blood. It is St. Albert who first explicitly connected devotion to the Sacred Heart with the Holy Eucharist. He sees the boundless love of Christ's heart as the motive which led to the institution of the Eucharist and all the other sacraments which flow to the Church from his heart opened on the Cross:

> Why was he wounded on the side near his Heart? In order that we may never tire in contemplating his Heart. (*In Joannem 20,20*)[67]
>
> By the blood of his side and of his Heart our Lord watered the garden of the Church, for with this blood he made the sacraments flow from his Heart. (*De Eucharistia* d. 2, tr. 2, c. 5)[68]

In an even more specific reference to the joy of our Lord's Sacred Heart at the institution of the Eucharist, he writes:

> His Heart overflowed with love and joy at being completely one with us and filling our hearts with joy and jubilation. (*De eucharistia* d. 2, tr. c2)[69]

Due to the writings of St. Albert, when the Feast of Corpus Christi was introduced in 1264, a firm bond was established between devotion to the Blessed Eucharist and devotion to the Sacred Heart of Jesus as the source of this most precious gift.

The Dominicans and Franciscans further strengthened the tie between

---

[66] Albertus Magnus, *Opera Omnia*, Vol. 29, *op. cit.*, p. 9.
[67] Albertus Magnus, *Opera Omnia,* Vol. 24, *op. cit.*, p. 683.
[68] Albertus Magnus, *Opera Omnia*, Vol. 38, *op. cit.*, p. 302.
[69] *Ibid.*, pp. 217-218.

the devotion to the Sacred Heart and Eucharistic liturgy with Masses of the Passion and Five Wounds which were used in both parish and monastery churches. Though these Masses were only of a local character, they greatly assisted the spread of the Devotion.

In 1353, Pope Innocent VI promulgated a Mass to the Catholic world on the occasion of the Holy See's reception of the relic of the Holy Lance of Longinus. The relic was returned by the Sultan Bajazet II. It was the first liturgical celebration of importance which dealt with the mystery of Christ's wounded Heart. The Mass contained three explicit references to the pierced Heart as did the hymn for Vespers and Lauds.

In the writings of St. Albert's illustrious student, St. Thomas Aquinas, it has generally been conceded that there is no direct reference to the devotion. Fr. Patrick O'Connell, however, offers the following "quote" from St. Thomas:

> Christ poured out his blood by the wound of his side and of his Heart that he might inflame the hearts of his doubting disciples and of many others grown cold and almost dead to faith, and having restored them to life, he wishes like a wounded stag to mark out for them the road to heaven with his own blood.[70]

Unfortunately, Fr. O'Connell fails to give a source for this quotation and it has been cited by other authors as authentic. The quotation is, in fact, taken from *Sermones de Venerabili Sacramenti Altaris* and is incorrectly attributed to St. Thomas.[71]

Despite this quote's lack of authenticity, the teaching of St. Thomas has always been referred to in support of the reverence which must be paid to the sacred humanity of Christ because of its hypostatic union with his divinity. St. Thomas, like St. Albert and the Fathers before him, also speaks of the Blessed Eucharist and the other sacraments as originating from the wounded side of our Lord:

> From the side of Christ there flowed water for the cleansing, blood for redeeming. Hence blood is associated with the sacraments of the

---

[70]Patrick O'Connell, *Devotion to the Sacred Heart, The Essence of Christianity and the Center of the Divine Plan of Redemption* (Wexford, Ireland: John English & Co., 1952), p. 113.

[71]cf. a. Walz, *De Veneratione Divini Cordis Iesu* (Rome: Pontificium Institutium Angelicum, 1937)

Eucharist, water with the sacrament of Baptism, which has its cleansing power by virtue of the blood of Christ.[72]

This period also witnessed a great rise in mystical phenomena relating to the Heart of Jesus. This was especially true at the great Cistercian monastery of Helfta near Eisleben in Germany. Here three great spiritual traditions met in this center of medieval culture and piety: 1) the Benedictine emphasis upon the solemn splendor of the liturgy; 2) St. Bernard's mystical love for Jesus; and 3) from the Dominicans at nearby Halle (who were their spiritual directors), a loving devotion for the Passion of our Lord. Of even greater importance than all these wonderful spiritual traditions was the outpouring of supernatural graces which made this monastery a center of fervent devotion to the Sacred Heart. Here, Mechthild of Madeburg, Mechthild of Hackeborn and Gertrude the Great were showered with mystical favors and revelations of our Lord's Sacred Heart. Volumes could be written on these three alone but here we must content ourselves with a brief sketch.

Mechthild of Madeburg originally lived as a Beguine who performed works of mercy. She entered the monastery of Helfta late in life (60 years old) in the year 1270. At the request of her Dominican confessor, she described her visions in her book *The Flowing Light* in which she speaks of the mystery of the Heart of Jesus:

> In my great sufferings God revealed himself to my soul, showed me the wound of his Heart and said: "See how they have made me suffer." Then my soul said: "Ah Lord, why didst thou suffer such great misery, why is thy holy blood shed so lavishly? By thy prayer alone all the world might surely have been easily saved and justice satisfied?" "No," he answered, "That would not have been sufficient for my Father. For all this poverty and toil, all this torment and shame, all this was but a knocking at heaven's gate until the hour when my Heart's blood ran down to the earth—only then was heaven opened."[73]

Mechthild understands the Sacred Heart as the interior life of Jesus. It is a vision dominated by our Lord's Passion. She sees the heart of Jesus as burning with love for sinful men who fail to love in return. This most naturally led her to share in the sufferings of our Lord's Heart and find her peace in him.

[72]Thomas Aquinas, *Summa Theologica* III, q. 66, a. 3. Leo Elders gives an insightful treatment of St. Thomas' teaching on the inner life of Jesus in *Faith in Christ and the Worship of Christ* (San Francisco: Ignatius Press, 1986), pp. 65-79.

[73]Mechthild of Madeburg, *Fliebendes Licht*, 6, 26; tr. Richstaetter, *op. cit.*, p. 91.

Do you truly wish to be converted?
Behold your Spouse, the whole world's Lord
See how he hangs there, high on the Cross,
Before the whole world all covered with blood,
His eyes dimmed and full of tears,
His sweetest Heart overflowing with love:
Remember the sharp spear's wound
Which pierced even to the depths of the Heart
And weep over that which you have done.[74]

Mechthild of Hackeborn was also favored with many special graces which she sought to hide from her fellow nuns. She confided only in St. Gertrude and another nun and this only after her sister, the abbess Gertrude, had died. At the request of the new abbess, the two nuns wrote *Liber Specialis Gratiae* in which they told of the special graces given to Mechthild of Hackeborn. When Mechthild heard that this book had been written she became distraught. Our Lord consoled her, however, and told her that the work would lead others to his Heart. Although Mechthild had led a life of intense suffering, she saw Christ not so much as the "Man of Sorrows" (as Mechthild of Madeburg) but as the glorified Lord of the Sacred Liturgy. In addition to the *Liber Specialis Gratiae*, Mechthild also left many prayers to the Sacred Heart. Josef Stierli mentions that these prayers were the "life-long favorites" of St. Peter Canisius, who made his own copy of them and carried it with him throughout his life, even clutching it on his deathbed. The following quotation gives testimony to her ardent love for the Heart of our Lord:

Hail sweetest Heart of Jesus most tuneful instrument of the Holy Trinity. Hail Heart of Jesus, flowing honey, living stream of all goodness and all grace. Hail, loving Heart of Jesus, most noble treasury of the riches of God. I bless and salute Thee a thousand and a thousand fold in the divine Goodness, that Thou art the Fountain and Source.[75]

St. Gertrude the Great had entered the monastery at the age of five. Despite a life of continuous suffering, she became one of the greatest saints of the Benedictine Order. Her spiritual life was filled with a superabundance of the most sublime heavenly graces in prayer which filled her with apostolic fervor. We have two of her best known Latin works which overflow with devotional love for the Sacred Heart. In *Legatus Divinae Pietatis* (*The Ambassador of Divine Love*) she associates the mystery of the Heart of Jesus with the

---

[74]*Ibid.*, pp. 91-92.
[75]Mechthild of Hackeborn, *Prayers*, (London: Burns & Lambert, 1861), pp. 76-77.

Passion. The following text points to this truth and also allows us to mention one of the greatest personal graces she received in 1288:

> O most loving Jesus by the pierced Heart, I pray thee wound my heart with that arrow of love; so that nothing of earth may abide in it more, but that it may be filled with thy glowing love alone forever. Amen.[76]

God answered this prayer in a mystical experience in which her heart was pierced. This special grace was similar to that which was later experienced by Teresa of Avila. St. Gertrude's other Latin work, *Exercitia Pietatis*, is a seven day spiritual exercise which includes numerous prayers to the Sacred Heart. She devotes the entire fifth day to a meditation on the Heart of Jesus. The following is a typical prayer to the Sacred Heart:

> Let thy all-resplendent soul, that precious pledge whereby my soul hath been redeemed, sing jubilantly unto Thee. Let Thy Divine and most sweet heart, which, in the hour of Thy death, love did pierce for my sake, sing jubilantly unto thee. Let Thy most loving and most faithful Heart, into which the lance did open a way for me, that my heart might enter and rest therein, sing jubilantly unto Thee. Let this Heart most sweet, the refuge of my earthly sojourning, which ever watcheth over me with such kindness, and which will never rest in its thirst for me until it taketh me eternally unto itself, sing jubilantly unto Thee.[77]

The teachings of St. Albert and the Dominican spirituality which guided the nuns at Helfta were continued most forcefully in the great German preachers, Meister Eckhart, John Tauler and Blessed Henry Suso.

Meister Eckhart (d. 1327) was truly one of the greatest preachers of the mystery of the Heart of Jesus. In keeping with the rich Dominican spiritual tradition, Eckhart approached this mystery through our Lord's passion:

> On the cross his Heart burnt like a fire and a furnace from which the flame burst forth on all sides. So was he inflamed on the Cross by his fire of love for the whole world.[78]

John Tauler (d. 1361), who was one of the greatest mystics and preachers the Church has known, held a deep veneration for the Apostle John with whom he bore a spiritual likeness:

---

[76]Gertrude the Great, *Prayers* (London: Burns & Lambert, 1861), p. 111.

[77]Gertrude the Great, *The Exercises of St. Gertrude*, trans., A Benedictine nun of Regina Laudis (Westminster, Maryland: The Newman Press, 1956), pp. 127-128.

[78]J. Stierli, ed., *op. cit.,* p. 80

If thou wilt rest with St. John on the lovely Heart of our Lord Jesus Christ, thou must devote thyself to the lovely example of our Lord Jesus Christ. Upon that thou must see his gentleness and humility, and the deep burning love which he bore towards his friends and his enemies, his obedience, and the submission which he showed on every occasion when his Father called him. Add to this the profound pity which embraced all mankind, and his poverty blessed.[79]

In his book entitled *Exercises*, which was traditionally attributed to Tauler, he offers deep and stirring meditations on the sufferings of Christ and speaks over fifty times of the Heart of Jesus. Here are a few examples of his meditations on the piercing of our Lord's side:

What more could he still do for us that he has not done? He has opened his very Heart to us, as the most secret chamber wherein to lead our soul, his chosen spouse. For it is his joy to be with us in silent stillness, and in peaceful silence to rest there with us. He gave us his Heart all wounded, that we may abide therein until we are wholly cleansed and without spot; until we are made like unto his Heart, and rendered fit and worthy to be led with him into the divine Heart of the Father. He gives us his Heart wholly and entirely, that it may be our home. Therefore he desires our heart in return that it may be his dwelling place. He gives us his Heart as a resting place, dyed with the purple of his blood, adorned with red roses. In return he asks for our heart, decked with the white lilies of good works.[80]

Blessed Henry Suso (d. 1295) was a disciple of Meister Eckhart. His great contribution was his extraordinary ability to foster the practice of devotion especially in terms of the reparatory value of suffering. Suso's writings, which include his *Autobiography*, his book on *Eternal Wisdom* and numerous meditations on the sufferings of Christ, had a tremendous influence. Signs of his ardent love and devotion to the Sacred Heart can be found on each page:

O Eternal Wisdom, my heart reminds thee how, after the Last Supper, on the Mount of Olives, thou wast bathed in thy bloody sweat because of the anguish of thy loving Heart.

O Lord, thy Heart bore all in tender love; O Lord, thy Heart, burning with love, must enkindle mine with love.[81]

In his book on *Eternal Wisdom*, we read:

---

[79] *Ibid.*, p. 80
[80] John Tauler, *Exercitia D. Ioannis Thauleri*, tr. Nicolao Eschio (Lugduni: S. B. Honorati, 1556) pp. 411-412; cf. Richstaetter, *op. cit.*, p. 127.
[81] J. Stierli, ed., *op. cit.*, p. 81.

110 Heart of the Redeemer

> O Lord, thou didst not only suffer death for me but thou didst also seek out the most intimate and secret depths of love in which suffering can or may be experienced. Thou didst really act as if thou hadst said: Behold, all your hearts, was ever a heart so full of love? Look on all my members; the noblest member I have is my Heart; my Heart I have allowed to be pierced through, to be slain and consumed, and crushed into small pieces, that nothing in me or upon me might remain unbestowed, so that you might know my love.[82]

That Blessed Henry Suso himself was spiritually blessed may be seen in his own words:

> One day it seemed to him that the Eternal Father's heart was, in a spiritual and ineffable manner, pressed tenderly, and with naught between them, upon his heart, as it lay open over against the Father's heart in longing desire, and it appeared to him that the Father's heart, in a way of love transcending all forms and images, spoke in his heart the uncreated Word, the Eternal Wisdom. Then he began to exclaim joyously in spiritual jubilee: Behold now my loveliest love! thus do I lay bare to Thee my heart, and in simplicity and nakedness with regard to all created things I embrace Thy formless Godhead.[83]

As might be expected, the Dominican nuns of the 14th century were subject to this influence and were deeply devoted to the Sacred Heart of Jesus. Among the thousands of nuns who practiced the devotion, several are worthy of mention: Bl. Margaret Ebner of Maria-Moedinger (d. 1351), Christina Ebner and Adelheid Langmann. All these saintly nuns left behind vivid testimonies in their writings to the strength of their devotion to the Sacred Heart of Jesus. Under the direct influence of Bl. Henry Suso, the Swiss Dominican convents at Oetenback, Toess and Katharinental became centers of fervent devotion to the Heart of Christ.

The devotion flowered in an extraordinary way in the life of St. Catherine of Siena (d. 1380). St. Catherine (a Third Order Dominican under the spiritual direction of Blessed Raymond of Capua) shared most deeply in the sufferings of Christ. She speaks constantly of the sufferings of Christ's Heart. St. Catherine not only bore in her body the wounds of Christ (though these remained invisible at her request) but also experienced the mystical exchange of hearts with Christ in 1370.

---

[82]*Ibid.*, p. 82.

[83]Henry Suso, *The Life of Henry Suso*, tr. T. F. Knox (London: Burns, Lambert & Oates, 1865), pp. 284-285.

Put your mouth at the heart of the Son of God, since it is a heart that casts the fire of charity and pours out blood to wash away your iniquities. I say that the soul that rests there and considers with the eye of the intellect the heart that is consumed and opened out of love, that soul receives in itself such conformity within, seeing itself so loved, that it cannot do anything but love.[84]

This great mystic of the Heart of Jesus, who was proclaimed a Doctor of the Church by Pope Paul VI, posed the following question to Christ and received his answer:

"Sweet and Immaculate Lamb, thou wert dead when thy side was opened. Why then didst thou want to be struck and have thy heart divided?" He said, "Because my desire towards the human generation was ended, and I had finished the actual work of bearing pain and torment, and yet I had not been able to show, by finite things, because my love was infinite, how much more love I had, I wished thee to see the secret of the Heart, showing it to thee open, so that thou mightest see how much more I loved than I could show thee by finite pain. I poured from it Blood and Water to show thee the baptism of water which is received in virtue of the Blood."[85]

Another fine example of this compassion for the suffering Heart of Christ is to be found in the devotional works of the great mystic St. Bridget of Sweden (1302-1373), who founded the Brigittines. Many more instances of the devotion could be cited but here we must be content with having attempted to sketch the major outlines of the golden age of medieval mysticism.

In the 15th century the devotion became very popular among the Carthusians. It entered this Order through Ludolf of Saxony who had spent 30 years as a Dominican with Eckhart, Tauler and Suso. Ludolf, in his *Vita Jesu Christi* (one of the two books which led to the conversion of St. Ignatius of Loyola), speaks of the pierced side of Christ:

The Heart of Christ was wounded for us with the wound of love, that through the opening of his side we may in return enter his Heart by means of love, and there be able to unite all our love with his divine love into one love, as the glowing iron is one with the fire. Therefore for the sake of this wound which Christ received for him on the Cross, when the dart of unconquerable love pierced his Heart, man should bring all his will into conformity with the will of God. But to fashion

---

[84]Catherine of Siena, *Letters*, 97.

[85]St. Catherine of Siena, *The Dialogue*, tr. A. Thorold (Rockford Ill.: Tan Books & Publ, Inc., 1974) pp. 171-172.

Figure 10: *Jesus transforming the heart of St. Catherine of Siena. Engraving by Francesco Vanni (1563-1610).*

himself into conformity with Christ's sufferings, he should consider what surpassingly noble love our Lord has shown us in the opening of his side, since through it he has given us the wide open entrance into his Heart. Therefore, let man make haste to enter into the Heart of Christ: let him gather up all his love and unite it with the divine love.[86]

There were many other Carthusians who distinguished themselves by their zeal for this devotion. Among the most famous are Heinrich Echer of Calcar (d. 1408) at the Charterhouse of Cologne, Dominic of Trier, Denis Ryckel, called "the Carthusian", Nicolaus Kemp, who originally was at the University of Vienna, Peter Blomevenna (d. 1536), Justus Landsberger and Ludwig Blosius, whose work *Monile Spirituale* was based on the writings of St. Gertrude and Mechthild and was translated into many languages. The devotion is also found during this period among the Augustinians[87] and English Mystics, such as Juliana of Norwich[88] and Richard Rolle.[89]

During this period (15th and 16th century), devotion to the Sacred Heart found lively expression in the writings of John Ruysbrock and the *Devotio Moderna*. Thomas à Kempis, the author of *The Imitation*, writes most fervently of the Sacred Heart of Jesus in his *Prayers and Meditation on the Life of Christ*:

> Enter then, enter thou, my soul, into the right side of thy crucified Lord, pass through the holy wound into the most loving Heart of Jesus, which out of love was pierced by the lance, that thou mayest rest in the clefts of the Rock (Cant. 2:14) from the trouble of the world. Enter then, O man, to the worshipful Heart, to the hidden Heart, to the silent Heart, to the Heart of God which opens to thee its portals. Enter, thou blessed of God; why standest thou without? Open to thee is the well of life, the way of salvation, the ark of heaven, whence issue many perfumes. There is the source of the divine stream to still the thirst of thy craving soul. Do thou also draw from the side of Jesus sweet consolations for life, that thou mayest no longer live to thyself, but in him who was wounded for thee. Give him thy heart who opens his Heart to thee.[90]

---

[86]Ludolphus de Saxonia, *Vita Jesus Christi*, ed. John Dadraeo (Venetiis: Valerium Bonellum, 1587), p. 1025; cf. Richstaetter, *op. cit.*, p. 177.

[87]Outstanding examples among the Augustinians would include Bl. Simon of Casia (d. 1348), Konrad of Waldhausen (d. 1369) and Bl. Alfonso de Orozco (d. 1591).

[88]Juliana of Norwich, *Revelations of Divine Love*, tr. M. L. del Mastro (Garden City, N.Y.: Image Books, 1977), p. 121.

[89]C. Horstman ed., *Richard Rolle of Hampole* (London, 1896) and C. Brown ed., *Religious Lyrics of the Fourteenth Century* (Oxford, 1924).

[90]Thomas à Kempis *Opera Omnia* Vol V, ed. Michael J. Pohl (Friburg, Brisigavorum: Herder, 1922), p. 197.

Towards the end of the Middle Ages, despite a widespread decadence among the clergy, there were many signs of a reforming spirit which was frequently united to a revival or renewal of the devotion to the Sacred Heart. The devotion in the Mendicant Orders, which had slackened somewhat during the 14th century, sprang forth anew. Among the Franciscans we find such famous names as St. Bernadine of Siena (d. 1444), the great German mystic Heinrich Herp, the great missionary Dietrich Coelde, Blessed Camilla Baptista of Varano (d. 1524), St. Joan of Valois (d. 1505), the tertiary who founded the Order of the Most Holy Annunciation, St. Peter of Alacantara (d. 1562), and St. Fidelis of Sigmaringen (d. 1622).

Among the Dominicans we find St. Antoninus of Florence (d. 1459), Jerome Savonarola (d. 1498), Louis Chardon (d. 1561), Louis of Granada (d. 1588) and Ignatius of Nente (d. 1648). There were also many Dominican nuns who were connected with the devotion. Those most worthy of mention would be Margaret of Savoy (d. 1464), St. Catherine de Ricci (d. 1590) and St. Rose of Lima (d. 1617).

These holy men and women all testify to the fact that devotion to the Sacred Heart had by this time become a fully acceptable form of Christian piety.

The young Society of Jesus from its very beginning played a major role in the theological development of the devotion. The foremost position among the German Jesuits who fostered the devotion is held by St. Peter Canisius (d. 1597). Canisius spent many years studying in Cologne where he came under the influence of the Carthusian tradition. This tradition, united with the *Spiritual Exercises* and the prayers of the German mystics, such as Bl. Mechthild of Hackeborn, laid a solid spiritual foundation for his fervent devotion to the Sacred Heart of Jesus. In 1549, while making his solemn profession (before his mission to Germany) in St. Peter's at the chapel of the Blessed Sacrament, he was favored with a mystical grace. He left the following description of this vision in his *Testament*:

> My soul fell prostrate before thee, my dull deformed soul, unclean and infected with many vices and passions. But thou, my Savior, didst open to me thy Heart in such a fashion that I seemed to see within it, and thou didst invite me and bid me to drink the waters of salvation from that fountain. Great at that moment was my desire that streams of faith, hope and charity might flow from it into my soul. I thirsted after poverty, chastity and obedience, and I begged to be clothed and adorned by thee. After I had thus dared to approach thy Heart, all full of sweetness, and to slake my thirst therein, thou didst promise me a robe woven of peace, love and perseverance, with which to cover my

Figure 11: *The Hours of Yolande de Lalaing, Crucifixion, c. 1450-60. Bodleian Library, Oxford.*

naked soul. Having this garment of grace and gladness about me, I grew confident again that I should lack for nothing, and that all things would turn out to thy glory.[91]

Famous passages on the Sacred Heart were written by many other Jesuits in the 16th century, including such illustrious men as Friedrich von Spee, Philip Kiecel, Ribadeneira, Alvarez, St. Alphonsus Rodriguez, Salmeron, Toledo, Maldonado and Suarez. Theological treatises on the Devotion to the Sacred Heart of Jesus were written by Druzbicki, John Baptist Saint-Juré (d. 1651) and Novet (d. 1680). Long before 1675 the Jesuits had spread the devotion not only in Europe but in Canada, Brazil (where the first church was dedicated to the Sacred Heart at Cuarpary in 1585), China and the Far East.

By the early 17th century, we find the devotion rising into prominence in France. The French school of spirituality at this time was profoundly Christocentric, affective and devotional. This school finds its origins principally in the writings of Cardinal Bérulle, St. Francis de Sales and St. John Eudes, who synthesized the spirituality of his two predecessors. This was the spiritual atmosphere that St. Margaret Mary was to breathe upon entering the Visitation convent at Paray-le-Monial.

Post-Reformation spirituality is aptly termed Roman Catholic rather than Christian, taking direction more from its fight against the supposed and real heresies of Protestants than from the sources of the entire Christian tradition. In such a context of reaction and defensiveness, the spiritual writers of the Post-Reformation period expressed themselves more than ever in the battle-and-combat imagery which the desert fathers had first popularized. In fact, it is not the meekness and openness of Francis de Sales' *Treatise on the Love of God* but the martial tactics of Lawrence Scupoli's *Spiritual Combat* (1589) that typify the period. It would be wrong, of course, to view Post-Reformation Catholic spirituality in simple negative terms. Actually, it exhibits considerable complexity and exuberance—what might be called the spirit of the Baroque.[92]

Considered the founder of this "Baroque Spirituality", Peter Cardinal Bérulle (1575-1629) was filled with a deep longing for God from early childhood. He was educated by the Jesuits and made the *Spiritual Exercises* of St. Ignatius Loyola early in life. He continued his studies at the Sorbonne and was finally ordained as a diocesan priest. Bérulle was a personal acquaintance of St. Francis de Sales. He had a special love for the writings of Sts.

---

[91]J. Broderick, *St. Peter Canisius*, (London: Sheed & Ward, 1938), p. 125.
[92]T. M. Gannon and G. W. Traub, *The Desert and the City* (London, 1969), pp. 227-228.

Augustine, Ignatius and Teresa of Avila. He played a key role in bringing the Spanish Carmelite nuns to France. In his systematic theology, he adhered to the teaching of St. Thomas Aquinas.

Bérulle's first work was published at Paris in 1597 and was entitled *Brief discours de l'abnegation interieure*. As can be seen from the title, he dealt with self-abnegation. Bérulle taught in this work that self annihilation was necessary for a Christian in order that he might totally commit himself to God. He taught that there were three degrees of self annihilation: 1) detachment from things indifferent to the spiritual life, 2) detachment from things useful for the spiritual life, and 3) detachment from things necessary for the spiritual life. The goal of total self-annihilation was to be achieved and sustained by the vow of holy slavery to Jesus and Mary.

His teaching concerning the need of total self renunciation aroused the opposition of Cardinal Richelieu, the Carmelite nuns and the professors at Louvain and Douai. These opponents saw in Bérulles' theology the seeds of Jansenism and Quietism. Bérulle defended his position by maintaining that the vow of slavery was nothing more than an attempt to live out the consequences of one's baptismal vows.

Due to his continual reading of the Church Fathers (especially St. Augustine), St. Teresa of Avila and the Spiritual Exercises of St. Ignatius (which he had made under Fr. Maggio), Bérulle shifted the doctrinal foundation of his teaching from man's misery and corruption to *the servitude of the sacred humanity of Christ in the hypostatic union*. It was this devotion to the sacred humanity of Christ which strongly influenced his disciples Bourgoing, Condren, Olier and St. John Eudes, who would summarize this spirituality in devotion to the Sacred Heart of Jesus. Bérulle died in 1629 while saying the Mass of the Incarnation.

St. Francis de Sales (1567-1622) profoundly influenced the spirituality of the 17th century and may be rightly considered a school of spirituality in himself. He was born in Savoy and studied under the Jesuits in Paris. He continued his studies at Padua and received doctorates in both civil and canon law. St. Francis was ordained to the priesthood in 1593 and eventually became Bishop of Geneva in 1602. In addition to administering his diocese, he dedicated himself with great fervor to preaching, spiritual writing and the direction of souls. He was proclaimed a Doctor of the Church by Pope Pius

IX in 1887.

His two most famous works are the *Introduction to the Devout Life*[93] and *Treatise on the Love of God*.[94] The doctrine contained in these works is nothing new but a return to one of the basic teachings of the Gospel: all Christians are called to holiness of life. His pastoral care for the laity did much to break down that restricted view of the spiritual life which saw the quest for perfection as proper only for the religious of the cloister. He also stressed the fundamental truth that charity is the essence of Christian perfection. St. Francis' theology is both Augustinian and Thomistic. His piety (which was strongly influenced by the *Spiritual Exercises* of St. Ignatius) was permeated with the mystery of the Heart of Christ:

> ...God's love is seated within the Savior's heart as on a royal throne. He beholds through the cleft of his pierced side all the hearts of the children of men. His heart is king of hearts, and he keeps his eyes fixed on our hearts. Just as those who peer through a lattice see clearly while they themselves are only half seen, so too the divine love within that heart, or rather that heart of divine love, always sees our hearts and looks on them with his eyes of love, while we do not see him, but only half see him. If we could see him as he is, O God, since we are mortal men we would die for love of him, just as when he was in mortal flesh he died for us, and just as he would still die for us were he not now immortal. Oh, if we could hear this divine heart singing with a voice infinitely sweet his canticle of praise to the divinity! What joy, ...what striving within our heart to spring up to heaven so as to hear it forever![95]

St. Francis de Sales, in turn, greatly influenced St. Jane Frances de Chantal, with whom he established the religious institute of the Visitation of the Blessed Virgin. On June 10, 1600 (the Friday after the octave of Corpus Christi—the day which our Lord later asked to be kept as the Feast of the Sacred Heart), St. Francis wrote to St. Jane:

> I thought, if you agree, that we ought to take as armorial bearings a single heart pierced by two arrows, and set in a crown of thorns. This plain heart could form the base of a cross inscribed with the sacred

---

[93]St. Francis de Sales, *Introduction to the Devout Life* (Garden City, N.Y.: Image Books, 1972)

[94]St. Francis de Sales, *Treatise on the Love of God*, 2 Vols. (Rockford, Ill.: Tan Books & Pub., Inc., 1975)

[95]*Ibid.*, Vol. I, Book V, chp. 11, p. 263.

Figure 12: St. Francis de Sales

names of Jesus and Mary. For truly, our little Congregation is the work
of the hearts of Jesus and Mary. By opening his Sacred Heart, the dying
Savior brought us to birth.[96]

This spiritual tradition, according to Stierli, was united to yet another tradition from the Society of Jesus. From this we can see that the devotion to the
Sacred Heart was known to the Order of the Visitation even before St.
Margaret Mary Alacoque. The knowledge of this devotion must have been
more limited than some suppose or it would be hard to explain the opposition
of the Saint's own community at Paray-le-Monial.

The liturgical development of the devotion continued throughout this
period. A feast of the Sacred Heart had been celebrated in the Dominican
monastery at Unterlinden in Colmar, Alsace in the 15th century. Numerous
Masses in honor of the Five Wounds, along with the Mass of the Holy Lance,
continued to be used with ever increasing popularity. The devotion reached
a new stage of development, thanks to the work of St. John Eudes (1601-
1680). St. John's lifelong apostolate was to popularize the devotion to the
Hearts of Jesus and Mary among the Catholic faithful. It was primarily due
to his fervent efforts that a wider and more specific liturgical cult of the Sacred
Heart came to be known in the Church. He wrote 15 separate Mass texts, the
last of which was composed in 1668 and officially celebrated on October 20,
1672. Pope St. Pius X called St. John Eudes the author and apostle of the
liturgical worship of the Sacred Heart. St. John also established the devotion
to the Sacred Heart on firmer theological foundations. He founded (with the
support of Cardinal Richelieu) the Congregation of Jesus and Mary in March
of 1643. His priests took no vows but dedicated themselves completely to the
two-fold task of 1) aiding the sanctification of the clergy through properly
rigorous seminary training and 2) preaching the Gospel to the laity. His first
Grand Seminary was opened at Caen in 1643, again with the support of
Richilieu and a generous endowment from the Cardinal's niece, the Duchess
of Aiguillon. Between 1650 and 1667, St. John happily saw four additional
Grand Seminaries open in Normandy: at Coustances, Lisieux, Rouen and
Evreux. During this period he constantly and fervently preached devotion to
the Hearts of Jesus and Mary. The members of his Congregations were
enjoined by the Saint to use "*Ave, Cor sanctissimum*" and "*Ave Cor amantis-
simum Jesu et Mariae*" as their familiar greetings. For his own followers he

---

[96]Vincent Kerns, ed. & trans., *The Autobiography of St. Margaret Mary* (London:
Darton, Longman & Todd., 1976), p. ix.

established two solemn feast days: one for the heart of Jesus and one for the heart of Mary. In his writings one may find a complete spirituality centered upon the Heart of Jesus "lovingly and willingly viewed and imitated from the Heart of Mary."[97]

> The heart of Christ is a temple of divine love. It is the uncreated and eternal love, namely, the Holy Spirit who has built this magnificent Temple and built it from the virginal blood of the Mother of love. This temple has been consecrated and sanctified through the anointing of Divinity. It is dedicated to Eternal love. It is infinitely holier than any temple, material or spiritual, ever built or ever to be built in Heaven or on earth. It is in that temple that God receives adorations, praises and glory really worthy of his infinite greatness. It is an eternal temple, the center of holiness.
>
> But the love of Jesus is not only a temple: it is also the altar of divine love. It is on that altar that the sacred fire of that same love is burning night and day. It is on that altar that our High Priest Jesus continually offers sacrifices to the most Holy Trinity.[98]

The inauguration of the feast of the Sacred Heart by St. John Eudes took place three years before the revelations to St. Margaret Mary at Paray-le-Monial. These two Saints did not even know each other, but we can see clearly the working of Divine Providence, leading to those climactic events that occurred in the Visitation monastery which would reverberate throughout the Catholic world.

Jean-Jacques Olier (1608-1657), the founder of the Sulpicians, was educated by the Jesuits and was guided to the priesthood by St. Francis de Sales. He was also deeply influenced later in life by St. Vincent de Paul. In his spiritual writings he emphasized self-abnegation and adherence to Christ. He did not expatiate at length on the Heart of Jesus, but we do have the following excerpt in which he refers to the Sacred Heart:

> In the Heart of Jesus you will enter into the enjoyment of all that he is.... Here in the Heart of the Son of God is the dwelling-place of the elect. It is in the Sacred Heart, in its adorable depth, that all mysteries are first wrought; it is here that God gives to his saints the most intimate communications and most perfectly expresses his divine mysteries.
>
> What can be said of the glory that God's majesty receives from

---

[97]Walter Kern, *Updated Devotion to the Sacred Heart* (Canfield, Ohio: Alba House Communications, 1975), p. 69.

[98]St. John Eudes, *Meditations on Various Subjects* (New York: P. J. Kennedy, 1947), p. 427-430.

the Heart of Jesus alone, that Heart which gives more homage to God than to all the saints? For saints and angels are made to express the feelings and thoughts of the Heart of Jesus....

All the praise and respect that the saints have ever rendered to God are drawn from the Heart of Jesus Christ, and from his fullness.... It is this great Heart that holds all that is poured out so lavishly in the Church.... O magnificent Heart of Jesus, adorable source of our religion, source too and plenitude of our homage to God, since all in us is drawn from you.[99]

Conclusion

In reviewing the six hundred years of the Medieval phase of the devotion to the Sacred Heart we can see conclusively that there was no sudden discovery of the devotion. It most certainly did not originate from the private revelation given to St. Margaret Mary Alacoque. The medieval forms of the devotion to the heart of Christ rested solidly upon patristic traditions as we have seen. It is primarily due to the work of preservation accomplished by the Benedictine monks that this vital link was forged.

From the Golden and Silver Ages of the Fathers down through each century of the Middle Ages we find constant references to the same recurring themes: the Heart of the crucified Savior as the source of the fountain of infinite graces; the Church as Christ's spotless Bride born of his Heart; the Eucharist and the other sacraments flowing from his opened side as streams of blood and water; and the Heart of Jesus as the sanctuary of rest and refuge where one may draw heavenly knowledge of God.

St. John the Beloved Disciple also played an important role in the piety of the Middle Ages. The disciple whom Jesus loved was seen as the intercessory guide who led the Christian to the Heart of the Savior. Here again we may see the influence of Origen's interpretation of St. John's reclining upon the bosom of our Lord at the Last Supper and drinking in the secrets of his Heart.

Medieval spiritual writers who commented upon the Canticle of Canticles also drew heavily from the patristic tradition which stressed the loving nuptial mystery between Christ and the soul.

Although the Christians of the Middle Ages depended upon the patristic

---

[99]Cf. M. Williams, *op. cit.*, p. 105. Among other famous witnesses to the devotion in the French School, we find the celebrated bishop and orator Jacques Bossuet (1627-1704) who was also trained by the Jesuits and had St. Vincent de Paul for his spiritual director; St. Louise de Marillac (d. 1659), foundress of the Daughters of Charity; St. Margaret of the Blessed Sacrament (d. 1648). Cf. Aumann, Mulhern, O'Donnell, *Devotion to the Heart of Jesus, op. cit.*, pp. 133-136.

foundation, they did build upon this edifice and make many contributions to the development of the devotion to the Sacred Heart. The ever increasing emphasis upon the Passion of Christ, especially in terms of his interior suffering added great depth to the devotion. This revealed the inner life of Christ, characterized by his love for his Father and sinful man. It was a burning love which was filled with infinite compassion and suffering. This form of profound meditation upon the Passion of our Lord was nourished by the Crusades and many pilgrimages to the Holy Land. The spiritual meditations of St. Bridget of Sweden (1302-1373), who visited the Holy Land, are a perfect example of this form of medieval piety which led to the fervent veneration of the Sacred Heart of Jesus.[100]

A strong bond was also established during this period between the Blessed Sacrament and the devotion to the Sacred Heart. This bond became more pronounced after the introduction of the feast of Corpus Christi. The Eucharist came to be seen with an ever increasing clarity as the supreme gift of the Heart of Jesus.

Despite the widespread destruction of monastic literature which resulted from the religious wars following the Protestant Revolt, enough remains to bear witness to the growth, development and vitality of the devotion into the 17th century. In this process of development we see the work of the Holy Spirit. From the moment the Spirit came forth from the opened Heart of the crucified Christ, he has been giving clearer shape to the revelation of the Sacred Heart of Jesus. The great mystery of the Heart of the Savior was heralded under his inspiration in the Sacred Scriptures and blossomed forth in the rich theology of the Fathers and early medievals. The Heart of our Lord was viewed as the inexhaustible source of all graces. The Holy Spirit sustained and developed this devotion during the High Middle Ages by directing fervent souls to a passionate meditation upon the Sacred Heart of Jesus. For our Modern era as well, this fiery Spirit of love was to give the devotion a new life. This life was to be given in the Spirit's own marvellous way—a way not envisaged by man, for those final days "when charity had grown cold."

---

[100]St. Bridget of Sweden, *The Magnificent Promises* (South Bend, Ind.: Marian Publications, 1971).

Figure 13: *Eighteenth century engraving from the oil-portrait of St. Margaret Mary in the Convent of Paray-le-Monial.*

III.

St. Margaret Mary Alacoque and Her Divine Mission

"Le coeur de Jesus etait brilliant come un soleil, aux dires de la Sainte de Paray."

("The Heart of Jesus shone like a sun, according to the saint of Paray.")

Her Life and Revelations

Our brief historical sketch has shown with sufficient clarity that the Church had a rather lengthy period of p reparation for accepting the message which our Lord entrusted to St. Margaret Mary Alacoque. The devotion was not established by the visions of the saint but goes back beyond the Medieval era to the patristic theology of the wounded side of Christ as the source of all graces. It would however be wrong to minimize the decisive role of these visions of our Lord who specifically revealed himself to St. Margaret Mary as the Sacred Heart for what Stierli calls "apologetic reasons." As a result of these visions and messages of our Lord, a special form was given to this traditional devotion by St. Margaret Mary. This special form has become intricately tied up with the devotion as it is taught and lived by the Church. It seems that in the case of St. Margaret Mary we may once again see our Lord's favorite way of doing things:

> ...the weakness of this world has God chosen...that which is despised...that which is nothing...lest any flesh should pride itself before Him. (1 Cor. 1:27-29)

This humble nun, hidden away in a cloistered Visitation convent in Paray-le-Monial, France became the clay in God's hands through which he communicated his redemptive plans for our age. Unlike the many mystical visions of the Sacred Heart which preceded those of St. Margaret Mary, her visions at Paray-le-Monial did not *center* upon a personal grace for her own growth in holiness but rather upon a mission to the Church. For these reasons we shall explore her own writings for a glimpse into her saintly life and a first hand account of our Lord's communications to her.

She was born on July 22, 1647, the youngest in a family of seven, which was moderately wealthy. She mentions in her autobiography that her father died while she was still a small child. His premature death brought severe hardships upon the family, especially on little Margaret and her mother. In her autobiography she speaks of her early spiritual development:

> From babyhood on you headed me off, claiming my heart for your very own—though you knew all along how difficult I was going to be. At the dawn of consciousness you showed me the ugliness of sin. So horrible was the impression it left on me, I simply couldn't bear the slightest stain.
>
> Over and over again I found myself saying something I couldn't understand: "To God I give my purity, and vow perpetual chastity." Once I said it at Mass between the two elevations. (I used to hear Mass on my bare knees, even in the coldest weather.) I'd no idea what I had done—neither "vow" nor "chastity" meant anything to me—but I knew what I wanted....
>
> The blessed Virgin always watched over me very carefully. I used to take all my needs to her, and she saved me from many a grave danger.[1]

Following the death of her father, Margaret was sent away to a boarding school of the Urbanists at Charolles. It was there that she received her first Holy Communion and felt an ever deepening desire for solitude and the life of prayer. She also developed a profound love for our Lord in the Most Blessed Sacrament. Margaret remained at the school for only two years due to a severe illness which kept her so weak that she couldn't walk for nearly four years. She was suddenly cured when she dedicated herself to the Virgin Mary, vowing to "be one of her daughters."

The rest of Margaret's life up to her entry into the Convent of the Visitation was spent at home with her mother. They both suffered severely because of the cruelty of relatives who lived in the same house. Margaret

---

[1]Vincent Kerns, ed. & trans., *The Autobiography of St. Margaret Mary, op. cit.,* pp. 3-5.

speaks of this suffering at home and her intense desire to be conformed to Christ crucified:

> I used to spend the nights, after all that, as I had spent the days—crying in front of my crucifix. There, though I didn't understand it at the time, our Lord explained that his aim was the undisputed mastery of my heart, and that my earthly life would be one of suffering like his. He would become my Master just for this: to make me aware of his presence, so that I'd behave as he did during his own cruel sufferings, which—he showed me—he had endured for love of me. (The effect on my soul was so deep, I wouldn't have had my sufferings cease, even for a moment.) He never left me afterwards, and I'd always see him crucified or carrying his cross. In the pity and love that filled my heart, all my own troubles seemed light. Besides, I wanted them; I wanted to take after Jesus in his sufferings.[2]

Margaret's mother soon became ill and the responsibility to nurse her back to health fell upon Margaret. Her mother had a repugnant ulcerated sore on her face and no one could stand the sight of it. It was during this period of domestic turmoil that Margaret advanced along the road of mental prayer as can be seen from her love of the Eucharistic Presence:

> Well, he kept me so hard at what I've just been describing that I lost all my taste for vocal prayers. I simply couldn't say any before the Blessed Sacrament; I used to be so intent on the Real Presence, I was never bored. Days and nights could have come and gone, food and drink forgotten—I wouldn't have noticed it, content to burn out there like a candle and give back love for love. I couldn't stay at the back of the church; I had to get as near the Blessed Sacrament as possible, in spite of the embarrassment I used to feel. The only people I envied were those who could go often to communion and be free to stay with the Blessed Sacrament—that was my idea of happiness.[3]

Although deeply spiritual, Margaret was also an attractive, vivacious young woman. When she came of age there were many young men who sought her hand in marriage. Her mother, with constant tears, would beg her to marry, saying that Margaret was her only hope for happiness.[4] This burden greatly increased her suffering to the point where the young girl felt herself

---

[2]*Ibid.*, p. 7.

[3]*Ibid.*, p. 11. A fine treatment of the centrality of the Eucharist in Margaret Mary's spirituality can be found in J. Dargaud, *The Eucharist in the Life of St. Margaret Mary* (Libertyville, Ill.: Franciscan Marytown Press, 1979).

[4]*Ibid.*, p. 13.

to be upon the rack. Despite these entreaties, our Lord drew her to "a deeper appreciation of the beauty of virtue—especially poverty, chastity and obedience, the three vows of religion."[5]

Finally this particular agony was brought to an end when on June 20, 1671 she entered the Order of the Visitation at Paray-le-Monial. As soon as she entered into the parlour she heard a voice inside her whisper: "This is where I want you." From that day onward, Margaret gave herself totally to the work of our Lord. On August 25 of the same year she completed her first probation and took the habit. During this period she was the recipient of many graces and favors from our Lord. On November 6, 1672 she made her simple religious profession and became even more intimate with the Savior. Several months before the revelations of the Sacred Heart, on October 4, 1673, Christ gave St. Francis of Assisi to Margaret as her guide:

> On the feast of St. Francis, our Lord let me see in prayer this great saint, clad in a garment of light and unspeakable brilliance. He had been raised above the other saints to an extraordinarily high degree of glory, because his life was so like that of the suffering Redeemer who is the life of our souls and the love of our hearts. His glory was the reward of his great love for the Passion of our Lord, a love which rendered him worthy of the sacred stigmata and made him one of the great favourites of Jesus' heart. By a very special favour he had been given great power in applying to the faithful the merits of the Precious Blood, a power which made him in a sense the mediator of this treasure.
>
> After I had seen all this, the Divine Bridegroom, as a token of his love, gave me St. Francis as my soul's guide. He was to lead me through all the pains and sufferings which awaited me.[6]

The first of the great visions in which our Lord revealed to Margaret Mary her role in the spreading of the devotion to the Sacred Heart occurred on the feast of St. John the Apostle, December 27, 1673. Here is her description of the vision:

> Once, however, when I happened to have a little more time to myself than usual, and I was spending it in front of the Blessed Sacrament, God's presence seemed to envelop me completely. I forgot all about myself, and where I was, it was so intense; I simply gave myself up to the Spirit of God—my heart, a willing prey to the

[5]*Ibid.*, p. 15.
[6]A. Hamon, *Vie de la Bienheureuse Marguerite-Marie* (Paris: Gabriel Beauchesne & Cie, 1908), p. 125.

Figure 14: Basilica of the Sacred Heart in Paray-le-Monial.

violence of his love. For a long time he kept me leaning on his breast, while he revealed the wonders of his love and the mysterious secrets of his Sacred Heart. Till then, he had always kept them hidden; but now, for the first time, he opened his Heart to me. The realistic and tangible way in which he did so, as well as the effects which this grace had on me, left no room for any doubt; still, I'm always afraid of being mistaken whenever I describe what goes on inside me. What happened, I think, was this....

"My divine Heart," he told me, "is so passionately fond of the human race, and of you in particular, that it cannot keep back the pent-up flames of its burning charity any longer. They must burst out through you and reveal my Heart to the world, so as to enrich mankind with my precious treasures. I'm letting you see them now; and they include all the graces of sanctification needed to snatch men from the very brink of hell. You are the one I have chosen for this great

Figure 15: The Monastery of the Visitation.

scheme—you're so utterly unworthy and ignorant, it will be all *my* work."

Next, he asked for my heart. I begged him to take it; he did, and placed it in his own divine Heart. He let me see it there—a tiny atom being completely burned up in that fiery furnace. Then, lifting it out—now a little heart-shaped flame—he put it back where he had found it. "There, my well-beloved," I heard him saying, "that's a precious proof of my love for you, hiding in your side a little spark from its hottest flames. That will be your heart from now on; it will burn you up—to your very last breath; its intense heat will never diminish—only blood-letting will cool it slightly. But I shall cast the shadow of my cross over your bleeding; so deeply, it will bring you more humiliation and suffering than relief. That is why I insist that you ask for this treatment in all simplicity; you will then be doing what you are told, as well as finding satisfaction in shedding your blood on the cross of humiliation. As a proof that the great grace I have just given you is not an illusion, but the basis of all those which I have still in store for you...although I've closed the wound in your side, you will always feel the pain of it. And how have you been describing yourself up to the present: my slave? Well, now I'm giving you a new name: the beloved disciple of my Sacred Heart."[7]

Following this vision, Margaret Mary felt on fire with love for the suffering Christ. On the first Friday of each month she received special graces along with the burning pain in her side. The second and third revelations occurred in 1674, although the exact date is uncertain. Here is Margaret's account:

One, from many, stands out....

The Blessed Sacrament was exposed, and I was experiencing an unusually complete state of recollection, my sense and faculties utterly withdrawn from their surroundings, when Jesus Christ, my kind Master, appeared to me. He was a blaze of glory—his five wounds shining like five suns, flames issuing from all parts of his human form, especially from his divine breast which was like a furnace, and which he opened to disclose his utterly affectionate and lovable heart, the living source of all those flames. It was at this moment that he revealed to me the indescribable wonders of his pure love for mankind: the extravagance to which he'd been led for those who had nothing for him but ingratitude and indifference. "This hurts me more," he told me, "than everything I suffered in my passion. Even a little love from them in return—and I should regard all that I have done for them as next to nothing, and look for a way of doing still more. But no; all my eager efforts for their welfare meet with nothing but coldness and

---

[7]Vincent Kerns, *op. cit.*, pp. 44-45.

Figure 16: *The Chapel of the Visitation, the site of the great revelations given to St. Margaret Mary.*

dislike. Do me the kindness, then—you, at least—of making up for all their ingratitude, as far as you can." When I pointed out my capacities, he replied: "Here you are! This will make good your deficiencies, every one of them!" His divine Heart opening as he spoke, such a scorching flame shot forth as I was sure would devour me. It went right through me; and when I could bear it no longer I begged him to take pity on my weakness. "I shall be your support," he told me; "Don't be afraid. Simply focus all your attention on my voice—on what I am asking of you so as to fit you for the fulfillment of my plans. First of all, you are to receive me in the holy Eucharist as often as obedience allows. Accept any mortification or humiliation that may result, as a token of my love. Besides this, you are to receive Communion on the first Friday of each month. Then, every Thursday night, I shall give you a share in that fatal sadness which I allowed myself to feel in the garden of olives; death couldn't be so hard as the agonized state to which this sadness will reduce you. You are to get up between eleven o'clock and midnight, to keep me company in humble prayer to my Father, exactly as I spent that night in agony. Lie face downwards with me for an hour—not only to allay God's anger by asking mercy for sinners, but also to soothe in some way the heartache I felt when my apostles deserted me, when I had to reproach them for being unable to watch with me even for an hour. And, during this hour, you are to do what I show you. But listen, child! Don't believe lightly in every inspiration, and don't be too sure of it—Satan is furiously bent on deceiving you. So don't do anything without the approval of those who are guiding you. As long as you have the sanction of obedience, he can never delude you; he is completely powerless over those who obey.[8]

The Visitation community of Paray-le-Monial received a new Superior, Mother Saumaise, to whom Margaret revealed the secrets of her soul to the best of her ability. Mother Saumaise firmly believed in the supernatural character of the visions and messages "on the strength of clear criteria."[9] She thought it best however to have them tested by wise theologians according to the sound principles of ascetical and mystical theology. Margaret agreed in obedience to this examination although this led to an increase of interior suffering and exterior embarrassment.

It was shortly after this that Bl. Claude de la Columbière (1641-1682) was sent to Margaret as a confessor. This holy, brilliant and cultured young Jesuit, who had tutored the sons of Colbert, was to play a central role in the future spread of the devotion. The coming of Fr. Columbière had been promised to

[8]*Ibid.*, pp. 46-47.
[9]J. Stierli, *op. cit.*, p. 118.

Figure 17: *Detail of the second great apparition by Luc Barbier in the Chapel of the Visitation in Paray-le-Monial.*

Margaret by our Lord, who in an apparition to St. Margaret Mary had referred to him as "my faithful servant and perfect friend." She poured out to him all that had been made known to her. The priest was used by Providence to strengthen and assure Margaret of the truth of her supernatural graces and commissions.[10]

This added support prepared the Saint for the Great Revelation of June, 1675:

> One day, kneeling before the Blessed Sacrament during the octave of Corpus Christi, I was deluged with God's loving favours. Inspired to make some return, and to give him love for love, I heard him say: "Do what I've already so often asked you; you can't show your love in a finer way than that! He disclosed his divine Heart as he spoke: "There it is, that Heart so deeply in love with men, it spared no means of proof—wearing itself out until it was utterly spent! This meets with scant appreciation from most of them; all I get back is ingratitude— witness their irreverence, their sacrileges, their coldness and contempt for me in this Sacrament of Love. What hurts me most is that hearts dedicated to my service behave in this way. That is why I am asking you to have the Friday after the octave of Corpus Christi set apart as a special feast in honour of my Heart—a day on which to receive me in Holy Communion and make a solemn act of reparation for the indignities I have received in the Blessed Sacrament while exposed on the altars of the world. I promise you, too, that I shall open my Heart to all who honour me in this way, and who get others to do the same; they will feel in all its fullness the power of my love.[11]

For the next ten years there was no public manifestation of the content of the visions. This was a period of intense suffering for Margaret. She was constantly subjected to humiliations by her fellow sisters but the Lord sustained her with a shower of graces—many of which were painful. In 1685 she was made mistress of novices and on the occasion of the celebration of her patronal feast, she directed the first outward reverence to the Sacred Heart, by having the novices erect a little altar upon which they placed a pen and ink drawing of the Sacred Heart. This action brought a storm of complaint upon

---

[10]Fr. Columbière was transferred to London in 1676 where he became chaplain to the young Mary Beatrice of Modena, the Duchess of York. This period during the dark reign of Charles II was one of spiritual joy and suffering for Bl. Claude. He brought many back to the ancient Faith by preaching the love of the Heart of Christ. Eventually, he was imprisoned and then driven out of England, a true confessor of the Faith. He returned to France in poor health and was able to spend only ten days in Paray. An excellent biography of Blessed Claude is Georges Guitton, SJ, *Perfect Friend* (St. Louis: B. Herder Book Co., 1956). See also Margaret Yeo, *These Three Hearts* (Milwaukee: The Bruce Pub. Co., 1940).

[11]Vincent Kerns, *op. cit.*, pp. 77-78.

Figure 18: Portrait of Bl. Claude de la Colombière.

the Mistress of Novices from the community who thought Margaret was seeking to introduce a new devotion.

Within a year, however, the entire community formally celebrated the first feast of the Sacred Heart on June 21, 1686. This remarkable change was due to the fact that two years after the death of Fr. Colombière (in 1684) four volumes of his sermons and one of his retreat notes were published in Lyons. In the holy priest's notes on the spiritual exercises given in London in 1677, he spoke of a highly favoured soul whom he knew personally. This chosen soul had received from the Lord himself, in a series of visions, the commission of spreading the devotion to the Sacred Heart. Despite the fact that neither person nor place were mentioned in the book, it was immediately understood as referring to Paray-le-Monial, where it was read during meals. With the authoritative backing of such a holy and deeply loved priest, all opposition ceased in the community. Paray-le-Monial became the first center of this devotion which rapidly spread out to the other houses of the Visitation. Margaret, after years of waiting, poured all her energies into apostolic activities by writing numerous letters [12] which she hoped would foster the devotion as the Lord had commanded her.

The remaining four years of Margaret Mary's life were filled by her efforts to spread the devotion. Hers was a life of intense suffering through which she was conformed to the image of her only love—Christ crucified. To the end of her life she spoke lovingly of "the precious treasure of the cross," "the delicious bread of humiliation and contempt." The world may love riches and honors but no such vain love could ever hope to surpass her in the degree of love for "the exact opposite of what the world loves and embraces." All of the suffering, humiliation and contempt heaped upon Margaret Mary served only to unite her ever more intimately to the Lord of Hearts. The beloved disciple of the Sacred Heart was called by her divine Master to her eternal reward on October 17, 1690. The following day she was buried in the chapel of the convent beneath the nuns choir. She was beatified by Pope Pius IX on September 18, 1864 and canonized by Pope Benedict XV on May 13, 1920.

The uniqueness of these visions as we have mentioned stems from the fact that they were directed beyond the saint to the universal Church. The content of these visions has shaped the external form of the Church's devotion to the Sacred Heart. This form of the devotion encompasses the First Friday Mass and Communion of Reparation, the Thursday night Holy Hour in memory of our Lord's bitter agony in Gethesemani, the liturgical feast for the

---

[12]See Clarence A. Herbst, S. J., trans., *Letters of St. Margaret Mary Alacoque* (Orlando, Florida: Men of the Sacred Heart, 1976).

Figure 19: The pen and ink drawing of the Heart of Jesus by St. Margaret Mary.

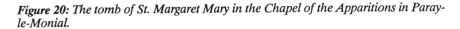

Figure 20: *The tomb of St. Margaret Mary in the Chapel of the Apparitions in Paray-le-Monial.*

Sacred Heart (the highest rank possible), and the heavy emphasis upon consecration and reparation. This fact, along with the canonization of St. Margaret Mary and subsequent papal encyclicals, all give an extraordinary and compelling testimony to the Church's belief in the authenticity of these visions and their message.

Some criticism has been directed against the devotion because of the "Promises" of the Sacred Heart to St. Margaret Mary. These promises were drawn out from the writings of the saint. Although other lists of the Promises existed as early as 1861 (if not earlier), the widespread publication of the Promises in tabular form dates back to 1882, when an American businessman from Dayton, Ohio, Philip Kemper, distributed the list throughout the world. By 1895, the Promises had been translated into 238 languages. On May 31, 1899, Pope Leo XIII sent Mr. Kemper a document of papal approbation and blessing for his "pious" and "useful" work. The list reads as follows:

1. I will give them all the graces necessary in their state of life.
2. I will establish peace in their homes.
3. I will comfort them in all their afflictions.
4. I will be their secure refuge during life, and above all, in death.
5. I will bestow abundant blessings upon all their undertakings.

6. Sinners will find in my Heart the source and infinite ocean of mercy.

7. Lukewarm souls shall become fervent.

8. Fervent souls shall quickly mount to high perfection.

9. I will bless every place in which an image of my Heart is exposed and honored.

10. I will give to priests the gift of touching the most hardened hearts.

11. Those who shall promote this devotion shall have their names written in my Heart.

12. I promise you in the excessive mercy of my Heart that my all powerful love will grant to all those who receive Holy Communion on the First Fridays in nine consecutive months the grace of final perseverance; they shall not die in my disgrace, nor without receiving their sacraments. My divine Heart shall be their safe refuge in this last moment.

Some modern Christians have been bothered by these promises as being "too easy," or "too automatic." For example, some have claimed "the Great Promise" of the nine First Fridays is merely a technique for gaining "power over God" or is a form of piety which will lead to presumption upon the mercy of God.[13]

All these clearly twist our Lord's intention in making these promises. We may accept Karl Rahner's appraisal of the promises as a valid answer to such criticism. He writes:

> Taken in their entirety, these promises affirm and offer no more than our Lord himself promised in the Gospel to absolute faith (Mt. 17, 20:21, 21f.; Mk. 16, 17f.; Jn. 14, 12f.). What is new in these promises is therefore not their content, but the circumstances of their fulfillment, the fact that what has already been promised in substance in the Gospels is now attached precisely to devotion to the Sacred Heart. To anyone with a proper grasp of the devotion, who practices it in the deep and unconditional faith that it demands, this "new" element in the promises will offer no special problem.
>
> Taken as a whole, these promises should be interpreted in the same way as those made in the Gospel to the prayer of faith. In neither case are we dealing with a technique or recipe for gaining a hold over God and the unconditioned sovereignty of his inscrutable will. The

---

[13]For an interesting textual, theological and pastoral study of the promises made to St. Margaret Mary, one may consult Paul Wenisch, S. J. *Promises of Our Lord to St. Margaret Mary* (India: The Nat'l. Office, Apostleship of Prayer, n.d.).

promises are made to man only in the measure in which he surrenders himself in unreserved faith and unquestioning love to the will of God, which is absolute, and for us unfathomable, love.[14]

According to Pope Benedict XV, private revelation should be accepted "with an assent of human belief according to the rules of prudence, when these rules present them as probable and devoutly believable."[15] The fact that Pope Benedict XV quoted the Great Promise in the Bull of canonization of St. Margaret Mary is a clear sign of its theological soundness.

Of course it must be remembered that there is nothing unusual at all about God making promises.[16] Sacred Scripture contains numerous conditional and unconditional promises. Examples of the unconditional promises can be seen in the following Scriptural passages: the promise of a redeemer (Gen. 3:15); of Peter's primacy and the indestructibility of the Church (Mt. 16: 17-19); and of the Holy Spirit (Jn. 3:37-39). For examples of conditional promises we may mention the promise of eternal life through the Eucharist. Many more could be given (Gen. 8:21-22; Gen. 12:1-3; Jer. 31:3; II Kings 7:10-16; Lk. 1:31-37; Mt. 5:3-12) but these will suffice for illustration.

The purpose of these promises was set forth by Pope Pius XII:

> For if Christ has solemnly promised them in private revelations it was for the purpose of encouraging men to perform with greater fervor the chief duties of the Catholic religion, namely, love and expiation, and thus take all possible measures for their own spiritual advantage.[17]

Is it true that we cannot be absolutely certain of the authenticity of these revelations, since we know of them through one individual? In such highly spiritual matters, human testimony is certainly not infallible. The witness in this case however is a canonized saint of the Church. The Church, in the process of beatification, examined all the writings of Margaret Mary which contained the detailed accounts of the revelations and She approved them. From this official approval on the part of the Church we may deduce that these revelations contain nothing against faith and morals which the Church always guards with a lively devotion.

The view taken by the Church of these revelations allows us to believe in

---

[14]Karl Rahner, "Some Theses on the Theology of the Devotion" in *Heart of the Savior*, ed. by J. Stierli, *op. cit.*, p. 155.

[15]Walter Kern, *Updated Devotion to the Sacred Heart, op. cit.*, p. 74.

[16]See Francis Larkin, *Understanding the Heart*, Orlando, Florida: Reconciliation Press, 1975), pp. 28-30. This is an excellent little book written by a holy priest who spent his life spreading devotion to the Sacred Heart. It has been republished by Ignatius Press.

[17]Pius XII, *Haurietis Aquas, op. cit.*, pp. 42-43.

their authenticity. Although the Church does not explicitly pronounce upon them with her infallible teaching authority, she has on numerous occasions expressed her belief in them.

Many popes, in a lengthy series of papal documents, speak of the revelations as undeniable realities.

Pope Pius IX, in the Brief of beatification of Margaret Mary, issued on September 18, 1864, writes:

> It was as she was praying with fervor before the august Sacrament of the Eucharist, that Christ our Lord intimated to her that it would be most pleasing to Him if the worship of His most Sacred Heart, burning with love for mankind, were established, and He wished the charge of this to be consigned to her. The humility of the Venerable Servant of God was greatly alarmed, as she deemed herself unworthy of such an office; nevertheless, in order that she might comply with the will of heaven and satisfy her desire of enkindling divine love in the hearts of men, she earnestly exerted herself both amongst the Religious of her own convent, and also, as far as she could, amongst all in general, to induce them to show every mark of honor, worship, reverence towards the most Sacred Heart, the seat of divine charity.[18]

Pope Leo XIII, in his Encyclical *Annum Sacrum*, issued on May 25, 1899, makes reference to "the mandate which Blessed Margaret Mary received from Heaven, that of propagating the cult of the divine Heart."

Pope Benedict XV, in the Bull of canonization of St. Margaret Mary issued on May 13, 1920, mentions the chief apparitions our Lord made to the Saint, along with the message He communicated to her.

Pope Pius XI, in his encyclical *Miserentissimus Redemptor*, issued on May 8, 1928, states:

> Since some Christians, perhaps, are ignorant of and others are indifferent to, the sorrows which the most loving Jesus revealed to St. Margaret Mary Alacoque in His apparitions to her, as well as His wishes and desires which He manifested to mankind, all of which in the last analysis work to man's advantage, it is our pleasure, Venerable Brothers, to write to you at some length of the obligation which rests upon all to make those amends which we owe to the Most Sacred Heart of Jesus....
>
> On the occasion when Jesus revealed himself to St. Margaret Mary, though He then insisted on the immensity of His love, at the same time, with sorrowful mien, He grieved over the great number of

---

[18]Msgr. Gauthey, ed. *Vie et Oeuvres de sainte Marguerite Marie* Vol. III (Paris: Poussielgue, 1930), p. 151.

horrible outrages heaped upon Him by the ingratitude of mankind. He used these words which should be graven on the hearts of all pious souls so as never to be forgotten by them: "Behold this Heart which has loved men so much, which has heaped upon them so many benefits. In exchange for this infinite love It finds ingratitude; instead It meets with forgetfulness, indifference, outrages, and all this at times even from souls bound closely to It in the bonds of a very special love."[19]

This attitude of belief taken by the Church has been adopted by successive Popes. Vatican Council II clearly acknowledged the existence of "most outstanding" charisms within the Church which are "extraordinary gifts."

It is not only through the sacraments and Church ministries that the same Holy Spirit sanctifies and leads the People of God and enriches it with virtues. Allotting His gifts " to everyone according as he will" (I Cor. 12:11), He distributed special graces among the faithful of every rank. By these gifts he makes them fit and ready to undertake the various tasks or offices advantageous for the renewal and upbuilding of the Church, according to the words of the Apostle: "The manifestation of the Spirit is given to everyone for profit" (I Cor. 12:7). These charismatic gifts, whether they be the most outstanding or the more simple and widely diffused, are to be received with thanksgiving and consolation, for they are exceedingly suitable and useful for the needs of the Church. Still, extraordinary gifts are not to be rashly sought after, nor are the fruits of apostolic labor to be presumptuously expected from them. In any case, judgment as to their genuineness and proper use belongs to those who preside over the Church, and to whose special competence it belongs, not indeed to extinguish the Spirit, but to test all things and hold fast to that which is good (cf. I Th. 5:12, 19-21). (*Lumen Gentium* 12)[20]

The revelations given to St. Margaret Mary, in their substance and in so far as they touch her divine commission, must unquestionably be included among those authentic "extraordinary gifts." This is certainly clear from the manner in which the competent authority of the Church has judged and acted. Certainly the extent to which the Church has approved and recognizes these revelations is unique. If there ever have been truly authentic extraordinary charisms in the Church, then without a doubt, those given to St. Margaret Mary must be counted among them.

---

[19]Pius XI, *Miserentissimus Redemptor*, AAS XX, 1928, p. 166; 173.

[20]Walter Abbott, *The Documents of Vatican II* (NY: American Press, 1966), p. 30; cf. *Sacrosanctum Oecumenicum Concilium Vaticanum II, op. cit.*, pp. 114-115.

After a lengthy period of intense examination the Church recognized all the essential elements of these revelations. Christ's request for the Feast of the Sacred Heart to be celebrated on the Friday after the Octave of Corpus Christi was acknowledged and the Magisterium further permitted and fostered throughout the universal Church the forms of devotion practised by St. Margaret Mary, including the Holy Hour, First Friday Communion, *et al.* The Church's belief is further seen in Her official liturgy for the various feasts associated with the Sacred Heart: the solemnity itself and the offices for the feasts of St. Margaret Mary and Bl. Claude de la Colombière (her confessor).

In the light of such a clear judgment, a believer would certainly be acting rashly and most temerariously if he were to place his personal opinion over that of the Church which moves with the utmost caution in these areas.

The character of Margaret Mary, as witnessed by her writings, the judgment of her superiors, her fellow religious and her spiritual directors, Bl. Claude and Ignatius Rolin, would also tend to preclude the possibility of illusion or hallucination. By officially canonizing Margaret Mary, the Church has acknowledged that she did not act imprudently in her attitude toward these revelations. Any sign of serious imprudence would argue against the virtue of the saint, and therefore preclude canonization. St. Margaret Mary showed no signs of premature credulity or craving for extraordinary experiences. The Saint, in her autobiography and numerous letters, reveals complete obedience and submission to her superiors, humility, circumspection and willingness to submit her revelations to the judgment of competent theologians and spiritual directors.

The phenomenal spread of the devotion throughout the Catholic world after the death of St. Margaret Mary speaks also in favor of the revelation's heavenly origin. Our Lord said that "a tree shall be known by its fruits." Certainly, regarding the devotion to the Sacred Heart of Jesus, the fruits of apostolic zeal, heroic sacrifice and growth in holiness witnessed in the lives of millions of Christians who practice the devotion have borne and continue to bear eloquent testimony to the spiritual truth of the visionary of Paray-le-Monial.

The Church's teachings concerning the revelations of the Sacred Heart furnish Christians with moral certainty so that they not only may, but even must, adopt a similar attitude of belief or be guilty of imprudence.

From this we may clearly see that the revelations made to St. Margaret Mary were offered by our divine Lord as a special grace for the general betterment of mankind. It is certainly true that salvation is possible without the acceptance of every special grace from God but the simple truth that God offers the grace because it is most *helpful* must strongly influence one's opinion of it. As St. Margaret Mary knew so well, the devotion to the Heart of Jesus is so intimately united to the essential Christian doctrines concerning God's redemptive love (as revealed in Christ) that it is necessary to ponder these matters with great care and openness of heart.

We shall fittingly conclude this section with the tribute paid to St. Margaret Mary by Pope Pius XII in *Haurietis Aquas*:

> But surely the most distinguished place among those who have fostered this most excellent type of devotion is held by St. Margaret Mary Alacoque who, under the spiritual direction of Blessed Claude de la Colombière who assisted her work, was on fire with an unusual zeal to see to it that the real meaning of the devotion which had had such extensive developments to the great edification of the faithful should be established and be distinguished from other forms of Christian piety by the special qualities of love and reparation. It is enough to recall the record of that age in which the devotion to the Sacred Heart of Jesus began to develop to understand clearly that its marvelous progress has stemmed from the fact that it entirely agreed with the nature of Christian piety since it was a devotion of love. It must not be said that this devotion has taken its origin from some private revelation of God and has suddenly appeared in the Church; rather, it has blossomed forth of its own accord as a result of that lively faith and burning devotion of men who were endowed with heavenly gifts, and who were drawn towards the adorable Redeemer and His glorious wounds which they saw as irresistible proofs of that unbounded love.
>
> Consequently, it is clear that the revelations made to St. Margaret Mary brought nothing new into Catholic doctrine. Their importance lay in this, that Christ Our Lord, exposing His Sacred Heart, wished in a quite extraordinary way to invite the minds of men to a contemplation of, and a devotion to, the mystery of God's merciful love for the human race. In this special manifestation Christ pointed to His Heart, with definite and repeated words, as the symbol by which men should be attracted to a knowledge and recognition of His love; and at the same time He established it as a sign or pledge of mercy and grace for the needs of the Church and our times.[21]

The Spread of the Devotion & the Response of the Church

It would be impossible here to give a complete history of the devotion to the Sacred Heart following the death of St. Margaret Mary. The devotion expanded so rapidly in so many areas, that all we may hope to achieve is a very broad outline which will necessarily involve many omissions. Our atten-

---

[21]*Ibid.*, pp. 35-36.

tion shall be focused upon the devotion as it spread among the faithful and
the early actions taken by the magisterium of the Church. We shall study the
contents of subsequent magisterial teaching in far greater depth in the
following section.

There are two individuals whose names are so intimately associated with
Margaret Mary and the early post-Paray period that they must be mentioned.

Fr. Jean Croiset (who was a spiritual son of Bl. Claude de la Colombière)
came to the assistance of Margaret Mary several years after Colombière's
death. He became her spiritual counselor and, at her request and direction,[22]
wrote a booklet in 1689 on the visions of Paray. He included in this work part
of Fr. Colombière's retreat notes. Fr. Croiset maintained an animated cor-
respondence with Margaret Mary until the saint's death. Upon her death, Fr.
Croiset published a larger work entitled *La Devotion au Sacré-Coeur de
Notre-Seigneur Jésus-Christ.* Fr. Croiset added in this book a brief account of
Margaret Mary's life and visions. The book was published in 1691 and quickly
went through numerous editions. Fr. Croiset suffered terribly because of this
book, for there were many, even within his own order, who opposed the
spread of the devotion. His Provincial, who had enthusiastically supported
him, was eventually replaced and the new Provincial established a commission of theologians to investigate his teachings. The commission ruled against
Fr. Croiset and he was removed from both his professorial chair in Lyon and
the Jesuit college in order that he would not influence young Jesuits. However, through the intervention of his former provincial and other friends
within the Society, he was eventually reinstated. Throughout this ordeal, Fr.
Croiset remained steadfast in both his obedience to his superiors and in his
love for the devotion to the Sacred Heart.

Unfortunately, in 1704, one of the numerous editions of Fr. Croiset's book
was placed on the Roman Index. This unexpected action evidently occurred
not because of the contents of the work but due to the book's lack of certain
formalities which were deemed necessary.[23] Despite this unfortunate event,
the book continued to be reprinted with some changes and was translated
into Italian. It greatly facilitated the spread of the devotion throughout
Europe. The prohibition, however, remained in effect until 1887, when the
Holy Office removed the work from the list and recommended its use as an
aid to foster genuine piety.

The other individual we must mention as perhaps the most influential

---

[22]Clarence A. Herbst, S. J., trans., *Letters of St. Margaret Mary Alacoque, op. cit.*, n.
130-131, pp. 188-193.
[23]Bainvel, J. V., S. J., *La Devotion au Sacré Coeur de Jésus* (Paris, 1930), p. 523.

helper of the cause of St. Margaret Mary is Fr. Joseph Francois Galliffet. He entered the Society of Jesus in 1678. In 1680, while studying philosophy at Lyon, he came under the influence of Fr. de la Colombière. Fr. Colombière was his spiritual director for over one year and introduced the young Jesuit to the spirituality of the Sacred Heart.

Ten years later Fr. Galliffet was sent to work in a hospital and there contacted a serious infection. His doctors believed death to be inevitable and gave up all hope of saving his life. At this point Fr. Croiset vowed in Fr. Galliffet's name that, if the young Jesuit's life was saved, the sick priest would dedicate himself to the propagation of the devotion to the Sacred Heart. Fr. Galliffet did in fact recover fully and accepted his fellow Jesuit's vow as binding.

For the rest of his life he labored unceasingly to spread the devotion. He held many influential positions within the Society as Superior at Grenoble, Lyons and Provincial. He was sent to Rome in 1723 as Assistant of the General of the Society. While in Rome, he worked tirelessly to advance the cause of devotion and specifically for the requests which our Lord made to Margaret Mary. In 1726 he published in Latin a comprehensive work on the devotion entitled *De Cultu Sacrosancti cordis Dei ac Domini Nostri Jesu Christi.* It was a brilliant work but was weakened in its impact because he defended the position that the physical heart was the source and center of man's emotional life. Those who opposed the devotion concentrated upon this weakness.

Opposition to the devotion came from many quarters. Foremost among the enemies of the devotion were the Jansenists, who thought the devotion to be a perversion of Christian doctrine, and referred to its devotées as "heart worshippers". Gallicans and philosophers of the "Enlightenment" also raised their voices in opposition to the devotion.

Within the Church herself many thought the devotion to be "new", particularly insofar as it sought a liturgical feast in honor of our Lord's heart. Although devout and learned pontiffs refused those petitions which sought the establishment of a special feast in honor of our Lord's Heart as requested at Paray, this did not constitute a fundamental rejection of the devotion. This can be clearly seen by the fact that the Holy See strongly encouraged and supported the birth and growth of numerous Sacred Heart confraternities in the first half of the 18th century, conferring upon them special indulgences and privileges. Between 1690 and 1740 (the nadir of the "new" devotion) Rome showed her warm approval by granting briefs which established over 700 Sacred Heart confraternities. The Jesuits, inspired by Fr. Galliffet's zeal and passionate love for the Heart of Jesus, took the lead in promoting these confraternities. In 1720 a terrible plague struck the city of Marseilles. Over 40,000 residents were to die. Bishop de Belsuce (who had visited the Visitation convent for prayers) and municipal leaders sought refuge in the Heart of Christ and consecrated their city to the Sacred Heart. Nearly 1,000 people died each day. Litanies to the Sacred Heart were prayed by the faithful as they walked in penitential processions through the streets of the city. From that moment on the plague halted. The litany used in Marseilles may have been derived in part from a litany composed by St.Margaret Mary herself.[24] It was also during this plague that Sacred Heart badges were used and due to the miraculous victory of Divine Mercy over the disease, they became extremely popular. These badges were used religiously for protection and were called "sauvegarde"—safeguard. At the time of the French Revolution they were an object of special hatred for the revolutionaries who referred to them as "the livery of fanaticism."[25]

Despite rapid growth of the devotion among the faithful, Rome cautiously continued to respond *"non expedit"* to those who requested a liturgical feast. As we have observed, this did not argue against the devotion itself but only against the form sought by the revelations of Paray-le-Monial. There were several reasons for this. First of all, the Church herself was uncertain and had not yet pronounced upon the supernatural character of Margaret Mary's visions. The Church always moves slowly and exercises great caution in this area and therefore did not yet feel obliged to initiate the feast. Secondly, there were still serious problems with the manner in which the devotion was presented.

Fr. Galliffet who, as Postulator, presented petitions to the Congregation of Rites for the institution of the liturgical feast, defended the physical heart as the seat of the emotions and love. In this he was following the teaching of Aristotle and St. Thomas. This was, however, an area of physiology which went beyond the competence of the Roman court. The cardinals were very much aware that there was another school of thought which held that it was the brain, not the heart, that was the seat of all human feeling. The Protector of the Faith at this time was the brilliant Cardinal Prospero Lambertini. It was his role at these hearings to argue as the devil's advocate. He focused

---

[24]Walter Kern, *Updated Devotion to the Sacred Heart, op. cit.*, p. 77.

[25]*Ibid.*, p. 77. Just before his deposition, Louis XVI consecrated his kingdom to the Sacred Heart. This marked the devotion as a special object of hatred for the revolutionaries, who viewed the devotion as a "fanatical and royalist cult." See Warren H. Carroll, *The Guillotine and the Cross* (Manassas: Trinity Communications, 1986) pp. 87, 90, 97, 118, 121, 175, 178-9. The image of our Lord's Heart was used as a symbol of the glorious rising of the Vendée and was hated by the bloody Fouquier-Tinville.

upon Fr. Galliffet's theory that the physical heart was the center of the emotions. He argued that the Church should abstain from this philosophical-scientific debate. If this petition was granted, would not this indicate that Rome was backing a particular position in the debate? He argued that it would not be prudent for the Church to make such a move at this time. Cardinal Lambertini had performed his duty well and on July 12, 1727 the Congregation of Rites issued its *"Non proposita"* decision. The decision was in truth one of adjournment and was not explicitly negative to the devotion. Despite this decision, the devotion continued to spread throughout Christendom. Providence was to reserve a special role in spreading the devotion to Cardinal Lambertini. In August of 1740, Cardinal Lambertini became Pope Benedict XIV. During his pontificate (1740-1758) he granted over 300 Briefs establishing confraternities of the Sacred Heart. It was also his distinct honor as "the Vicar of Christ" to bestow the title of "Venerable" upon Margaret Mary Alacoque.

Fr. Galliffet returned to France in 1732, where he continued to preach and zealously promote the devotion. He translated his work on the Sacred Heart into French and it went through numerous editions.

The widespread growth and success of the devotion infuriated the Jansenists. The fierce opposition of this group, who labelled the devotion Nestorian, was eventually to bring triumph for the devotion and destruction for the followers of Saint-Cyran. Two actions taken by the Church in 1765 and 1794 brought mankind closer to the Heart of the Savior.

In the three decades that followed the Sacred Congregation of Rites' rejection of Fr. Galliffet's petition, pressure continued to mount for approval of the feast. The fervent requests poured in from all over the Christian world: the nobility, including the Queen of France, the kings of Poland Augustus III and Stanislaus, Clement Francis, the Duke of Bavaria, over 150 bishops, as well as numerous confraternities and religious, implored the Holy See to establish the feast. Alphonsus Liguori, in 1758, sent a copy of his *Novena to the Sacred Heart of Jesus* to Pope Clement XIII (1758-1769) and in his preface spoke of his ardent hope that Fr. Galliffet's petition would soon be approved. Clement was most favorable to the devotion, for he himself had been a member of one of its confraternities.

The moment of decision came via a *Memoriale* from the Polish bishops who clearly and forcefully presented the value of the Feast and the devotion. As a matter of prudence they did not request the Feast and Office for the Universal Church as had Fr. Galliffet and his associates, but only for Poland and the Archconfraternity. The *Memoriale* of the bishops concluded with a request that the Feast be placed on the Friday following the Octave of Corpus

Christi.[26] The sacred Congregation received the petition on January 26, 1765 and responded favorably to it at that very session. Pope Clement XIII happily approved the decree and it was issued on February 6, 1765. The text reads as follows:

> Having been requested to grant a Mass and an Office of the Sacred Heart by the greater part of the most Reverend Bishops of Poland and by the Roman Archconfraternity erected under this title, the Sacred Congregation of Rites, in its session of January 26th, 1765, recognizing that the cult of the Heart of Jesus is already spread in almost all parts of the Catholic world, favoured by Bishops and enriched by the Apostolic See with a thousand Briefs of indulgences granted to nearly inumerable Confraternities canonically erected in honour of the Heart of Jesus; moreover, understanding that by allowing this Mass and Office nothing else is aimed at than to develop a cult already established and renew symbolically the memory of the divine love by which the Only-begotten Son of God took upon Himself a human nature and, obedient unto death, wished to prove to men by His example that He was, as He had said, meek and humble of heart; for these reasons, acting on the report of His Eminence Cardinal Bishop of Sabinum, after hearing the Right Reverend Cajetanus Fortis, promoter of the Faith, and putting aside the decisions of July 30th, 1729, the said Sacred Congregation has deemed it right to accede to the request of the Bishops of the Kingdom of Poland and of the said Roman Archconfraternity. It will later on make a decision as to the Mass and Office which can be fittingly approved. This prescription of the Sacred Congregation has been submitted to our Holy Father, Pope Clement XIII. His Holiness, having given it his attention, has approved it in every respect.[27]

The approval of the Feast and Office of the Sacred Heart was a posthumous triumph for Fr. Galliffet since the defense and arguments used by the Polish bishops were taken (at times even verbatim) from Fr. Galliffet's book.[28]

Rome had given here a new and even more powerful impetus to the devotion which spread like wildfire. Every pope from Clement XIII on enthusiastically approved the devotion. On May 11, 1765 the Congregation specifically approved the Mass and Office for Poland and the Archconfrater-

---

[26]The Latin text may be found in Nicholas Nilles, S. J., *De rationibus festorum Beatissimi Cordis Jesu et purissimi Cordis Mariae* (Oeniponte, 1873), Liber I, cap. iii, p. 134.

[27]Louis Verheylezoon, S. J., *Devotion to the Sacred Heart* (Rockford, Ill.: Tan Books & Pub., Inc. 1978), p. xxxviii-ix.

[28]A. Hamon, S. J., *Histoire de la Devotion au Sacré-Coeur* (Paris: Rue de Rennes, 1925), Vol. IV, p. 207-213.

nity in Rome. Within two months the Visitandines were granted the feast for their order. A flood was loosed and petitions poured in from all over the Catholic world. By the year 1856 the Congregation observed that virtually every diocese had received the same privilege. Pope Pius IX in that very year received a special request from the Bishops of France for an extension of the Feast to the universal Church. The Holy Father acknowledged the truly Catholic longing for the Feast and extended it to the universal Church with a rank of *duples maius.* [29]

The second great victory for the devotion to the Heart of Jesus occurred in 1794 with the Bull *Auctorem Fidei* of Pope Pius VI. It was this Bull which mortally wounded the Jansenists.

We may briefly trace here the Jansenist's attitude towards Christ's humanity and devotion to the Sacred Heart. The Jansenist position seems to stem from a truncated view of the Redemption. They held that it was not the intention of our Lord in his sacrificial suffering and death to save all mankind. Accordingly, it was the will of Christ to save only the predestined few with the mass of humanity preordained to everlasting fire. With such a narrow view of salvation one can readily see why the chief proponents of Jansenism questioned the ancient and widespread devotion to the humanity of Christ. This devotion focused attention upon the merciful heart of Jesus and found widespread support. In response to this popular fervor they attacked the devotées as spiritual inferiors who were "heart idolators." The Church had defended the adoration of Christ's Sacred Humanity on many occasions but events led her to speak out again and this time in defense of the devotion to the Sacred Heart of Jesus.

A staunch and ardent Jansenist, Scipione de Ricci, became bishop of the diocese of Pistoria in the Italian duchy of Tuscany. As bishop he maintained that it was a rule of faith that few men will be saved. Because of this, priests were instructed to constantly harangue the faithful with this "truth" in order that they might be led from spiritual death to repentance. To impress this upon the minds of the people, he urged his priests to stop giving sacramental absolution to every penitent and to withhold Holy Communion from most of the faithful.

The wayward bishop sought to regiment his diocese by calling for a synod. This pseudo-Synod of Pistoia was opened on September 18, 1786 and had 234 participants, including 171 priests and 13 religious. The Synod held

---

[29] Pope Leo XIII elevated the Feast of the Sacred Heart to the high rank of "Double of the First-class". In the 20th century Pope Pius XI gave the Feast the highest possible rank "Double of the First Class with Octave". Since that time the Feast has continued to be given the highest liturgical rank by the Church.

sessions over a ten day period and published a vast number of decrees. Ricci, however, did not have the support of the Tuscan hierarchy and his efforts at implementing the synod so outraged popular piety that he was driven out of the city. When the bishop's cathedral chapter joined the popular protest, Ricci was forced to resign on June 3, 1790. This synod of Jansenists viciously attacked the devotion to the Sacred Heart of Jesus. It claimed that 1) by adoring Christ's humanity or any part thereof, one was giving divine worship to a creature; 2) the devotion to the Heart of Jesus was a novelty, false or at least dangerous; 3) it was wrong for the faithful to adore the Heart of Christ, separate or apart from His divinity. Some within the Church hoped to delay an official evaluation of the synod by the Holy See but Pope Pius VI "to fulfill his apostolic and pastoral duty" selected 85 different statements from the decrees of the synod and evaluated each individually to avoid any ambiguity. On August 28, 1794 the Holy Father issued his Bull *Auctorem Fidei* in which he quoted the erroneous statements of the synod and gave the appropriate censure. There are three propositions in this Bull which are of great importance for our study here:

> *Proposition 61:* The proposition which asserts that the "direct adoration of the humanity of Christ, and above all a part of this humanity, is always the rendering to a creature of an honor due to God Alone," insofar as by the word "direct" is meant to blame the cult of adoration which the faithful pay to the humanity of Christ; as if it could be said that the adoration rendered to the humanity and living flesh of Christ, not considered in itself and as mere flesh, but as united with the Divinity, was divine honor paid to a creature, and not rather one and the same adoration by which the Word Incarnate with its own flesh is adored: this proposition is false, fallacious, injurious and offensive to the pious cult which is due to the humanity of Christ and which the faithful have always rendered to it and are bound to render it.

> *Proposition 62:* The doctrine which rejects the devotion to the most sacred Heart of Jesus among the devotions which it qualifies as new, erroneous, or at least dangerous; if this devotion is understood, to be such as is approved by the Apostolic See: [this doctrine] is false, temerarious, pernicious, offensive to pious ears, and injurious against the Apostolic See.

> *Proposition 63:* Likewise, the devotées of the Heart of Jesus are reproached with paying no heed to the fact that neither the most sacred flesh of Christ, or any part of it, nor even the whole human nature if separate or apart from the Divinity, may be adored with the highest worship (*cultu latriae*); as though the faithful adored the Heart

of Jesus, separate or apart from the Divinity, whereas they adore it as the Heart of Jesus, that is, as the Heart of the Person of the Word, with whom it is inseparably united, in the same way as the bloodless body of Christ, in the three days of death, was adorable in the tomb not as separate nor as apart from the Divinity: this doctrine is fallacious, injurious to the devout worshippers of the Heart of Christ.[30]

This bull firmly established the devotion within the Catholic family. The Jansenists, in their effort to protect the divinity of Christ, were not merely angered that Christ's human nature was given divine worship. The cause of this opposition ran more deeply. It was that the heart of Christ symbolized his universal love for mankind. In their narrow vision of redemption (the few elect), they felt that the view which attributed to the divine nature universal merciful love for all mankind was the real evil of the devotion.

In this bull, the Church defined the divine honor which is to be paid to Christ's sacred humanity because of its substantial union to the Word of God. In so doing, the full *Auctorem Fidei* transcended the limitations of the Jansenists controversies and acknowledged the constant tradition based upon Sacred Scripture: the man Jesus is to be imitated by all believers in their pursuit of Christian perfection. In truth, by living a life in imitation of the virtues of Jesus, they are more fully conformed to the image of God because Jesus is God.

The devotion blossomed forth in a brighter and healthier atmosphere as a result of the Bull. The devotion was practiced throughout the Church by her greatest saints and the faithful at large. Thousands of churches, religious, congregations and monasteries throughout the world were founded and dedicated to the Sacred Heart of Jesus. Under the leadership of President Maréchal de MacMahon, the French people erected the Basilica of Montmartre (Sacré Coeur) in Paris, dedicated "To Christ and His Most Sacred Heart from a Penitent and Devout France." The Apostleship of Prayer was formed and spread to every continent. The papal magisterium propagated the devotion with great fervor. Briefs, encyclicals and exhortations poured forth from the See of Peter. The expansion of the devotion truly took on the form of a triumphal procession. In our own modern era, every pope from Leo XIII to John Paul II has called upon mankind to turn and fix their gaze upon the Heart of Christ. We shall closely examine this magisterial teaching in the next section. Although the devotion, along with all other devotions, went through a brief period of decline after the excitement of the Second Vatican Council, it is now once again showing new signs of vitality

---

[30]Denzinger-Schönmetzer, *Enchiridion Symbolorum, op. cit.*, (2661-2663), p. 535-536.

Figure 21: *The Basilica of the Sacred Heart on Montmartre. Here perpetual adoration is offered to the Eucharistic Heart of Christ.*

and a strong resurgence of interest.

Deep within their souls, all men by nature long for and seek happiness. To the extent that a man shall find love in this life he shall be happy. The ultimate satisfaction and completion of this longing is to be found for all men only in the Heart of Christ Jesus. Yet in the eyes of the world this has never been deemed news worth reporting.

Even at the birth of the Incarnate Word, heralded by the angels, we find only ignorant shepherds and three wise men taking any interest. These terrestrial events which are most important never make headlines in the world press. God usually does not speak in the roar of the hurricane but in the softness of a gentle wind. Such was His method in the stillness of the Visitation chapel of Paray-le-Monial. From this site of silent tranquility, far removed from the cares of the world, a divine spark issued forth which became a raging conflagration of love. It is the ultimate goal of this Divine Love to melt the hearts of all men by enkindling within them this heavenly fire of love. He who came to save the world by casting the fire of his Divine love upon it beckons and draws all men to his heart which is the *fornax ardens caritatis* (burning furnace of charity).

IV.

The Devotion to the Sacred Heart of Jesus and the Magisterium in Modern Times

Can a form of devotion surpassing that to the most Sacred Heart of Jesus be found which corresponds better to the essential charac-ter of the Catholic Faith or which is more capable of assisting the present day needs of the Church and the human race?
                    Pius XII, *Haurietis Aquas*

In this section we turn our attention to the magisterial teaching concern-ing the devotion to the Sacred Heart of Jesus. Although some persons have branded the devotion as "dated", or even "out-dated", this most certainly has not been the attitude taken by the See of Peter. Every Pope of the 20th century has exhorted the faithful to turn to the loving Heart of Christ. It is there that they shall find the healing love which alone is the cure for the many ills which so afflict our modern age.

The Holy See has undoubtedly given the devotion an extraordinary place in the life of the Church.[1] This is due not only to the requests our Lord made to St. Margaret Mary but also because of the devotion's sound doctrinal base and its timeliness.

---

[1]Cardinal Ciappi argues that there exists an intimate union between the See of Peter and devotion to the Sacred Heart since Peter, the Head of the Apostolic College, was first in the love of Christ. Cf. *The Heart of Christ, the Center of the Mystery of Salvation* (Rome: CdC Pub., 1983), pp. 65-88.

The Center for Applied Research in the Apostolate (CARA), based in Washington, D.C. was hired by the International Institute of the Heart of Jesus to study the present state of devotion to the Sacred Heart of Jesus and to make recommendations as to the best means of strengthening the devotion. One of the most important of the recommendations made was that the faithful should become familiar with the teaching of the papal magisterium concerning the devotion. The study urged that the papal documents be "published and strategically disseminated" observing that religious who were familiar with the papal documents were the "most alert, most interested, and the most motivated regarding the devotion."[2] For this reason we have sought to present this teaching as completely as possible.

Pope Leo XIII (1878-1903)

The first document which we shall examine is Pope Leo XIII's encyclical letter *Annum Sacrum*. This Pope, who is universally acknowledged by historians to be one of the greatest popes in history (his social encyclicals continue to form the basis for the modern Church's understanding of social justice), referred to this encyclical as "the greatest act of my pontificate." In this encyclical the Holy Father consecrated the entire human family to the Sacred Heart of Jesus (*communitatem generis humani devovere augustissimo cordi Jesu*).

The Pontiff was strongly influenced in this matter by Blessed Maria Droste Zu Vischering.[3] In a series of apparitions our Lord had made known to her his desire that the Holy Father should consecrate the world to his Sacred Heart. The encyclical was published on May 25, 1899 and is most significant in that it was issued in preparation for the Holy Year which was to usher in the 20th century. This consecration of humanity to the Heart of the Savior was to be the high point of the Holy Year. It is a tragedy that the

---

[2]CARA, *The Sacred Heart Devotion: A Christocentric Spirituality for Our Time* (Washington, D.C.: IIHJ. 1977), pp. 216-217.

[3]Maria Droste was beatified by Pope Paul VI in 1975. She was born on September 8, 1863 in Munster, Germany. She came from a deeply pious family and at the age of 25 she became a Sister of Our Lady of Charity of the Good Shepherd. She received the name "Sister Mary of the Divine Heart." She was later transferred to Portugal and at the age of 31 was appointed superior of the congregation's convent in Oporto. Although very active, she experienced an intense mystical union with God. At the end of her brief life, our Lord made known to her his desire to have the entire universe consecrated to his Heart and she was to request this of the Pope. Leo XIII was deeply moved and requested a theological investigation. Sister Maria suffered terribly at the end of her life from an excruciatingly painful spinal disease. She died on June 8, the day before the Feast of the Sacred Heart. On June 11, the Pope solemnly consecrated the universe to the Heart of Jesus.

world today is not that familiar with or even aware of this great encyclical. At that time however it did educe an overwhelming response. The Holy Father begins:

> But a short time ago, as you well know, We, by letters apostolic, and following the custom and ordinance of Our predecessors, commanded the celebration in this city, at no distant date, of a Holy Year. And now, today in the hope and with the object that this religious celebration shall be more devoutly performed, We have traced and recommended a striking design from which, if all shall follow it out with hearty good-will, We not unreasonably expect extraordinary and lasting benefits for Christendom in the first place, and also for the whole human race.
>
> Already more than once We have endeavored, after the example of Our predecessors Innocent XII, Benedict XIII, Clement XIII, Pius VI, Pius VII and Pius IX devoutly to foster and bring out into fuller light that most excellent form of devotion which has for its object the veneration to the Sacred Heart of Jesus: this We did especially by the decree given June 28, 1889, by which We raised the feast under that name to the dignity of the first class. But now We have in mind a more signal form of devotion which shall be in a manner the crowning perfection of all the honors that people have been accustomed to pay to the Sacred Heart, and which We confidently trust will be most pleasing to Jesus Christ, our Redeemer. This is not the first time, however, that the design of which we speak has been mooted. Twenty-five years ago, on the approach of the solemnities of the second centenary of the blessed Margaret Mary Alacoque's reception of the divine command to propagate the worship of the Sacred Heart, many letters from all parts, not merely from private persons but from bishops also, were sent to Pius IX, begging that he would consent to consecrate the whole human race to the most Sacred Heart of Jesus. It was thought best at the time to postpone the matter in order that a well-considered decision might be arrived at: meanwhile permission was granted to individual cities which desired it thus to consecrate themselves and a form of consecration was drawn up. Now, for certain new and additional reasons, We consider that the plan is ripe for fulfillment.[4]

It is important to take note here of two things: 1) that the Pope praises

---

[4]Leo XIII, Encyclical *Annum Sacrum*, 25 May 1899, *Acta Leonis*, Vol. XIX, 1900, pp. 71-72. A complete English text of all the papal encyclicals in this chapter can be found in Claudia Carlin, *The Papal Encyclicals*, V Vols. (McGrath Pub. Co.,1981). The Vatican English texts, which we for the most part have followed, may be obtained from the Libreria Editrice Vaticana, Vatican City, and also in the United States from the Daughters of St. Paul, Boston, Massachusetts.

Figure 22: *Interior of the Basilica of the Sacred Heart on Montmartre. This mosaic by Olivier Merson is one of the largest in the world. The figures surrounding Christ represent the Blessed Mother, Leo XIII (in the act of consecrating the human race to the Sacred Heart), St. Joan, France personified (offering the crown), and St. Michael.*

the devotion as "most excellent" and 2) that he expects the consecration shall bring "extraordinary and lasting benefits." The Pontiff then develops the twofold basis for Christ's Kingship over all creatures. First he speaks of his natural right as the Son of God:

> This world-wide and solemn testimony of allegiance and piety is especially appropriate to Jesus Christ, who is the Head and supreme Lord of the race. His empire extends not only over Catholic nations and those who, having duly washed in the waters of holy Baptism, belong of right to the Church, although erroneous opinions keep them astray, or dissent from her teachings cuts them off from her care; it comprises also all those who are deprived of the Christian faith, so that the whole human race is most truly under the power of Jesus Christ. For He who is the only-begotten Son of God the Father, having the same substance with Him and being the brightness of His glory and figure of His substance, necessarily has everything in common with the Father, and therefore sovereign power over all things.[5]

In addition to our Lord's natural right to sovereignty as Son of God, he also acquired the right by his universally redemptive suffering and death which was offered for the salvation of all men.

> For, He it was who snatched us from the powers of darkness, and gave Himself for the redemption of all. Therefore not only Catholics, and those who have duly received Christian Baptism, but also all men, individually and collectively, have become to Him a purchased people. St. Augustine's words are therefore to the point when he says: "You ask what price He paid? See what He gave and you will understand how much He paid. The price was the blood of Christ. What could cost so much but the whole world, and all its people? The great price He paid for all."[6]

The Holy Father next speaks of the boundless love of Christ which allows us to give ourselves fully in an act of personal consecration:

> He graciously allows us, if we think fit, to add voluntary consecration. Jesus Christ, our God and our Redeemer, is rich in the fullest and perfect possession of all things: we, on the other hand, are so poor and needy that we have nothing of our own to offer Him as a gift. But yet, in His infinite goodness and love, He in no way objects to our giving and consecrating to Him what is already His, as if it were really our own; nay, far from refusing such an offering, He positively desires it

---

[5]*Ibid.*, p. 72-73.
[6]*Ibid.*, p. 74-75.

and asks for it: "My son, give Me thy heart." We are, therefore, able to be pleasing to Him by the good-will and the affection of our soul. For by consecrating ourselves to Him we not only declare our open and free acknowledgment and acceptance of His authority over us, but we also testify that if what we offer as a gift were really our own, we would still offer it with our whole heart. We also beg of Him that He would vouchsafe to receive it from us, though clearly His own. Such is the efficacy of the act of which We speak, such is the meaning underlying Our words.[7]

The Pope then speaks of the appropriateness of the faithful's personal consecration to the Sacred Heart of Jesus, since it is the "symbol and sensible image of the infinite love of Jesus Christ which moves us to love one another." By this consecration each Christian offers himself to Jesus Christ and in so doing unites himself to Christ, since "whatever honor, veneration, and love is given to this divine Heart is really and truly given to Christ Himself." It was the hope of the Pope that this act would re-enkindle the fires of charity within Christians.

As Christ's Vicar on earth, the Holy Father next speaks of his paternal solicitude for all those living in the world who have not yet received the light of Christian truth. He reminds Christians everywhere that Christ died for all men and as an aid to the missionary effort of the Church the Holy Father writes "in pity for their lot, with all Our soul We commend them, and as far in us lies We consecrate them to the Sacred Heart of Jesus."[8]

The Pontiff then expresses his hope that this public act of consecration to the Heart of Jesus will stem the tide of an ever menacing hostile secularization of life:

> In these latter times especially, a policy has been followed which has resulted in a sort of wall being raised between the Church and civil society. In the constitution and administration of States the authority of sacred and divine law is utterly disregarded, with a view to the exclusion of religion from having any constant part in public life. This policy almost tends to the removal of the Christian faith from our midst, and, if that were possible, of the banishment of God Himself from the earth. When men's minds are raised to such a height of insolent pride, what wonder is it that the greater part of the human race should have fallen into such disquiet of mind and be buffeted by waves so rough that no one is suffered to be free from anxiety and peril?

[7]*Ibid.*, p. 75-76.
[8]*Ibid.*, p. 77-78.

Hence the abundance of evils which have now for a long time settled upon the world, and which pressingly call upon us to seek for help from Him by whose strength alone they can be driven away. Who can he be but Jesus Christ, the only-begotten Son of God? For there is no other name under heaven given to men whereby we must be saved. We must have recourse to Him who is the Way, the Truth, and the Life. We have gone astray and we must return to the right path: darkness has overshadowed our minds, and the gloom must be dispelled by the light of truth: death has seized upon us, and we must lay hold of life. It will at length be possible that our many wounds be healed and all justice spring forth again with the hope of restored authority; that the splendors of peace be renewed, and swords and arms drop from the hand when all men shall acknowledge the empire of Christ and willingly obey His word, and every tongue shall confess that the Lord Jesus Christ is in the glory of God the Father.[9]

Here Pope Leo clearly acknowledges the timeliness of the devotion which is so firmly grounded in Christian truth and may effectively counter those influences which would seek to weaken and destroy the Christian faith. For this reason he calls upon all men of good will to rally around a standard in which the Christian faith shall ultimately triumph over the evils of the modern age. The Vicar of Christ, in the most famous passage of the encyclical offers the standard of our Lord's Heart:

When the Church, in the days immediately succeeding her institution, was oppressed beneath the yoke of the Caesars, a young emperor saw in the heavens a cross, which became at once the happy omen and cause of the glorious victory that soon followed. And now, today, behold another blessed and heavenly token is offered to our sight— the most Sacred Heart of Jesus, with a cross rising from it and shining forth with dazzling splendor amidst flames of love. In that Sacred Heart all our hopes should be placed, and from it the salvation of men is to be confidently sought.[10]

The Holy Father ends his encyclical by calling for special prayers to be said by the faithful in every principal church throughout Christendom on the ninth, tenth and eleventh of June. In addition to these special prayers, the Pope also asked that the Church's official Litany of the Sacred Heart (which had just recently been approved on April 2, 1899) be recited. We shall shortly examine this beautiful prayer in greater detail. On the last day a special prayer of consecration was to be said by all the faithful. This Act of Consecration

---

[9]*Ibid.*, p. 78.
[10]*Ibid.*, p. 78-79.

was published with *Annum Sacrum*. In this prayer, written by Pope Leo himself, after calling attention to the evils of the modern age, the Holy Father urges all men to join with him in a complete act of self surrender and dedication to the loving heart of Christ:

> Most sweet Jesus, Redeemer of the human race, look down upon us, humbly prostrate before Thy altar. We are Thine and Thine we wish to be. But, to be most surely united with Thee, behold each of us freely consecrates himself today to Thy most Sacred Heart.
> Many indeed have never known Thee. Many, too, despising Thy precepts, have rejected Thee. Have mercy on them all, most merciful Jesus, and draw them to Thy Sacred Heart. Be Thou King, O Lord, not only of the faithful who have never forsaken Thee, but also of the prodigal children who have abandoned Thee. Grant that they may quickly return to their Father's house, lest they die of wretchedness and hunger. Be Thou King of those who are deceived by erroneous opinions, or whom discord keeps aloof, and call them back to the harbor of truth and unity of faith, so that soon there may be but one flock and one Shepherd. Be Thou King also of all those who sit in the ancient superstition of the Gentiles, and refuse not to deliver them out of darkness into the light and kingdom of God. Grant, O Lord, to Thy Church, assurance of freedom and immunity from harm. Give peace and order to all nations, and make the earth resound from pole to pole with one cry: Praise to the Divine Heart that wrought our salvation— to It be glory and honor forever! Amen.[11]

The Church's Litany of the Sacred Heart of Jesus has always been extremely popular with the faithful and is without a doubt one of the most beautiful. The litany in its present form was approved for the universal Church by Pope Leo XIII on April 2, 1899. Through this solemn and universal approval (*"urbi et orbi"*) the Litany became part of the official liturgical cult of the universal Church and thus became a rich source of profound doctrinal value (*lex orandi, lex credendi*). Few are aware that much of the litany's beauty and constant appeal are due to the striking biblical language and imagery contained in nearly every invocation. Every Litany begins, after seeking mercy from the Lord, with an invocation of the Most Holy Trinity.

> Lord have mercy on us—Christ have mercy on us.
> Lord have mercy on us. Christ hear us:
> Christ graciously hear us.
> God the Father of heaven, have mercy on us
> God the Son, Redeemer of the world, have mercy on us

---

[11]*Ibid.*, p. 80.

> God the Holy Spirit, have mercy on us
> Holy Trinity one God, have mercy on us

The Litany shows forth the Trinitarian nature of the devotion by focusing upon the relation of the Heart of the Lord to God as Father and Holy Spirit.

> Heart of Jesus, Son of the Eternal Father, (Mt. 16:16, 6:9)
> Heart of Jesus, formed by the Holy Spirit in the Virgin Mother's womb, (Mt. 1:20, Lk. 1:26)

After the Father and Holy Spirit, the Litany focuses attention upon the Person of the Word. Here the doctrinal edifice built by the Councils of Nicea, Constantinople, Ephesus and Chalcedon are referred to. These early councils, as we have seen, set forth with great clarity the Church's understanding of the Person of Christ and formed the foundation of the veneration of our Lord's Heart which through the hypostatic union with the Word is the Heart of God.

> Heart of Jesus, substantially united to the Word of God, (Jn. 1:14)
> Heart of Jesus, of infinite majesty, (Mt. 25:31, Mt. 16:27, 26:64; Ps. 71:19; Col. 1:15; Heb. 1:3)
> Heart of Jesus, holy temple of God, (Jn. 2:19-21, Jn. 4:23)
> Heart of Jesus, tabernacle of the Most High, (Heb. 9:11-12; Jn. 1:14; II Pet. 1:13:14)
> Heart of Jesus, house of God and gate of heaven, (Gn. 28:17; Jn. 1:51)

The next group of invocations turns our attention to the glorious treasures of our Lord's heart in itself:

> Heart of Jesus, glowing furnace of charity, (Eph. 3:19; Prov. 27:21; Wis. 3:6)
> Heart of Jesus, vessel of justice and love, (Heb. 1:19; Rom. 3:26, 5:5)
> Heart of Jesus, abyss of all virtues, (Eccles. 1:2; Heb. 1:9)
> Heart of Jesus, most worthy of all praise, (Heb. 1:6; Rev. 5:9)
> Heart of Jesus, King and center of all hearts, (Heb. 2:8; Ez. 11:19; Jer. 32:39)
> Heart of Jesus, wherein are all the treasures of wisdom and knowledge, (Col. 2:3)
> Heart of Jesus, wherein dwell all the fullness of Godhead, (Col. 2:9)
> Heart of Jesus, in whom the Father is well pleased, (Mt. 3:17, 17:5)

The third group of invocations turns to the Heart of the Lord as the *source* and *fount* of all goodness. These prayers beautifully convey a great Christian truth: to the extent to which a man will empty himself he shall be enabled to be filled with Christ Jesus.

> Heart of Jesus, of whose fullness we have all received, (Jn. 1:16)
> Heart of Jesus, desire of the everlasting hills, (Gn. 49:26; Ps. 120:1)
> Heart of Jesus, patient and rich in mercy, (II Thes.3:5; Ex. 34:6)
> Heart of Jesus, rich unto all who call upon you, (Rom. 10:12)
> Heart of Jesus, fount of life and holiness, (Is. 12:3; Ps. 35:10; Jn. 7:38; I Cor. 10:4; Apoc. 7:17, 21:6, 22:1)
> Heart of Jesus, propitiation for our offenses, (I Jn. 2:2; Rom. 3:25)
> Heart of Jesus, overwhelmed with reproaches, (Jer., Lam. 3:30; Ps. 21)
> Heart of Jesus, bruised for our iniquities, (Is. 53:5)
> Heart of Jesus, obedient even unto death, (Phil. 2:8; Heb. 5:8)
> Heart of Jesus, pierced with a lance, (Jn. 19:34; Cant. 2:14)
> Heart of Jesus, source of all consolation, (Mt. 11:28; Lk. 2:25; Cor. 1:3)
> Heart of Jesus, our life and resurrection, (Jn. 11:25, I Jn. 1:2)
> Heart of Jesus, our peace and reconciliation, (Col. 1:20; Lk. 2:14; Jn. 20:19)
> Heart of Jesus, victim for our sins, (Ps. 128:3; Mt. 26:28)
> Heart of Jesus, salvation of those who hope in You, (Rom. 10:13)
> Heart of Jesus, hope of those who die in You, (I Thes. 4:13; Col. 1:5, 27)
> Heart of Jesus, delight of all the saints, (Rev. 21:23)

This group of invocations obviously speaks a great deal of sin and reparation for sin. Unfortunately, the terrible reality of sin has been all too characteristic of man throughout his history, beginning with the fall of Adam. Through his suffering and death, however, Christ has triumphed over sin and death. For this reason the litany concludes by calling our attention to salvation and the new paradise at the end of time. That paradise shall be in the Heart of Jesus which is "the delight of all the saints." The Heart of Christ is the focal point since it speaks most eloquently of the bloody immolation which reveals that infinite love which brought about our salvation.

> Lamb of God, who takes away the sins of the world,—spare us, O Lord
> Lamb of God who takes away the sins of the world,—graciously hear us, O Lord
> Lamb of God, who takes away the sins of the world,—have mercy on us.
> V. Jesus meek and humble of heart,
> R. Make our hearts like unto thine.

To enhance the solemnity of the act of consecration to the Most Sacred Heart of Jesus, a triduum of prayer was prescribed during which the Litany was recited. It remains today as one of the most sublime of all the litanies officially recommended by Holy Mother Church.

Pope Benedict XV (1914-1922)

Both Pope St. Pius X and Benedict XV continued with great enthusiasm to foster and encourage the growth of this devotion.[12] Of particular interest is a letter by Pope Benedict to Fr. Mateo Crawley-Boevey. Fr. Mateo initiated the movement of Enthronement of the Sacred Heart of Jesus in the homes of Christian families. It is a letter of great importance because it deals with a subject of vital interest today—the survival of the Christian family. The contribution which the devotion to the Sacred Heart of Jesus can make to the renewal and strengthening of the family is stressed by the Holy Father.

> We have read your letter with interest and likewise the documents that accompanied it. From them we have learned of the diligence and zeal with which for many years you have devoted yourself to the work of consecrating families to the Most Sacred Heart of Jesus, in such a way that while His image is installed in the principal place in the home as on a throne, our Divine Savior Jesus Christ is seen to reign at each Catholic hearth.
>
> Our Predecessor, Leo XIII, of happy memory had already consecrated the entire human race to the Divine Heart, and his noteworthy Encyclical, *Annum Sacrum*, on this subject is well known. Notwithstanding that general and collective consecration, however, the devotion as applied to each family in particular is not without purpose. On the contrary, it is perfectly in accord with the former, and can only contribute to the religious aim of that Pontiff. For what concerns each one in particular affects us more deeply than the interests we share with others. Therefore we rejoice at the thought that your work has borne abundant fruit in this direction, and we exhort you to persevere with diligence in the apostolate you have begun.
>
> *Nothing, as a matter of fact, is more suitable to the needs of the present day than your enterprise.* To pervert, both in private and in

---

[12]Pius X, in speaking to Fr. Mateo Crawley-Boevey concerning the priest's desire to spread the practice of enthroning the Sacred Heart in the home, said: "No, no, my son. I do not permit you, I command you, do you understand? I order you to give your life for this work of salvation. It is a wonderful work; consecrate your entire life to it." quoted in Fr. Marcel Bocquet, SSCC, *The Firebrand: The Life of Fr. Mateo Crowley-Boevey, SSCC* (Washington, D. C.: Corda Press, 1966) p. XX. Pius X also encouraged the devotion by granting partial and plenary indulgences *in perpetuam* to the Association of Priests established in honor of the Sacred Heart (see Apostolic Letter in *AAS*, II (1910), pp. 318-320). He also approved the Decree of the Sacred Congregation of Rites which established the First Friday of each month as solemn (see *AAS*, III (1911), pp. 322-323).

public life, the concept of morality engendered and fostered by the Church, and, after having almost effaced the last vestige of Christian wisdom and decency, to lead human society back to the miserable institutions of paganism, such is the plan which too many are trying to realize today. Would that their efforts were fruitless! Moreover, the attacks of the wicked are directed primarily against the family, for, containing within itself as it does the principles and, as it were, the germ of all human society, they clearly see that the change, or rather the corruption, which they are trying to bring about in human society will necessarily follow, once the corruption of the family itself has been accomplished. Hence divorce laws are introduced to put an end to the stability of marriage; children are forced to follow an official teaching for the most part estranged from religion, thus eliminating the authority of parents in a matter of the highest importance; moreover, countenance is given to the spread of a shameful course of selfish indulgence which contravenes the laws of nature, and, striking a blow at the human race at its very source, stains the sanctity of marriage with impure practices.

You do well, then, dear son, while taking up the cause of human society, to arouse and propagate above all things a Christian spirit in the home by setting up in each family the reign of the love of Jesus Christ. And in doing this you are but obeying our Divine Lord Himself, who promised to shower His blessings upon the homes wherein an image of His Heart should be exposed and devoutly honored.

It is assuredly, therefore, a holy and salutary work to secure for our beloved Redeemer such worship and honor. But that is not everything. It is of the utmost importance to know Christ, to know His doctrine, His life, His Passion, His glory. For to follow Him does not consist in allowing ourselves to be swayed by a superficial religious sentiment that easily moves weak and tender hearts to tears, but leaves vices intact. To follow Christ is to be permeated with a lively and constant faith, which not only acts upon the mind and heart, but likewise governs and directs our conduct. Moreover, the real reason why Jesus is neglected by so many and but little loved by others is to be found in the fact that He is almost entirely unknown to the former and not known sufficiently by the latter. Continue therefore, beloved son, in your efforts to enkindle in Catholic homes the flames of love for the most Sacred Heart of Jesus: but likewise and before all else, and this is our wish, endeavor to make this love result from a knowledge of Christ the Lord, and from a greater and deeper understanding of the truths and laws which He Himself has given us.

For our part, in order to encourage the piety of the faithful in this matter, we extend to all families of the Catholic world that consecrate themselves to the Most Sacred Heart of Jesus all those spiritual favors which our predecessor, Pius X, of happy memory, granted with Pontifical liberality in 1913, at the instance of the bishops of Chile to the families of that republic consecrated to the Sacred Heart.

As a pledge of divine favors and as a mark of our paternal goodwill, we impart to you affectionately, beloved son, the Apostolic blessing.[13]

The Pope here acknowledges the great value of the devotion and in particular the enthronement ritual itself as a means of reinvigorating Christian morality in the family. Through the moral renewal of the basic unit of society, men of faith may counteract those secularizing influences which seek to lead mankind "back to the miserable institutions of paganism."[14]

Pope Pius XI (1922-1939)

In one of his early encyclicals, *Quas Primas*, Pope Pius XI established the universal feast of Christ the King and inseparably united this feast with the devotion to the Sacred Heart of Jesus. Europe was still recovering from the effects of World War I when the great Pontiff proclaimed the Holy Year in 1925. It was at the end of the year's solemnities that Pope Pius published this encyclical in response to the overwhelming number of requests from cardinals, bishops and faithful throughout the Catholic world. Many of the petitions were collected by the Apostleship of Prayer. Through the institution of this feast, Pope Pius XI hoped to promote the establishment of *"pax Christi in regno Christi."*

Echoing the teaching of Pope Leo XIII in *Annum Sacrum* concerning the twofold basis for the kingship of Christ, Pius called upon Christians to let

---

[13]Benedict XV, *Acta Apostolicae Sedis* 7 (1915), pp. 203-205 (27 April 1915). See also the excellent biography written by Fr. Marcel Bocquet, SS.CC., *The Firebrand: The Life of Father Mateo Crawley-Boevey SS.CC., op. cit.* Pope Benedict's letter is discussed on pp. 74-77.

[14]On May 13, 1920 it was the joy and honor of Pope Benedict to officially proclaim Margaret Mary Alacoque a saint of the Church; see Bull of Canon., *Acta Apostolicae Sedis* 12 (1920) pp. 486-573. The same Pope also sent a joyous letter to the Archbishop of Paris, Cardinal Amette, on the occasion of the solemn consecration of the Basilica of the Sacred Heart of Montmartre (*AAS* 11 (1919) pp. 412-414). Montmartre is the sacred site where the first martyrs of Paris, St. Denis and companions, died for Christ. It is also the location of an illustrious abbey of Benedictine nuns visited by such spiritual giants as St. Bernard, St. Joan of Arc, St. Ignatius Loyola, St. Francis Xavier, Berulle and Olier.

The basilica itself, constructed in a striking Romano-Byzantine style, dominates the Parisian skyline. The Church was built as a result of a vow made in 1870, with contributions received from all over Catholic France. St. Thérèse of Lisieux, Charles de Foucauld, Card. Pacelli (Pius XII), and Card. Roncalli (John XXIII) frequently prayed there.

Devotion to the Sacred Heart and the Holy Eucharist are perfectly united in this spiritual center where perpetual adoration has continued without interruption since the dedication of the basilica.

Christ reign over their minds, wills and hearts. Our Lord is to reign as King of our hearts because of his infinite love "which surpasses all knowledge."

After expounding upon the scriptural foundations for our Lord's title as King, the Pope quotes from *Annum Sacrum* to demonstrate the universality of Christ's kingship. It was Leo XIII who, in *Annum Sacrum*, had initially united the Kingship of Christ with the devotion to the Sacred Heart. As the King of all Hearts, Christ must reign in individual hearts before his social kingship may be established. It is only through the living hearts of men filled with divine faith that this reign may be established. Pope Pius sees the rise of secularism as the great obstacle to the reign of Christ:

> The plague of the age is what is called secularism, with all its attendant errors and impious purposes. You know, Venerable Brothers, that such impiety does not spring up over night. For a long time it has been eating its way into the very vitals of society. As a matter of fact, the rule of Christ over mankind has been denied, the Church has been refused the right, which comes from the very law of Jesus Christ, to teach all peoples, to make her own laws for the spiritual government of her subjects in order to bring them to eternal happiness. Little by little the Christian religion has been made the equal of other and false religions and has been lowered to their level. The Catholic religion has been made subject to the civil power and has been given over to the control of rulers and statesmen. This error went still further; an attempt was made to substitute a certain vague natural religion for the truth of the religion of Christ. There were not wanting governments which imagined they could do without God altogether and cover up their lack of religion by irreligion and disrespect for God Himself.[15]

To help counter the growth of this secularism, which is so hostile to Christian order, Pope Pius instituted the Feast of Christ the King. In so doing, the Holy Father speaks of the special bond between this Solemnity and the devotion to the Heart of Jesus:

> Certainly it appears to Us that an annual celebration of the Feast of Christ Our King will greatly assist all nations towards a condemnation of and a reparation for those public apostasies which secularism, with so much harm to society, has given birth to. In fact, the more the dear name of Our Redeemer is passed over in shameful silence, be it at international meetings, be it in chancelleries, so much the more necessary it is to acclaim Him King and announce everywhere the rights of His royal dignity and power.
> All can see that since the end of the last century the way was being

---

[15]Pius XI, *Quas Primas*, AAS 17, (1925), pp. 604-605.

prepared for the long desired institution of this new feast. No one can be ignorant of how this cult was spread and defended in books written in all the languages of the civilized world. The supremacy of the Kingdom of Christ was also recognized in the pious practice of those who dedicated, even consecrated, their families to the Sacred Heart of Jesus. Not only families but even whole nations and kingdoms were likewise consecrated. Due to the desire of Leo XIII, the human race, during the Holy Year of 1900, was solemnly consecrated to the Divine Heart.[16]

On the day of the Feast all the faithful were to renew their consecration to the Sacred Heart of Jesus using the prayer of Pope Leo XIII.

Therefore, in virtue of Our Apostolic authority, We institute the Feast of Our Lord Jesus Christ, King, and decree that it be celebrated everywhere and annually on the last Sunday in October, that is, on the Sunday preceding the Feast of All Saints. Likewise We decree that on this same day, annually, there is to be renewed the consecration of mankind to the Sacred Heart of Jesus, an act of consecration which Our Predecessor of holy memory, Pius X, had previously commanded to be made every year. This year We wish the consecration to take place on the thirty-first of this month, on which occasion We Ourselves will celebrate solemn Pontifical Mass in honor of Christ the King. At that time the consecration to the Sacred Heart will be made in Our presence. Moreover, it seems to Us that it would be impossible in any more fitting way to close and crown this Holy Year than to signify Our gratitude and that of all Catholics to Christ, "Eternal King of the Ages," for the benefits conferred upon Us, the Church, and the whole Catholic world during the Holy Year just ended.[17]

Appropriately enough the reign of Christ will be accomplished through his most Sacred Heart. The fire of his divine love alone can reenkindle the cold indifferent hearts of men who ignore and hold in contempt the Redeemer of mankind, who purchased our salvation "not with perishable things, with silver or gold, but with his precious blood" (I Pet. 1:18).

On May 9, 1928 Pope Pius XI issued his encyclical *Miserentissimus Redemptor* which dealt with the reparation due to the Sacred Heart. This beautiful encyclical reveals a great deal concerning the attitude of the magisterium towards the devotion. The Pope's teaching concerning the duty of making acts of reparation is a logical development of the act of consecration initiated by Leo XIII in *Annum Sacrum*.

---

[16]*Ibid.*, p. 606.
[17]*Ibid.*, pp. 607-608.

Pope Pius begins by reminding the faithful of Christ's abiding presence within the Church. Throughout her long history, especially during times of extreme crisis, Christ has remained with his Bride. He observes that today many erroneous doctrines are being taught and spread throughout the world. These false teachings threaten to dry up the sources of the Christian life and are even leading men to forsake the love of God. In this age, with all its evil, the Savior's presence remains with his Church. Our Lord's gift of the devotion to his Sacred Heart is a sign of his continuing presence within his Church. The Pope, after this brief introduction, states the purpose of the encyclical:

> Since some Christians, perhaps, are ignorant of, and others are indifferent to, the sorrows which the most loving Jesus revealed to St. Margaret Mary Alacoque in His apparitions to her, as well as His wishes and desires which He manifested to mankind, all of which in the last analysis work to man's advantage, it is Our pleasure, Venerable Brothers, to write you at some length of the obligation which rests upon all to make those amends which we owe to the Most Sacred Heart of Jesus.[18]

It is important to note here that reparation to the Sacred Heart is stressed as *obligatory for all Christians*. The devotion to the Heart of Jesus is described by Pius XI as "the very summary of our religion" (*totius religionis summa*) which if practiced "will most surely lead us to know intimately Jesus Christ and will cause our hearts to love more tenderly and to imitate Him more generously."[19]

It would certainly be difficult to imagine a greater tribute to the theological richness and ascetical value of the devotion. These words of the Holy Father reveal not only the extraordinary value of the devotion but also the unsurpassed esteem in which the Holy See holds this "devotion of devotions" which provides a complete synthesis of the Faith.

The Pontiff then speaks of the solicitude of his predecessors who have praised the devotion "most highly" and have promoted it "with the greatest possible zeal." The wondrous spread of the devotion among the faithful is due, according to the Pope, to nothing less than the inspiration of God. The Pope also singles out for praise the practice of receiving Holy Communion on the First Friday of the month as "a custom which had its origin in the wish of Jesus Christ Himself."[20] The Holy Father continues:

---

[18]Pius XI, *Miserentissimus Redemptor*, AAS XX, 1928, p. 166
[19]*Ibid.*, p. 167
[20]*Ibid.*, p. 167

Moreover, to all these expressions of veneration, and especially to that most fruitful one, the act of consecration, which by means of the institution of the Feast of Christ the King has been, as it were, again confirmed, it is expedient that another be added, and of this last, Venerable Brothers, We wish to speak now somewhat at length. We refer to the act of expiation or of reparation, as it is called, to be made to the Sacred Heart of Jesus.

If in the act of consecration the intention to exchange, as it were, for the love of the Creator the love of us creatures stands out most prominently, there follows almost naturally from this another fact, namely, that if this same Uncreated Love has either been passed over through forgetfulness or saddened by reason of our sins, then we should repair such outrages, no matter in what manner they have occurred. Ordinarily, we call this duty reparation. If we are held to the duty of making reparation by the most powerful motives of justice and of love of justice, in order to expiate the injury done God by your sins and to reestablish, by means of penance, the Divine order which has been violated; and of love, in order to suffer together with Christ, patient and covered with opprobrium, so that we may bring to Him, in so far as our human weakness permits, some comfort in His sufferings.[21]

United to our act of consecration must be acts of reparation. Reparation, in the general sense in which it is used by Pope Pius, is an act of restoring something which had been damaged or destroyed i.e., the divine order. This is repaired by either doing away with the thing damaged and restoring it to its previous state of integrity or by substituting something else of equal value. Of course, after man had separated himself from God, he was incapable of either form of reparation. Man could have remained in this state of desperate impotence since God in his transcendent glory had no need of ever receiving homage from his creatures. God, however, freely chose in the divine economy to bestow upon us full reconciliation through universal reparation. This free and loving act manifests his nature as infinite goodness. St. Thomas beautifully illustrates this point:

It belongs to the nature of goodness to communicate itself to others.... Hence it belongs to the nature of the highest good to communicate itself in the highest manner to the creature, and this is brought about chiefly by...God becoming man.[22]

The Son of God, made Man, through his suffering, love and obedience unto

---

[21]*Ibid.,* p. 169
[22]Thomas Aquinas, *Summa Theologica* III, q. 1, a. 1

death, is the first and only Repairer of God's honor. The Second Adam as Head of all mankind gave far more than was necessary to compensate for the universal sinfulness of mankind. Through this superabundance of merits, Christ recreated and elevated man, bestowing upon him the supernatural life of grace. Man once again united to God became capable of sharing in the objective and subjective reparation achieved by Christ. Objectively, Christ redeemed man without his cooperation; subjectively, however, man is not saved without his voluntary and individual acceptance of Christ's redemptive graces.

> Though the ample redemption of Christ more than abundantly satis-
> fied for all our offenses, nevertheless, by reason of that marvelous
> disposition of Divine Wisdom by which we may complete those "things
> that are wanting of the sufferings of Christ in our own flesh, for His
> body, which is the Church," we are able, in fact we should, add to the
> acts of praise and satisfaction which "Christ in the name of sinners has
> presented to God," our own acts of praise and satisfaction. However,
> we must always remember that the expiatory value of our acts depends
> solely on the bloody sacrifice of Christ.[23]

Through our intimate union with Christ, we continue the appropriation of His reparation which must be continued throughout human history by the individual restoration of all the harm inflicted upon souls by sin.

> The Apostle admonished us that "bearing about in our body the
> mortification of Jesus" and "buried together with him by Baptism unto
> death," not only should we "crucify our flesh the corruption of that
> concupiscence which is in the world," but also that the "life of Jesus
> be made manifest in our bodies," and having become partakers in His
> holy and eternal priesthood, we should offer up "gifts and sacrifices
> for sins."[24]

In explaining the theological and ascetical character of reparation, the Holy Father stressed its universal obligation as based upon a desire for justice and love. The divine justice, united with divine mercy, reveals the whole work of redemption as a work of God's infinite love for mankind. Reparation must spring from a childlike trust in the merciful justice of God, in which man returns love to his heavenly Father.

The Pope then adds another aspect of the spirit of reparation or expiation by noting that the consolation of Christ has always been a major element in

---

[23]Pius XI, *Miserentissimus Redemptor, op. cit.,* pp. 170 - 171
[24]*Ibid.,* pp. 171 -172

the devotion to the Sacred Heart of Jesus. The desire to console the suffering Savior has always existed in devout souls from the beginning of Christianity. This longing on the part of those who meditate upon the passion of our Lord is a natural one. It is a beautiful expression of love for Him who suffered so greatly for love of us. Pius quotes from the revelations given by Jesus to St. Margaret Mary. These words of Our Lord "which should be graven on the hearts of all pious souls so as to never be forgotten"[25] reveal Christ's intense love for sinful men and his desire for their love in return:

> "Behold the Heart which has loved men so much, which has heaped upon them so many benefits. In exchange for this infinite love It finds ingratitude; instead it meets with forgetfulness, indifference, outrages, and all this at times even from souls bound closely to it in the bonds of a very special love."[26]

To make reparation for such faults, our Lord requested that the faithful should 1) make a "Communion of Reparation", and 2) in remembrance of his suffering in Gethsemane, make the "Holy Hour" during which time they would offer acts and prayers of reparation. The Pope acknowledges that the Church has not only approved these pious exercises, but has enriched them with "special spiritual favors." Thus we may clearly see that the form of the devotion as practiced by St. Margaret Mary and requested by our Lord has been and shall continue to be fully incorporated into the life of the Church.

The Holy Father then turns his attention to the question of consoling Christ. He asks: "How can we...believe that Christ reigns happily in Heaven if it is possible to console Him by such acts as those of reparation?"[27] The Pope responds with the words of St. Augustine: "The soul which truly loves will comprehend what I say." These sentiments of Augustine found an echo in the words of Pascal centuries later: "The heart has its reason about which the reason knows nothing!" The profound truth of this statement is revealed in the proper understanding of consolation which is *essentially an act of love*. Authentic consolation finds its origin in the intellect of a loving person who sees a friend suffering. From this knowledge comes an act of the will motivated by charity which seeks to comfort the friend in distress. Since this is essentially an act of charity it is quite natural that the appropriate affections accompany such an act. Because of the love revealed, this loving consolation gives a certain pleasure to the suffering person. This truth concerning con-

[25]*Ibid.*, p. 173
[26]*Ibid.*, p. 173
[27]*Ibid.*, p. 173

solation is defended by St. Thomas:

> When one is in pain, it is natural that the sympathy of a friend should afford consolation. The Philosopher indicates a twofold reason for this. The first is because, since sorrow has a depressing effect, it is like a weight of which we strive to unburden ourselves, so that when a man sees others saddened by his own sorrow, it seems as though others were bearing the burden with him, striving, as it were, to lessen its weight; and so the load of sorrow becomes lighter for him, just as also occurs in the carrying of bodily burdens. The second and better reason is because when a man's friends console with him, he sees that he is loved by them, and this affords him pleasure, as stated above. Consequently, since every pleasure assuages sorrow, as stated above, it follows that sorrow is mitigated by a sympathizing friend.[28]

Christ, in his human nature, was most certainly consoled by his contemporaries. (This is known as *historical consolation* which extended from his birth till his death.) Since Christ was fully man, those who loved him could offer to him, personally, compassionate consolation while he was suffering pain in body and soul. Our Lord must have sorely grieved at seeing his sorrowing Mother suffering at the foot of the cross with his beloved disciple witnessing his agonizing death. Knowing, however, that this heartrending sorrow sprang from their great love, he certainly accepted this true act of love as a great consolation during his final agony. Beyond this limited "historical consolation" which could occur only during Christ's temporal existence, the Pope beckons the faithful to a deeper understanding of their present acts of consolation.

> Every soul which burns with true love of God, if it but turns its thoughts to the past, sees in meditation and can contemplate Jesus suffering for mankind, afflicted by grief in the midst of sorrows suffered "for us men and for our salvation," weighed down by agony and reproaches, "bruised for our sins," in the very act of healing us by His bruises. With so much the more understanding can pious souls meditate upon these mysteries if they appreciate that the sins and crimes of men, no matter when committed, were the real reason why the Son of God was condemned to death and that even sins committed now would be able of themselves to cause Christ to die a death accompanied by the same sufferings and agonies as His death on the cross, since every sin must be said to renew in a certain way the Passion of Our Lord, "crucifying again to themselves the Son of God and making Him a mockery." And if, in view of our own future sins,

---

[28] Thomas Aquinas, *Summa Theologica* I - II, q. 38, a. 3

foreseen by Him, the soul of Jesus became sad even unto death, there can be no doubt that by His prevision at the same time of our acts of reparation He was in some way comforted when "there appeared an angel from heaven" to console that Heart of His bowed down with sorrow and anguish.

At the present time, we too, in a marvelous but no less true manner, may and ought to console that Sacred Heart which is being wounded continually by the sins of thoughtless men, since—and we read this also in the sacred liturgy—Christ Himself grieved over the fact that He was abandoned by His friends. For He said, in the words of the Psalmist, "My heart hath expected reproach and misery. And I looked for one that would grieve together with Me, and I found none."[29]

This form of consolation of which the Pope speaks is possible because our Lord's knowledge and ability to receive consolation transcended the narrow horizons of his historical condition. In his comprehensive knowledge and all encompassing love he experienced all the consolation of the entire human family during his lifetime when he was still capable of suffering and of being consoled. As God, of course, he possessed divine omniscience, knowing all of mankind's good and evil acts even before creation. In his human soul, which was hypostatically united to his divine Person, he received the irradiation of the beatific vision.[30]

In addition to this, he possessed an infused knowledge which gave him a comprehensive view of the souls of all men past, present and future. Accordingly, just as he allowed himself to be saddened by the vision of the sins of mankind, so did he also allow himself to be consoled by all the human acts of compassionate consolation throughout history until the end of time. So, despite the fact that the future consolers of our Lord were not *personally*

---

[29]Pius XI, *Miserentissimus Redemptor, op. cit.,* pp. 173 - 174.

[30]Thomas Aquinas, *Summa Theologica* III, q. X, a.1-4; cf. Decr. S. Officii, 5 June 1918, *De scientia animae Christi, Acta Apostolicae Sedis* 10 (1918), p. 282. This teaching, although unpopular in some theological circles, is *central* to the teaching of this encyclical and has been stated and restated in numerous other documents by the magisterium which can be easily found in Denzinger-Schönmetzer: cf. Decr. S. Offici, 3 July 1907 *Lamentabili* D.S. 3432, 3433, 3434; 5 June 1918 *De Scientia animae Christi* D.S. 3645-47; Pius XI *Miserentissimus Redemptor* AAS 20, p. 174; Pius XII, *Mystici Corporis* D.S. 3812; *Sempiternus Rex* D.S. 3905; *Haurietis Aquas* D.S. 3924; Sacred Congregation for the Doctrine of the Faith AAS 58 (1966) pp. 659 - 660.

A number of prominent theologians have developed the Church's teaching: cf. Card. Luigi Ciappi, OP, *The Heart of Christ the Center of the Mystery of Salvation* (Rome: CdC 1983); Rev. William G. Most, *The Consciousness of Christ* (Front Royal: Christendom College Press 1980); Rev. Bertrand de Margerie, S.J., *The Human Knowledge of Christ* (Boston: Daughters of St. Paul 1980); see also Rev. Bertrand de Margerie, S.J., "The Double Consciousness of Christ" in *Faith & Reason* Vol. XIV no. 1.

Figure 23: *Pinacothèque Vannucci, Crucifix of German School from the second half of the fifteenth century.*

present during the passion, the reparatory value of their foreknown actions did in fact console Christ. This loving consolation was received by our Lord not in an ever-growing sequence, but instantaneously in his *nunc stans*—everlasting now. This is the great truth which many artists have sought to communicate down through the ages by painting various saints from different time periods standing at the foot of the cross. Although separated by time, their great love for Christ did in fact console him in his agony, since our Lord foresaw all their acts of loving consolation.

Although Christ *is* now in glory and incapable of suffering he still is the same divine Person who suffered for us. Through offering a loving consolation to our Lord in appreciation for his past sufferings, we attempt a return of love for his infinite love which he manifested on the cross. If one were to refuse to return to the mortal life of Christ in a loving remembrance of his suffering, it would truly reveal a shocking lack of love. It is this horrible ingratitude and forgetfulness which caused our Lord to complain to various mystics. In seeking to console the Sacred Heart, we are not turning to events which no longer have any effect upon us. The effects of our Lord's passion possess an eternal value which do not diminish with the passage of time; i.e., man's reconciliation with God, the continual application of Christ's sacrifice in Holy Mass, etc. Consoling our Lord for his past suffering leads to an ever more profound understanding of and participation in our Lord's work of redemption. Those who console the Sacred Heart of Jesus are returning love for love at their particular time in salvation history, adding to the universal consolation which Christ accepted during his mortal life. This retrospective intention of compassionate love is true consolation. For Christ, now in glory, these acts of consolation become reparation which brings everlasting joyful satisfaction to him as he sees his Father honored by the faithful who appropriate the merits of redemption for their own salvation.

The Pope next speaks of a third aspect—the value of consoling Christ, who "suffers" in his mystical body, which is the Church:

> To the above we may add that the expiatory passion of Jesus Christ is renewed and in a certain manner continued in His mystical body, the Church. To use again the words of St. Augustine, "Christ suffered all that He had to suffer: nothing at all is lacking to the number of His sufferings. Therefore His sufferings are complete, but in Him as in the head; there remain even now sufferings of Christ to be endured in the body." In fact, Christ Himself made the same statement, for to Saul "breathing out threatenings and slaughter against the disciples of the Lord," he said, "I am Jesus whom thou persecutest." By this He plainly affirmed that persecutions visited on the Church are in reality directed

against the Head of the Church. Therefore, Christ, suffering in His mystical body, with reason desires to have us as companions in His own acts of expiation. He asks to be united with us for since we "are the body of Christ, and member for member," in so far as the Head suffers so also should the members suffer with it.[31]

The Holy Father then turns his attention to the tremendous need in our present age for expiation or reparation to the Sacred Heart of Jesus. He speaks of the numerous evils in which men have "shamefully abandoned Christ burdened with sorrows and attacked by the satellites of Satan":

- rulers and governments have openly attacked the Church;
- religious dedicated to the service of the Lord have been persecuted;
- human and Divine rights have been overthrown;
- grievous assaults have been made on the purity of youth;
- apostasy has become commonplace.

Within the Church herself the Pope decries the fact that many of the faithful are ignorant of Catholic truth and have been poisoned by false doctrines. Many live sinful lives, wandering far from their Father's house. They deprive themselves of the light of the true Faith and the strength and comfort to be found in Christ's love. He speaks further of the evils afflicting the Church:

- disrespect for Church discipline and tradition;
- the assault on the sanctity of marriage;
- the education of children has become based upon false theories;
- the virtue of modesty has been virtually forgotten;
- materialism has become an uncontrollable desire;
- the authority of the Word of God is now publicly despised.

These evils described so vividly by Pope Pius XI have not diminished in the decades that have followed this encyclical, but have increased in magnitude and intensity at an alarming rate. Certainly the need for loving reparation to the Heart of Jesus is even greater today, especially when one considers the widespread slaughter of the millions of innocent unborn children by abortion, the facility of divorce, the glorification of promiscuity and many other evils.

---

[31]*Ibid.*, p. 174

To stress the apocalyptic dimensions of these evils, Pope Pius writes:

> There thus comes to mind, almost involuntarily, the thought that we have arrived at the hour prophesied by Our Lord when He said: "And because iniquity has abounded, the charity of many shall grow cold."[32]

To battle these evils which grievously injure the majesty of God and the welfare of souls, the Pope calls upon the faithful to enkindle with their hearts the fire of divine love and to make reparation to the loving Heart of Jesus.

> If the faithful, burning with love for the suffering Christ, should meditate on all these considerations, it would be unthinkable that they should not expiate with greater zeal both their own and the faults of others, that they should not repair the honor of Christ, be filled with zeal for the eternal salvation of souls. Assuredly, We may adapt to our own age to describe it what the Apostle wrote: "When sin abounded, grace did more abound," for even though the sinfulness of man has greatly increased, by the grace of the Holy Ghost, there has also increased the number of the Faithful who most gladly try to make satisfaction to the Divine Heart of Jesus for the numerous injuries heaped on Him. What is more, they joyfully offer themselves to Christ as victims for sin.
>
> Anyone who has been considering in a spirit of love all that has been recalled to his mind up to this, if he has impressed these thoughts, as it were, upon the fleshy tablets of his heart, such a one assuredly cannot but abhor and flee all sin as the greatest of evils. He will also offer himself whole and entire to the will of God and will strive to repair the injured majesty of God by constant prayer, by voluntary penances, by patient suffering of all those ills which shall befall him; in a word, he will so organize his life that in all things it will be inspired by the spirit of reparation.[33]

The Pope ends his encyclical expressing his "most ardent desire" that the devotion of reparation to the Sacred Heart, which possesses "the seal of highest approval of Our Apostolic authority" shall "come to be practiced *universally* and in a most solemn manner by *all* Christian peoples."[34] The Pope then orders that each year on the Feast of the Sacred Heart a solemn act of reparation be made to our most loving Redeemer in all the churches of the world. The purpose of the act was to make reparation for the personal sins of the Faithful and restore the sovereign rights of Christ "the King of Kings

---

[32]*Ibid.,* p. 176
[33]*Ibid.,* p. 176
[34]*Ibid.,* p. 177

and our most loving Master" which have been viciously assaulted. The formula of reparation to be used in all the churches on the Feast was included in the encyclical. It is a beautiful prayer which seeks to effect a change of heart within the believer and to renew his fervor:

> O sweet Jesus, Whose overflowing charity for men is requited by so much forgetfulness, negligence and contempt, behold us prostrate before Thy altar eager to repair by a special act of homage the cruel indifference and injuries, to which Thy loving Heart is everywhere subject.
>
> Mindful alas! that we ourselves have had a share in such great indignities, which we now deplore from the depths of our hearts, we humbly ask Thy pardon and declare our readiness to atone by voluntary expiation not only for our own personal offences, but also for the sins of those, who, straying far from the path of salvation, refuse in their obstinate infidelity to follow Thee, their Shepherd and Leader, or, renouncing the vows of their baptism, have cast off the sweet yoke of Thy law.
>
> We are now resolved to expiate each and every deplorable outrage committed against Thee; we are determined to make amends for the manifold offences against Christian modesty in unbecoming dress and behaviour, for all the foul seductions laid to ensnare the feet of the innocent, for the frequent violation of Sundays and holidays, and the shocking blasphemies uttered against Thee and Thy Saints. We wish also to make amends for the insults to which Thy Vicar on earth and Thy priests are subjected, for the profanation, by conscious neglect or terrible acts of sacrilege, of the very Sacrament of Thy divine love; and lastly for the public crimes of nations who resist the rights and the teaching authority of the Church which Thou has founded.
>
> Would, O divine Jesus, we were able to wash away such abominations with our blood. We now offer, in reparation for these violations of Thy divine honour, the satisfaction Thou didst once make to Thy eternal Father on the cross and which Thou dost continue to renew daily on our altars; we offer it in union with the acts of atonement of Thy Virgin Mother and all the Saints and of the pious faithful on earth; and we sincerely promise to make recompense, as far as we can with the help of Thy grace, for all neglect of Thy great love and for the sins we and others have committed in the past. Henceforth we will live a life of unwavering faith, of purity of conduct, of perfect observance of the precepts of the gospel and especially that of charity. We promise to the best of our power to prevent others from offending Thee and to bring as many as possible to follow Thee.
>
> O loving Jesus, through the intercession of the Blessed Virgin Mary our model in reparation, deign to receive the voluntary offering we make of this act of expiation; and by the crowning gift of per-

severance keep us faithful unto death in our duty and the allegiance we owe to Thee, so that we may all one day come to that happy home, where Thou with the Father and the Holy Ghost livest and reignest God, world without end. Amen.[35]

Through this solemn act, which seeks to renew the fire of love which had grown cold, the Holy Father expected

> ...many signal blessings, not only for individuals, but for society itself, domestic and civil, since Christ Himself promised to St. Margaret Mary that "He would shower abundantly His graces upon those who rendered this honor to His Sacred Heart." Assuredly sinners "looking on Him whom they pierced," stricken by the sorrow of the Church, detesting the injuries offered to the King of Kings, "will return to themselves," for they cannot become obstinate in sin in the presence of Him whom they have wounded "coming in the clouds of heaven."[36]

Four years later Pope Pius XI was moved to write a second encyclical on the need to offer prayer and expiation to the Sacred Heart of Jesus. It was written during the period known as the Great Depression. *Caritate Christi Compulsi* was promulgated on May 3, 1932, and issued a clarion call to the faithful of Christ for prayer and penance. The Holy Father eloquently reechoed the message of St. Margaret Mary: the Heart of Jesus is offered as the sign of salvation for an apostate age in which the love of men has grown cold and millions have closed their hearts to God. He speaks of the devotion to the Sacred Heart as "the extraordinary remedy for the extraordinary needs of our time."

The Pope draws attention to the evils which are responsible for the spiritual and material distress which had become so deep and widespread. Men and nations are moved primarily by a selfish egoism which manifest itself in brazen greed, excessive individualism and an exaggerated nationalism. Above all else, the Pope speaks of the forces of organized atheism which seek to profit from the world-wide suffering:

> Profiting by so much economic distress and so much moral disorder, the enemies of all social order, be they called Communists, or any other name, boldly set about breaking through every restraint. This is the most dreadful evil of our times, for they destroy every bond of law, human or divine; they engage openly and in secret in a relentless struggle against religion and against God Himself; they carry out the

---

[35]*Ibid.*, p. 179; pp. 184 - 185
[36]*Ibid.*, pp. 177 -178

diabolical program of wresting from the hearts of all, even of children, all religious sentiment; for well they know that when once belief in God has been taken from the heart of mankind they will be entirely free to work out their will. Thus we see today, what was never before seen in history, the satanic banner of war against religion brazenly unfurled to the winds in the midst of all peoples and in all parts of the earth. [37]

The Holy Father acknowledges the fact that the world has never been lacking impious men but rightfully observes that these had always been few in number. They were, for the most part, isolated and did not openly profess disbelief. Today, however, atheism has spread through large masses of people:

>...well organized, it works its way even into the common schools; it appears in theaters; in order to spread it makes use of its own cinema films, of the gramophone and the radio; with its own printing presses it prints booklets in every language; it promotes special exhibitions and public parades; it has formed its own political parties and its own economic and military systems. This organized and militant atheism works untiringly by means of its agitators, with conferences and projections, with every means of propaganda secret and open, among all classes, in every street, in every hall; it secures for this nefarious activity the moral support of its own universities, and holds fast the unwary with the mighty bonds of its organizing power. At the sight of so much activity placed at the service of so wicked a cause, there comes spontaneously to Our mind and to Our lips the mournful lament of Christ: "The children of this world are wiser in their generation than the children of light."[38]

This militant atheism is directed not only against the Catholic Faith but against all who acknowledge God as the Creator of heaven and earth. Pius XI well understood the apocalyptic dimension of this struggle and called upon all Christians to unite for the inevitable battle:

>It is necessary, therefore, Venerable Brethren, that without faltering we "get up a wall for the house of Israel," that we likewise unite all our forces in one solid, compact line against the battalions of evil, enemies of God not less than of the human race. For in this conflict there is really a question of the fundamental problem of the universe and of the most important decision proposed to man's free will. For God or

---

[37]Pius XI, *Caritate Christi Compulsi*, AAS Vol. XXIV, (1932), pp. 177 - 180
[38]*Ibid.*, pp. 180 - 181

against God, this once more is the alternative that shall decide the destinies of all mankind, in politics, in finance, in morals, in the sciences and arts, in the state, in civil and domestic society. In the East and in the West, everywhere this question confronts us as the deciding factor because of the consequences that flow from it.[39]

In addition to political efforts to promote social justice through Catholic Action, the major weapons to be used by the People of God are prayer and penance, offered in a spirit of love to the Sacred Heart of Jesus. The Pope calls prayer and penance "the two most mighty weapons of the spiritual life." He laments the fact that today in the Church expiation and penance have "lost in great part the power of rousing enthusiasm of heart and heroism of sacrifice." With profound insight, the Holy Father observes that the faithful's belief in the need of penance and expiation is lost "in proportion as belief in God is weakened, and the idea of original sin and of the first rebellion of man against God becomes confused and disappears."[40]

This provides a deeper understanding of the contemporary difficulty which exists among many Christians concerning concepts of penance and expiation. We shall deal with this problem in greater detail in the final section.

Prayer and penance offered to the Heart of Christ are further described by the Holy Father as "the two potent inspirations sent to us at this time by God that we may lead back to Him mankind that has gone astray and wanders about without a guide; they are the inspirations that will dispel and remedy the first and principal cause of every revolt and every revolution, the revolt of man against God."[41]

The Pope ends this appeal by calling all Christians to unite in prayer and reparation on the Feast of the Sacred Heart of Jesus:

> Let therefore this year the Feast of the Sacred Heart be for the whole Church one of holy rivalry of reparation and supplication. Let the faithful hasten in large numbers to the Eucharistic Table, hasten to the foot of the altar to adore the Redeemer of the world, under the veils of the Sacrament, that you, Venerable Brethren, will have solemnly exposed that day in all the churches; let them pour out to that most Merciful Heart that has known all the griefs of the human heart, the fullness of their sorrow, the steadfastness of their faith, the trust of their hope, the ardor of their charity.
>
> The Divine Heart of Jesus cannot but be moved at the prayers

---

[39]*Ibid.,* pp. 183 - 184
[40]*Ibid.,* p. 189
[41]*Ibid.,* p. 191

and sacrifices of His Church, and He will finally say to His spouse, weeping at His feet under the weight of so many griefs and woes: "Great is thy faith; be it done to thee at thou wilt."[42]

It is most certain, in view of the aggravated situation in which the world finds itself today, that many Christians did not heed the call of the Holy Father to reform their lives in the spirit of the devotion to the Sacred Heart. There were certainly, however, many pious souls who did answer the call. The heroic sacrifices of these individuals are a source of many hidden graces which we, in our hasty and superficial judgments, often would fail to acknowledge.

Pope Pius XII (1939-1958)

One pious soul who was deeply touched and responded with his whole heart was Eugenio Pacelli, the future Pope Pius XII. On October 20, 1939, only seven months after his election to the See of Peter, he issued his first encyclical, *Summi Pontificatus*. In this encyclical, Pius XII speaks of his deep devotion to the Sacred Heart of Jesus as evidenced by his tribute to Leo XIII's encyclical *Annum Sacrum*. The Pope speaks of the encyclical's impact on his priesthood and pontificate. He also recalls the great work of his immediate predecessor, Pius XI, who, motivated by a devout love for the Sacred Heart of Jesus, sought to extend the universal sovereignty of Christ the King over all men:

> In the year which marks the fortieth anniversary of the consecration of mankind to our Redeemer's Most Sacred Heart the inscrutable counsel of the Lord, for no merit of Ours, has laid upon Us the exalted dignity and grave care of the Supreme Pontificate—for that consecration was proclaimed by Our immortal predecessor, Leo XIII, at the beginning of the Holy Year which closed the last century. And We, as a newly ordained priest, then just empowered to recite "I will go in to the altar of God," hailed the Encyclical *Annum Sacrum* with genuine approval, enthusiasm and delight as a message from Heaven. We associated Ourselves in fervent admiration with the motives and aims which inspired and directed the truly providential action of a Pontiff so sure in his diagnosis of the open and hidden needs and sores of his day.
>
> It is only natural, then, that We should today feel profoundly grateful to Providence for having designed that the first year of Our Pontificate should be associated with the memory so precious and so dear of Our first year of priesthood; and that We should take the

---

[42]*Ibid.*, pp. 192 - 194

opportunity of paying homage to the King of Kings and Lord of Lords as a kind of Introit Prayer to Our Pontificate, in the spirit of Our renowned predecessor and in the faithful accomplishment of his designs; and that, in fine, We should make of it the alpha and omega of Our aims, of Our hopes, of Our teaching, of Our activity, of Our patience and of Our sufferings, by consecrating them all to the spread of the Kingdom of Christ. [43]

The spreading of the devotion to the Divine Heart of Christ our King and Savior was to be the beginning and the end of the new Pope's pontificate.

Just as Pope Pius XI had emphasized the moral obligation resting upon all Christians to make reparation, so Pope Pius XII during his pontificate stressed this duty as necessary for salvation:

No other than Christ could make full satisfaction to almighty God for the sins of the human race; and therefore He willed to be immolated on the Cross, being "the atonement made for our sins, and not only for ours, but for the sins of the whole world." But this purchase does not take full effect immediately. Having bought the world with this great price which is Himself, Christ has yet to take actual possession of men's souls. And so, in order that the redemption and salvation of individuals in all ages until the end of the world may become effective and be ratified by God, it is necessary for each member of the human race to get vitally in touch with the Sacrifice of the Cross, so that the merits that flow from it may be bestowed upon him. We might say that on Calvary Christ has provided a bath of expiation and salvation, filled with the blood He has shed for us; but unless men plunge into it and there wash away the stains of their sins, they cannot be cleansed and saved.

Therefore if individual sinners are to be purified in the blood of the Lamb, Christians themselves must co-operate. Although Christ, universally speaking, has reconciled the whole human race to the Father by His death, yet He has willed that all men should come and be brought to His Cross, especially by means of the Sacraments and the Mass, and so take possession of the fruits which through the Cross He has won for them. By this active and personal co-operation, the members become ever more and more like their Head, and at the same time the salvation that flows from the Head is applied to the members themselves; so that each of us can repeat the words of St. Paul: "With Christ I hang upon the Cross; and yet I am alive; or rather, not I; it is Christ that lives in me." To quote what We wrote on another occasion in dealing more fully with this subject: Christ Jesus "dying on the Cross, bestowed upon His Church the boundless treasure of the

---

[43]Pius XII, *Summi Pontificatus*, AAS 37 (1939), p. 413-414

Redemption without any co-operation on her part; but in the distribution of that treasure He not only shares this work of sanctification with
His spotless Bride, but wills it to arise in a certain manner out of her
labour." [44]

Elsewhere in his great encyclical, *Mediator Dei*, Pius XII speaks specifically of the intimate union which exists between the devotion to the Heart of
Jesus and the sacred liturgy.

In speaking of the need to offer a prolonged thanksgiving after receiving
Holy Communion, the Holy Father reminds the faithful that "The divine
Redeemer loves to listen to our entreaties, to speak with us familiarly, and to
give us a refuge in His Heart which burns with love for us."[45]

The Pope also speaks of adoration of the Blessed Sacrament and those
eucharistic devotions intimately associated with the devotion to the Sacred
Heart of Jesus. He stresses the vital role which these devotions play in living
a full liturgical life:

> In the course of time the Church has introduced various forms of
> this cult, forms ever growing in beauty and usefulness. Such are, for
> example, devout and even daily visits to the Blessed Sacrament;
> solemn processions through towns and villages, especially at Eucharis-
> tic Congresses; adoration of the Blessed Sacrament exposed. Some-
> times such expositions last only for a short time, sometimes for hours,
> even forty hours; in certain places they continue, each church taking
> its turn, the whole year round; and in some cases perpetual adoration
> is conducted day and night in religious communities, the faithful often
> taking part.
>
> These devotional practices have contributed greatly to increasing
> the faith and the supernatural life of the Church on earth, which
> indeed by this perpetual worship is giving echo to the hymn of praise
> which the Church triumphant sings everlastingly to God and the Lamb
> "that was slain." These devotions therefore, which in the course of
> ages have become universal, the Church has not only approved but
> has even made her own and commended by her authority. They have
> their origin in the spirit of the liturgy; and therefore, so long as they
> are conducted with due seemliness and with faith and devotion that is
> required by the sacred ritual and the instructions of the Church, they
> undoubtedly contribute greatly to the living of a liturgical life.[46]

In addition, the Holy Father gives a special word of commendation at the

---

[44]Pius XII, *Mediator Dei*, AAS 39 (1947), pp. 549 - 551
[45]*Ibid.*, p. 567
[46]*Ibid.*, pp. 569 - 570

conclusion of this encyclical to the devotions to the Sacred Heart of Jesus and the Blessed Mother, and speaks of their liturgical value:

> There are certain other pious practices, which though not belonging strictly to the liturgy, nevertheless enjoy a special importance and dignity, such that they are regarded as raised to liturgical rank, and have received approval from this Apostolic See and the Episcopate. Among these are special devotions to the Virgin Mother of God during the month of May, and to the Sacred Heart of Jesus during the month of June....
>
> These practices incite the faithful to receive the Sacrament of Penance more frequently, to take their part devoutly in the Eucharistic Sacrifice and to receive Holy Communion, and also to meditate on the mysteries of our Redemption and to imitate the examples of the Saints; they therefore cause us to take part in the liturgy with greater spiritual profit.[47]

On May 15, 1956 Pope Pius XII issued the Sacred Heart encyclical, *Haurietis Aquas*. With the publication of this masterful encyclical, a new era in the history of the devotion was ushered in. The Holy Father examined the foundations and values of the devotion. He invited scholars to delve more deeply into the matter and begin a more thorough study of its riches. *Haurietis Aquas* is by far the most important of the magisterial documents which we shall examine concerning the devotion to the Heart of Jesus. For this reason it is vitally important to our present study that we examine this teaching of the Sovereign Pontiff in great detail.

The encyclical itself may be divided into four basic sections: 1) an introduction which provides an overall view of the devotion, recalling previous papal teachings and certain prevalent errors concerning the devotion; 2) a survey of the origin and foreshadowing of the devotion in the Old Testament, the New Testament, and in the tradition of the Church; 3) a description of the development of the devotion within the life of the Church; and 4) a statement on the supreme importance of the devotion and an appeal for study, meditation and practice of the devotion to the Sacred Heart.

The Pope begins with the prophecy of Isaiah, "You shall draw waters with joy out of the Savior's fountain" (Is. 12:3). Using this highly significant imagery, the prophet foretells the abundant graces which were to flow during the Christian era.

---

[47]*Ibid.*, pp. 586 - 587. A fine theological exposition of the relationship between the Sacred Heart and the Liturgy can be found in Abbot Gueranger's *The Liturgical Year*, vol. X (Westminster, MD: The Newman Press, 1949) pp. 413-444.

Pius speaks of the devotion as a "priceless gift" which our Divine Lord has given to the Church:

> It is altogether impossible to enumerate the heavenly gifts which devotion to the Sacred Heart of Jesus has poured out on the souls of the faithful, purifying them, offering them heavenly strength, rousing them to the attainment of all virtues.[48]

The Pope states that the devotion will enable us to love Christ in a more generous and effective way. It will help us to respond to our Lord's invitation to drink of his saving waters (Jn. 7:31-37). (Pope Pius here uses the Ephesian punctuation which sees the waters of salvation as flowing directly from the Heart of Christ.)

If one considers the true nature of this devotion which concentrates upon Divine Love, its power and efficacy are made manifest.

> If we consider its special nature it is beyond question that this devotion is an act of religion of high order; it demands of us a complete and unreserved determination to devote and consecrate ourselves to the love of the divine Redeemer, Whose wounded Heart is its living token and symbol. It is equally clear, but at a higher level, that this same devotion provides us with a most powerful means of repaying the divine Lord by our own. [49]

The Holy Father next speaks of the solicitude which the Church continues to have for devotion to the Most Sacred Heart of Jesus. Because of the Church's high esteem for the devotion, she has always sought to protect it from false opinion. Despite the fact that the devotion has "completely penetrated the Mystical Body"[50] some persons, even within the Church, have little regard for it. The Holy Father rejects those who would brand the devotion as taught by the Church as a kind of "sentimentalism" or "naturalism". He likewise rejects the criticism that the devotion is ill-adapted or harmful to the modern needs of the Church and humanity. Pope Pius also speaks of the error of some men who believe that they may accept or reject the devotion according to their own whim. This false belief stems from a fundamental misunderstanding of the nature of the devotion: "There are some who, confusing and confounding the primary nature of this devotion with various individual forms of piety which the Church approves and en-

---

[48]Pius XII, *Haurietis Aquas*, AAS 48 (1956), p. 309

[49]*Haurietis Aquas, op. cit.*, p. 311

[50]*Ibid.*, p. 312

courages but does not command, regard this as a kind of additional practice which each one may take up or not according to his own inclination."[51]

The Pontiff goes on to say that all these false opinions are contrary to the explicit teaching of the Holy See, particularly the magisterium of Leo XIII, Pius XI and Pope Pius XII himself:

> Who does not see, venerable brethren, that opinions of this kind are in entire disagreement with the teachings which Our predecessors officially proclaimed from this seat of truth when approving the devotion to the Sacred Heart of Jesus? Who would be so bold as to call that devotion useless and inappropriate to our age which Our predecessor of immortal memory, Leo XIII, declared to be "the most acceptable form of piety?"[52]

To avoid such errors the Holy Father undertook the task of writing this encyclical. In addition, he calls upon the faithful to study in greater depth this "priceless gift":

> We are absolutely convinced that not until we have made a profound study of the primary and loftier nature of this devotion with the aid of the light of the divinely revealed truth, can we rightly and fully appreciate its incomparable excellence and the inexhaustible abundance of its heavenly favors.[53]

The Pope again stresses that the infinite love of God for the human race is the principal object of the devotion. Before examining the foundation for the devotion in Sacred Scripture and tradition, the Holy Father explains precisely why the Church gives the highest form of worship (*latria*) to the Heart of the Divine Redeemer. The reasons are two in number: 1) Our Lord's Heart, "the noblest part of human nature," is hypostatically united to the Person of the Divine Word. Because of this, the highest worship of adoration with which the Church honors the Person of the Incarnate Son of God is called for. The Pope reminds the faithful that "we are dealing with an article of faith" which had been solemnly defined at the General Council of Ephesus in 431 and again at the Second General Council of Constantinople in 553. 2) The Heart of Christ itself calls for, in a special way, the highest form of worship since His Heart, more than all the other members of His body, "is the natural sign and symbol of his boundless love for the human race."[54]

---

[51] *Ibid.,* p. 312
[52] *Ibid.,* p. 313
[53] *Ibid.,* p. 315
[54] *Ibid.,* p. 316

Although the Sacred Scriptures do not explicitly speak of a special worship of and love for the physical Heart of our Lord as the symbol of his love,

> ...it cannot cause us surprise nor in any way lead us to doubt the divine love for us which is the principal object of this devotion; since that love is proclaimed and insisted upon in the Old and in the New Testament by the kind of images which strongly arouse our emotions. Since these images were presented in the Sacred Writings foretelling the coming of the Son of God made man, they can be considered as a token of the noblest symbol and witness of that divine love, that is, of the most Sacred and Adorable Heart of the divine Redeemer.[55]

In his examination of the foundation of the devotion in the Old Testament as it *touches upon its principal object*, the Pope draws upon the beautiful imagery used by Moses, Osee, Isaiah, Jeremiah and the Canticle of Canticles. (Deut. 6:46; Os. 11:1,3-4; 14:5-6; Is. 49:14-15; Cant. 22:2; 6:2; 8:6; Jer. 31:3, 33-34). By means of these illustrations Pius shows that the covenant between God and the Jews was based on love. In turning his attention from the Old Testament to the New Testament, the Holy Father speaks of the manifest superiority of the latter:

> This most tender, forgiving and patient love of God, though it deems unworthy the people of Israel as they add sin to sin, nevertheless at no time casts them off entirely. And though it seems strong and exalted indeed, yet it was only an advance symbol of that burning charity which mankind's promised Redeemer, from His most loving Heart, was destined to open to all and which was to be the type of His love for us and the foundation of the new covenant.
>
> Assuredly, when He who is the only begotten of the Father and the Word made flesh "full of grace and truth" had come to men weighed down with many sins and miseries, it was He alone, from that human nature united hypostatically to the divine Person, Who could open to the human race the fountain of living water which would irrigate the parched land and transform it into a fruitful and flourishing garden.[56]

The mystery of our divine redemption as described in the New Testament is primarily and essentially a mystery of love. It is a mystery which reveals the two movements of love within Christ. Our Lord, by his excruciating suffering upon the cross, revealed his perfect love for his Father in Heaven. This also

---

[55]*Ibid.,* p. 317
[56]*Ibid.,* pp. 319 - 320

reveals the mystery of the love of the Holy Trinity and the divine Redeemer for mankind. The grandeur of the mystery of divine love is enhanced when we realize that humanity, left to itself, could never have made adequate satisfaction for all its sins and that God has no need to receive the love of his creatures. Christ, through his loving death, restored completely and elevated the covenant between God and man, broken by the fall of our first parents.

In examining the nature of Christ's love, the Holy Father acknowledges the fact that the Incarnate Word did indeed love mankind with a spiritual love proper to God insomuch as "God is a Spirit" (Jn. 4:24). This is the love with which God loved our ancestors and the Jews in the Old Testament. The many expressions of intimate paternal love contained in the Old Testament are "tokens" and "symbols" of the true but completely spiritual love of God. In the New Testament, however, we find an added dimension:

> On the other hand, the love which breathes from the Gospel, from the letters of the Apostles and the pages of the Apocalypse, all of which portray the love of the Heart of Jesus Christ, expresses not only divine love but also human sentiments of love. All who profess themselves Catholics accept this without question.[57]

This great and wondrous truth concerning our Savior guards against any return to a Docetic or Gnostic Christology. The human nature which the Word of God united to Himself lacked nothing. From this we may conclude that He possessed a fully human intellect and will and those other internal and external faculties with the desires and all the natural impulses of the senses. These are the essentials of Catholic teaching concerning the humanity of Christ as proclaimed by the Popes and General Councils of the Church. Since we have already dwelt upon this particular aspect in some detail in the doctrinal section, we shall not concentrate upon it here. The main point stressed by the Holy Father is that Jesus took a human nature with a heart capable of suffering and death because, out of love, he longed to offer himself in a bloody immolation for man's salvation.

> Hence, since there can be no doubt that Jesus Christ received a true body and had all the affections proper to the same, among which love surpassed all the rest, it is likewise beyond doubt that He was endowed with a physical heart like ours; for without this noblest part of the body the ordinary emotions of human life are impossible. Therefore the Heart of Jesus Christ, hypostatically united to the divine Person of the Word, certainly beat with love and with the other emotions; but these,

---

[57]*Ibid.,* p. 323

joined to a human will full of divine charity and with the Father and the Holy Spirit, were in such complete unity and agreement that never among these three loves was there any contradiction of or disharmony. However, even though the Word of God took to Himself a true and perfect human nature, and made and fashioned for Himself a heart of flesh, which, no less than ours could suffer and be pierced, unless this fact is considered in the light of the hypostatic and substantial union and in the light of its complement, the fact of man's redemption, it can be a stumbling block and foolishness to some, just as Jesus Christ, nailed to the Cross, actually was to the Jewish race and to the Gentiles.[58]

The Holy Father turns to the writings of the Fathers of the Church (St. Justin, St. Basil, St. John Chrysostom, St. Ambrose, St. Jerome, St. Augustine and St. John Damascene) who universally acclaim the fully human love of our Savior as evidenced by the Incarnation and Redemption. The Son of God took to himself a human nature in order to manifest the burning love of his twofold wills in a human manner. To help demonstrate this truth, Pius calls upon the teaching of St. Thomas Aquinas:

> ...His divine love and the sense emotions which accompany it; that is, desire, joy, weakness, fear and anger, as shown by His face, words or gesture. The face of our adorable Savior was especially the guide, and a kind of faithful reflection, of those emotions which moved His soul in various ways and like repeating waves touched His Sacred Heart and excited its beating. For what is true of human psychology and its effects is valid here also. The Angelic Doctor, relying on ordinary experience, notes: "An emotion caused by anger is conveyed to the external members, and particularly to those members in which the heart's imprint is more obviously reflected, such as the eyes, the face, and the tongue."[59]

The Heart of Jesus is therefore the "chief sign and symbol" of the threefold love with which the Son of God unceasingly loves His Father and sinful men. The Holy Father writes that our Lord's heart symbolizes the following aspects of his love:

1) the divine love which he shares with the Father and the Holy Spirit. But only the Word became man; therefore, He alone manifested this love in a perishable body;

2) the fiery love infused into his human soul, which enriched the will and

---

[58]*Haurietis Aquas*, op. cit., pp. 323 - 324

[59]*Ibid.*, p. 327; Thomas Aquinas, *Summa Theologica* I-II, q. 48, a. 4

Figure 24: *Giovanni Bellini, "Christ's Blessing," c. 1460. The Louvre.*

governed it acts through "the most perfect knowledge" drawn from the beatific vision and that which was directly infused;

3) his sensible love, since he possessed complete powers of feelings and perception "in fact moreso than any other human body."

> Since, therefore, Sacred Scripture and the official teaching of the Catholic faith instruct us that all things find their complete harmony and order in the most holy soul of Jesus Christ, and that He has manifestly directed His threefold love for the securing of our redemption, it unquestionably follows that we can contemplate and honor the Heart of the divine Redeemer as a symbolic image of His love and a witness of our redemption and, at the same time, as a sort of mystical ladder by which we mount to the embrace of "God our Savior."[60]

Everything that our Lord did during his sojourn on earth—his journeys, teachings, miracles, etc.—all manifest this threefold love. In addition, Pope Pius XII singles out those works which show forth most clearly his love for us. He mentions in particular the institution of the Eucharist, His suffering and death, the gift of his Mother, the founding of the Church and finally, the sending of the Holy Spirit. Later in the encyclical he speaks of these acts of love in greater detail as gifts which spring from the loving Heart of Jesus.

The Holy Father concludes this section of the encyclical by calling upon the faithful to meditate upon the mystery of our Lord's Heart *which will never cease to symbolize his threefold love:*

> Likewise we ought to meditate most lovingly on the beating of His Sacred Heart by which he seemed, as it were, to measure the time of His sojourn on earth until that final moment when, as the Evangelists testify, "crying out with a loud voice, 'It is finished', and bowing His Head, He yielded up the ghost." Then it was that His heart ceased to beat and His sensible love was interrupted until the time when, triumphing over death, He rose from the tomb. But after His glorified body had been re-united to the soul of the divine Redeemer, conqueror of death, His most Sacred Heart never ceased, and never will cease, to beat with calm and imperturbable pulsations. Likewise, it will never cease to symbolize the threefold love with which He is bound to His heavenly Father and the entire human race, of which He has every claim to be the mystical Head.[61]

Pius XII next draws many illustrations of our Lord's human and divine

---

[60]*Ibid.,* p. 328
[61]*Ibid.,* pp. 328 - 329

love from the Gospels. He speaks of the love Jesus manifested in his life with the Holy Family in Nazareth, in his public life with his teachings, arduous journeys and countless miracles, and, lastly, in his loving suffering and death upon the cross.

The greatest gifts of our Lord to men sprang from his most loving Heart. Chief among these gifts are the Eucharist, the Priesthood and the Blessed Virgin Mary, to be our Mother.

> But who can worthily depict those beatings of the divine Heart, the signs of His infinite love, of those moments when He granted men His greatest gifts: Himself in the Sacrament of the Eucharist, His most holy Mother, and the office of the priesthood shared with us?
>
> Even before He ate the Last Supper with His disciples Christ Our Lord, since He knew He was about to institute the sacrament of His body and blood by the shedding of which the new covenant was to be consecrated, felt His heart roused by strong emotions, which He revealed to the Apostles in these words: "With desire have I desired to eat this Pasch with you before I suffer." And these emotions were doubtless even stronger when, "taking bread, He gave thanks, and broke, and gave to them, saying, 'This is My body which is given for you, this do in commemoration of Me.' Likewise the chalice also, after He had supped, saying, 'This chalice is the New testament in My blood, which shall be shed for you'."
>
> It can therefore be declared that the divine Eucharist, both the sacrament which He gives to men and the sacrifice in which He unceasingly offers Himself "from the rising of the sun till the going down thereof," and likewise the priesthood, are indeed gifts of the Sacred Heart of Jesus.
>
> Another most precious gift of His Sacred Heart, is, as We have said, Mary the beloved Mother of God and the most loving Mother of us all.[62]

In addition, the Holy Father, re-echoing a great patristic theme, speaks of the Church as being born from the opened Heart of Christ.

> Hence, from the wounded Heart of the Redeemer was born the Church, the dispenser of the Blood of the Redemption—whence flows that plentiful stream of Sacramental grace from which the children of the Church drink of eternal life, as we read in the sacred liturgy: "From the pierced Heart, the Church, the Bride of Christ, is born.... And He pours forth grace from His Heart."[63]

---

[62]*Ibid.*, pp. 331 - 332
[63]*Ibid.*, p. 333

The Pope points out that this great and mysterious symbol was known to the earliest Fathers and ecclesiastical writers, as we have seen in our study of the early Patristic phase of the devotion. Pope Pius stresses, however, that whatever was written of the side of Christ opened by the soldiers "should also be said of the Heart which was certainly reached by the stab of the lance, since the soldier pierced it precisely to make certain that Jesus Christ crucified was really dead."[64]

After his Ascension into heaven, our Lord's Heart, now gloriously reigning, continues to love His Church:

> After our Lord had ascended into heaven with His body adorned with the splendors of eternal glory and took His place by the right hand of the Father, He did not cease to remain with His spouse, the Church, by means of the burning love with which his Heart beats. For He bears in His hands, feet and side the glorious marks of the wounds which manifest the threefold victory won over the devil, sin and death.
>
> He likewise keeps in His Heart, locked as it were in a most precious shrine, the unlimited treasures of His merits, the fruits of that same threefold triumph, which He generously bestows on the redeemed human race.[65]

The Holy Spirit's infusion of divine charity also has its origin in the Heart of our Divine Savior. This divine charity "is the most precious gift of the Heart of Christ and of His Spirit."[66] It is this fire of divine charity which gave fortitude to the martyrs to shed their blood for Christ, implanted zeal in the Doctors of the Church to defend and explain the truth of the Catholic Faith, nurtured and stirred the many virtues of the confessors and moved virgins to deny themselves earthly pleasures and consecrate themselves to Christ for the sake of the Kingdom.

Because of these truths, Pius XII reaffirms the teaching of the Church that Christians should adore the Most Sacred Heart of Jesus as the symbol and source of love:

> Nothing therefore prevents our adoring the Sacred Heart of Jesus Christ as having a part in and being the natural and expressive symbol of the abiding love with which the divine Redeemer is still on fire for mankind. Though it is no longer subject to the varying emotions of this mortal life, yet it lives and beats and is united inseparably with the Person of the divine Word and, in Him and through Him, with the

---

[64]*Ibid.*, p. 334; P. Barbet, *op. cit.*
[65]*Ibid.*, p. 334
[66]*Ibid.*, p. 335

divine Will. Since then the Heart of Christ is overflowing with love both human and divine and rich with the treasure of all graces which our Redeemer acquired by His life, sufferings and death, it is therefore the enduring source of that charity which His Spirit pours forth on all members of His Mystical Body.[67]

The Holy Father continues his praise for the devotion stating that in the Heart of Jesus the Christian can find *the summary of the entire mystery of redemption (summa totius mysterii nostrae redemptionis)*. This truth, proclaimed by Pope Pius XII, harks back to the teachings of his immediate predecessor Pius XI:

And so the Heart of our Savior reflects in some way the image of the divine Person of the Word and, at the same time, of His twofold nature, the human and the divine; in it we can consider not only the symbol but, in a sense, the summary of the whole mystery of our redemption. When one adores the Sacred Heart of Jesus Christ, we adore in it and through it both the uncreated love of the divine word and also its human love and its other emotions and virtues, since both loves moved our Redeemer to sacrifice Himself for us and for His Spouse, the Universal Church.[68]

The Pope concludes the second section of the encyclical by speaking of the Heart of Jesus, "always living to make intercession for us" (Heb. 7:25), as a most powerful advocate with his heavenly Father. He turns to the Seraphic Doctor, St. Bonaventure, to illustrate this truth:

He shows His living Heart, wounded as it were, and throbbing with a love yet more intense than when it was wounded in death by the Roman soldier's lance: "[Thy Heart] has been wounded so that through the visible wound we may behold the invisible wound of love."
It is beyond doubt, then, that His heavenly Father, "Who spared not even His own Son, but delivered Him up for us all," when appealed to with such loving urgency by so powerful an Advocate, will, through Him send down on all men an abundance of divine graces.[69]

In the third part of the encyclical, which deals with the historical development of the devotion, the Holy Father begins by briefly summarizing his conclusions concerning the inner nature of the devotion to the Sacred Heart of Jesus as derived from Sacred Scripture:

---

[67]*Ibid.*, p. 336
[68]*Ibid.*, p. 336
[69]*Ibid.*, p. 337

Figure 25: Here Christ as "The Man of Sorrows" shows his wounded heart to his heavenly Father. German altar piece, 1479.

We think that Our comments, which are guided by the light of the Gospel, have proved that this devotion, summarily expressed, is nothing else than devotion to the divine and human love of the Incarnate Word and to the love by which the heavenly Father and the Holy Spirit exercise their care over sinful men. For, as the Angelic Doctor teaches, the love of the most Holy Trinity is the origin of man's redemption; it overflowed into the human will of Jesus Christ and into His adorable Heart with full efficacy and led Him, under the impulse of that love, to pour forth His blood to redeem us from the captivity of sin: "I have a baptism wherewith I am to be baptized, and how am I straitened until it be accomplished?"[70]

The Pope states emphatically that this devotion to the love of God and to Christ's love for men, by means of the "revered symbol" of the wounded Heart, *"has never been altogether unknown to the piety of the faithful."*[71] The Pope does acknowledge that it has become more clearly known and has spread in a remarkable manner in recent times. He observes that this was even more true after Christ himself revealed this "divine secret" to chosen and elevated souls through a superabundant outpouring of divine grace. The devotion developed within the Church as an outgrowth of devotion to the Sacred Humanity of Christ. A devotion of thanksgiving, adoration and love towards the sacred human nature of Christ, especially his holy wounds, was practiced by the Blessed Virgin Mary, the Apostles, the great Fathers of the Church and all Christians down through the ages. We have dealt extensively in the historical section with the countless holy men and women who contributed to the devotion's development. Of particular importance, the Holy Father mentions by name St. Bonaventure, St. Albert the Great, St. Gertrude, St. Catherine of Siena, Blessed Henry Suso, St. Peter Canisius, St. Francis de Sales and St. John Eudes.

Of course, by far the most important individual in the history of the development of the devotion is St. Margaret Mary Alacoque:

> But surely the most distinguished place among those who have fostered this most excellent type of devotion is held by St. Margaret Mary Alacoque who, under the spiritual direction of Blessed Claude de la Colombière who assisted her work, was on fire with an unusual zeal to see to it that the real meaning of the devotion which had had such extensive developments to the great edification of the faithful should be established and be distinguished from other forms of Christian piety by special qualities of love and reparation.[72]

The wondrous progress which the devotion to the Heart of Jesus has made in recent times stems from the fact "that it entirely agreed with the nature of the Christian religion since it was a devotion of love."[73]

The Holy Father emphatically states that it must not be said that this devotion originated from a private revelation.

---

[70]*Ibid.,* pp. 337 - 338
[71]*Ibid.,* p. 338
[72]*Haurietis Aquas, op. cit.,* p. 339
[73]*Ibid.,* p. 340

> It must not be said that this devotion has taken its origin from some private revelation of God and has suddenly appeared in the Church; rather, it has blossomed forth of its own accord as a result of that lively faith and burning devotion of men who were endowed with heavenly gifts, and who were drawn towards the adorable Redeemer and His glorious wounds which they saw as irresistible proofs of the unbounded love.[74]

This is a sharp rebuke of a criticism which is still all too frequently leveled against the devotion. Our Lord's revelations to St. Margaret Mary added nothing to Catholic doctrine. Their importance, according to the Pope, lies in the fact that

> Christ Our Lord, exposing His Sacred Heart, wished in a quite extraordinary way to invite the minds of men to a contemplation of, and a devotion to, the mystery of God's merciful love for the human race. In this special manifestation Christ pointed to His Heart, with definite and repeated words, as the symbol by which men should be attracted to a knowledge and recognition of His love; and at the same time He established it as a sign or pledge of mercy and grace for the needs of the Church of our times.[75]

To further stress the fact that the devotion is based upon the solid foundation of Christian truth and is not a purely private revelation, the Pontiff recalls the fact that the liturgical feast of the Sacred Heart was approved by the Holy See before the writings of St. Margaret Mary received approbation.

Pope Pius exhorts the faithful to turn again to Scripture, tradition and the liturgy in study and pious meditation to gain a deeper understanding of the inner nature of this devotion. If the faithful practice the devotion with this knowledge and deeper understanding they will most certainly "attain to the sweetest knowledge of the love of Christ which is the perfection of the Christian life." This was the very prayer of St. Paul which he uttered in his epistle to the Ephesians:

> "For this cause I bow my knees to the Father of our Lord Jesus Christ...that He may grant you, according to the riches of His glory, to be strengthened by His Spirit with might unto the inward man; that Christ may dwell by faith in your hearts; that, being rooted and founded in charity...you may be able to know also the charity of Christ

---

[74]*Ibid.,* p. 340
[75]*Ibid.,* p. 340

which surpasseth all knowledge, that you may be filled unto all the fullness of God." The clearest image of this all-embracing fullness of God is the Heart of Christ Jesus Itself.[76]

Concerning those who would characterize devotion to the Sacred Heart of Jesus as crass materialism that would hinder truly spiritual and interior love of God, Pius XII forcefully and with great eloquence asserts the contrary. The Holy Father bases his defense upon three basic points: 1) the divine Person as the final object of the devotion; 2) the proper and vital role played by religious symbol and images; and 3) the hypostatic union by which the two natures are united in one Person.

> Quite the contrary is the thought and teaching of Catholic theologians, among whom St. Thomas writes as follows: "Religious worship is not paid to images, considered in themselves, as things; but according as they are representations leading to God Incarnate. The approach which is made to the images as such does not stop there, but continues towards that which is represented. Hence, because a religious honor is paid to the images of Christ, it does not therefore mean that there are different degrees of supreme worship or of the virtue of religion." It is, then, to the Person of the divine Word as to its final object that that devotion is directed which, in a relative sense, is observed towards the images whether those images are relics of the bitter sufferings which our Savior endured for our sake or that particular image which surpasses all the rest in efficacy and meaning, namely, the pierced Heart of the crucified Christ.
>
> Thus, from something corporeal such as the Heart of Jesus Christ with its natural meaning, it is both lawful and fitting for us, supported by Christian faith, to mount not only to its love as perceived by the senses but also higher, to a consideration and adoration of the infused heavenly love; and finally, by a movement of the soul at once sweet and sublime, to reflection on, and adoration of, the divine love to the Word Incarnate. We do so since, in accordance with the faith by which we believe that both natures—the human and the divine—are united in the Person of Christ, we can grasp in our minds those most intimate ties which unite the love of feeling of the physical Heart of Jesus with that twofold spiritual love, namely, the human and the divine love. For these loves must be spoken of not only as existing side by side in the adorable Person of the divine Redeemer but also as being linked together by a natural bond insofar as the human love, including that of the feelings, is subject to the divine and, in due proportion, provides us with an image of the latter. We do not pretend, however, that we

[76]*Ibid.,* pp. 341 - 342

must contemplate and adore in the Heart of Jesus what is called the formal image, that is to say, the perfect and absolute symbol of His divine love, for no created image is capable of adequately expressing the essence of this love. But a Christian in paying honor along with the Church to the Heart of Jesus is adoring the symbol and, as it were, the visible sign of the divine charity which went so far as to love intensely, through the Heart of the Word made Flesh, the human race stained with so many sins.

It is therefore essential, at this point, in a doctrine of such importance and requiring such prudence that each one constantly hold that the truth of the natural symbol by which the physical Heart of Jesus is related to the Person of the Word, entirely depends upon the fundamental truth of the hypostatic union. Should anyone declare this to be untrue he would be reviving false opinions, more than once condemned by the Church, for they are opposed to the oneness of the Person of Christ even though the two natures are each complete and distinct.[77]

From this great truth of our faith we can see that the Heart of Jesus is the heart of a divine Person, the Word who has given us this rich image to symbolize his all-embracing love. The Pontiff concludes this third section by calling the devotion the *highest expression of piety* because it centers upon *Christ the Mediator:*

Consequently, the honor to be paid to the Sacred Heart is such as to raise it to the rank—so far as external practice is concerned—of the highest expression of Christian piety. For this is the religion of Jesus which is centered on the Mediator who is man and God, and in such a way that we cannot reach the Heart of God save through the Heart of Christ, as He Himself says: "I am the Way, the Truth and the Life. No one cometh to the Father save by Me."[78]

In the final section the Holy Father calls upon all Catholics to promote the devotion with "vigorous zeal." He stresses the vital importance of the devotion, leaving no room for doubt or ambiguity since the devotion is no ordinary form of piety:

In truth, if the arguments brought forward which form the foundation for the devotion to the pierced Heart of Jesus are duly pondered, it is surely clear that there is no question here of some ordinary form of piety which anyone at his own whim may treat as of little consequence

---

[77] *Ibid.,* pp. 343 - 344
[78] *Ibid.,* pp. 344 - 345

or set aside as inferior to others, but of a religious practice which helps very much towards the attaining of Christian perfection. ...is it possible that there is any service of God more obligatory and necessary, and at the same time more excellent and attractive, than the one which is dedicated to love? For what is more pleasing and acceptable to God than service which pays homage to the divine love and is offered for the sake of that love—since any service freely offered is a gift in some sense and love "has the position of the first gift, through which all other free gifts are made."[79]

The devotion itself was *proposed by Christ* and approved by the Holy See and therefore one must hold it in high esteem or else *offend Almighty God Himself.*

That form of piety, then should be held in highest esteem by means of which man honors and loves God more and dedicates himself with greater ease and promptness to the divine charity; a form which our Redeemer Himself deigned to propose and commend to Christians and which the Supreme Pontiffs in their turn defended and highly praised in memorable published documents. Consequently, to consider of little worth this signal benefit conferred on the Church by Jesus Christ would be to do something both rash and harmful and also deserving of God's displeasure.[80]

Because of this the Supreme Pontiff urges *all the Christian faithful* to practice the devotion. Once again the Pope emphasizes the need to study the devotion since this study will lead all the faithful to see the solid foundation of the devotion, its warm approval by the Apostolic See and the great grace which it bestows:

We therefore urge all Our children in Christ, both those who are already accustomed to drink the saving waters flowing from the Heart of the Redeemer and, more especially those who look on from a distance like hesitant spectators, to eagerly embrace this devotion. Let them carefully consider, as We have said, that it is a question of a devotion which has long been powerful in the Church and is solidly founded on the Gospel narrative. It received clear support from tradition and the sacred liturgy and has been frequently and generously praised by the Roman Pontiffs themselves. These were not satisfied with establishing a feast in honor of the most Sacred Heart of the Redeemer and extending it to the Universal Church; they were also responsible for the solemn acts of dedication which consecrated the

---

[79]*Ibid.,* p. 346
[80]*Ibid.,* p. 346

whole human race to the same Sacred Heart.

Moreover, there are to be reckoned the abundant and joyous fruits which have flowed therefrom to the Church: countless souls returned to the Christian religion, the faith of many roused to greater activity, a closer tie between the faithful and our most loving Redeemer. All these benefits particularly in the most recent decades, have passed before Our eyes in greater numbers and more dazzling significance.[81]

After joyfully thanking those who are tirelessly working for the spread of the devotion, Pope Pius XII speaks of the urgent need of this devotion in the Church and contemporary society. The Church herself lacks perfection in many of her members and stands in need of renewal. Many people in distant lands have yet to receive the saving truth of Christ Jesus. In civil society also a militant atheism continues to spread destroying countless souls. Evil men "as if instigated by Satan himself" openly and with great vehemence direct their hatred against God, the Church and Christ's Vicar. In addition, a false materialism and "an unbridled license for unlawful desires" appears to be engulfing the world. The Pope laments that love, the highest law of the Christian Faith which alone can secure the foundations for true peace and justice, has lost its warmth in the hearts of many. As our Lord forewarned his followers, "Because iniquity has abounded, the charity of many will grow cold" (Mt. 24:12).

Like his predecessors, the Holy Father proclaims the devotion to the Most Sacred Heart of Jesus as the cure best suited to the needs of our present age.

When so many evils meet Our gaze—such as cause sharp conflict among individuals, families, nations and the whole world, particularly today more than at any other time—where are We to seek a remedy, venerable brethren? Can a form of devotion surpassing that of the most Sacred Heart of Jesus be found, which corresponds better to the essential character of the Catholic faith, which is more capable of assisting the present-day needs of the Church and the human race? What religious practice is more excellent, more attractive, more salutary than this, since the devotion in question is entirely directed towards the love of God itself? Finally, what more effectively than the love of Christ—which devotion to the Sacred Heart of Jesus daily increases and fosters more and more—can move the faithful to bring into the activities of life the Law of the Gospel.[82]

---

[81]*Ibid.,* pp. 347 - 348
[82]*Ibid.,* p. 350

The Pontiff again draws attention to the continuity of the Papal teaching on this point:

> And so, following in the footsteps of Our immediate predecessor, We are pleased to address once again to all Our dear sons in Christ those words of exhortation which Leo XIII, of immortal memory, towards the close of the last century addressed to all the faithful and to all who were genuinely anxious about their own salvation and that of civil society: "Behold, today, another true sign of God's favor is presented to our gaze, namely, the Sacred Heart of Jesus...shining forth with a wondrous splendor from amidst flames. In it must all our hopes be placed; from it salvation is to be sought and hoped for."[83]

The Heart of Christ, the great "sign of God's favor," is the outstanding symbol and source of unity, salvation and peace for all Christians. Because of this the Holy Father speaks of its great value for the Blessed Sacrament:

> It is likewise Our most fervent desire that all who profess themselves Christians and are seriously engaged in the effort to establish the kingdom of Christ on earth will consider the practice of devotion to the Heart of Jesus as the source and symbol of unity, salvation and peace. Let no one think, however, that by such a practice anything is taken from the other forms of piety with which Christian people, under the guidance of the Church, have honored the divine Redeemer. Quite the opposite. Fervent devotional practice towards the Heart of Jesus will beyond all doubt foster and advance devotion to the Holy Cross in particular, and love for the Most Holy Sacrament of the Altar. We can even assert—as the revelations made by Jesus Christ to St. Gertrude and to St. Margaret Mary clearly show—that no one really ever has a proper understanding of Christ crucified to whom the inner mysteries of His Heart have not been made known. Nor will it be easy to understand the strength of the love which moved Christ to give Himself to us as our spiritual food save by fostering in a special way the devotion to the Eucharistic Heart of Jesus, the purpose of which is—to use the words of Our predecessor of happy memory, Leo XIII—"to call to mind the act of supreme love whereby our Redeemer, pouring forth all the treasures of His Heart in order to remain with us till the end of time, instituted the adorable Sacrament of the Eucharist." For "not the least part of the revelation of that Heart is the Eucharist, which He gave to us out of the great charity of His own Heart."[84]

---

[83]*Ibid.*, pp. 350 - 351
[84]*Ibid.*, p. 351

208 Heart of the Redeemer

In concluding the encyclical, the Holy Father calls the devotion to the Sacred Heart of Jesus "the most effective school of the love of God" and urges that the faithful unite to this devotion veneration for the Immaculate Heart of Mary. He ends with a prayer that "the love of the faithful may grow daily more and more towards the Sacred Heart of Jesus and its sweet and sovereign kingdom be extended more widely to all in every part of the world."[85]

Summary

The teaching of the Papal Magisterium concerning the devotion to the Sacred Heart of Jesus possesses a marvellous unity. Here we may see with radiant clarity the mind of the Church.

The successors of St. Peter proclaim the devotion to be a divine gift offered to the Church by the Lord himself. In a veritable litany of superlatives the Holy See has given the devotion its "highest seal of approval," calling it a "most excellent form of piety" and "the highest expression of the Catholic religion." As to the devotion's spiritual benefits, it has been described as the "best school of divine love." It most certainly will lead to growth in holiness since the Heart of the Savior is a "mystical ladder" which leads to the bosom of the Most Holy Trinity. The sovereign Pontiffs unequivocally stated that if the devotion is practiced countless blessings will flow with lasting benefits for individuals and society.

The devotion did not spring from a private revelation but grew with the aid of divine grace from the strength of its doctrinal foundation. It is so intimately united to Catholic doctrine that the Popes have referred to the devotion as "the very summary of our faith," "the summary of the whole mystery of redemption" and as a complete synthesis of faith.

So perfectly does the devotion contain and teach the truths of the Catholic Faith that it must be held in high esteem by all Christian people. Acts of reparation to the Sacred Heart of Jesus are called obligatory for all Catholics. In fact, if the inner nature of the devotion is correctly understood, its practice is not left to personal taste. The Holy See warns that to treat such a "priceless gift" with indifference would be a rash and detrimental act "deserving of God's displeasure."

Because of this intimate union between doctrine and the devotion, the Heart of Jesus is and *always shall remain* the "most appropriate and excellent symbol and sensible image" of the infinite love of Jesus Christ which moves us to love God and our fellow man. The devotion's ability to show forth the

---

[85]*Ibid.*, p. 353

truths of Christology can be seen in the Papal teaching that our Lord's Heart reveals "most perfectly" the threefold love of Christ with which he loves his Father and sinful men.

The Holy See has also emphatically taught that the practice of the devotion is intimately connected to and strengthens the liturgical life of the Church since the Eucharist is "the outstanding gift of the Heart of Jesus." In addition to strengthening love for our Lord in the Eucharist, the devotion, with its emphasis upon prayer, loving reparation, and penance will also lead to a more frequent reception of the Sacrament of Penance.

The Holy See has offered to the world the Sacred Heart of Jesus as a sign of victory for our age. Ours is an age confronted with tremendous evils. At the same time, however, it is an age filled with great hope. If men would again turn to Christ, placing their trust in his most loving, merciful Heart, society may be built upon the secure foundations of His peace and justice. With an ominous sense of urgency, the See of Peter has spoken time and time again of the devotion as the "extraordinary remedy for the extraordinary needs of our time." It has been heralded as being most capable of saving souls and society as it is "best adapted" to meet the pressing needs of our modern age.

It is also "most suitable" to meet the needs of the Christian family which is being assaulted on all sides by the forces of paganism. It can effectively counter the rapid moral decline of society which is characterized by the widespread attack upon the unborn. The nearly universal approval of selfish egoism, self-interest and crass materialism can be battled through prayer, penance and loving reparation which will in turn vivify the social apostolate. Most importantly, since the devotion centers upon love of God and seeks to enkindle the fire of love upon the earth, the Holy See has declared it to be best suited to halt the advance of militant atheistic communism throughout the world. The power and efficacy of the devotion in this particular area of grave concern was made manifest by the Spanish Communists who, during Spain's bloody civil war sent out a battalion of soldiers who, firing numerous rounds, publicly "executed" the statue of our Lord revealing his Sacred Heart. (The statue had been erected to commemorate Spain's consecration to the Heart of the Savior.)

This consistency and urgency of the Papal Magisterium's teachings is of tremendous importance for all Christians who desire to *sentire cum Ecclesia*. The evils listed by the Popes have not abated but have increased in their extension and intensity. This being the case, is it possible that the devotion to the Sacred Heart of Jesus no longer possesses any value? On this point we may unhesitatingly assert that Rome has spoken—*Roma locuta est*. The veneration of the Most Sacred Heart of Jesus is a devotion whose time has just arrived. Its need has never been so great since ours is truly an age in which iniquity abounds and charity has grown cold.

The Holy See has proclaimed the Heart of Jesus as the source of that heavenly fire of divine charity which alone can save humanity and ensure the victory of love.

V.

The Second Vatican Council and Subsequent Papal Teaching

Following the death of Pope Pius XII, the Cardinals, on October 28, 1958, elected Angelo Roncalli, the Patriarch of Venice, to the See of Peter. On January 25, 1959, Pope John XXIII travelled to the basilica of St. Paul's Outside the Walls and there announced to the world his intention to convoke a General Council of the Church. Few knew at this time the profound impact which this Council would have upon the Church and the world.

At the time of his ordination to the priesthood, Pope St. Pius X spoke to Father Roncalli of his prayer for the future Pope:

> I will ask the good Lord to grant a special blessing on these good intentions of yours, so that you may really be a priest after his own heart.[1]

The decision to call a Council was certainly inspired by the Spirit in the heart of this man who so beautifully mirrored the meekness and humility of the Lord. Pope John's spirituality had always centered around the Heart of Christ and His most priceless gift of the Eucharist. In his spiritual autobiography, *Journal of a Soul*, Pope John's intense love for the Heart of Jesus breathes forth from nearly every page:

> Every time I hear anyone speak of the Sacred Heart of Jesus or of the Blessed Sacrament, I feel an indescribable joy....
> These are loving appeals from Jesus who wants me wholeheartedly there at the source of all goodness, his Sacred Heart, throbbing mysteriously behind the Eucharistic veils.

---

[1]Francis Larkin, *Understanding the Heart, op. cit.*, p. 34

The devotion to the heart of Jesus has grown with me all my life.

I want to serve the Sacred Heart today and always. It is to the heart of Jesus that I must look for a solution of all my troubles.

I want the devotion to his Heart, concealed within the sacrament of love, to be the measure of all my spiritual progress.

I am determined to give myself no peace until I can truly say I am absorbed into the Heart of Jesus. [2]

Such was the spirituality and love of the man from Sotto il Monte near Bergamo, who summoned the Second Vatican Council and is called the Pope of Unity.[3]

Vatican Council II

There are some who believe that somehow the Second Vatican Council invalidated all previous magisterial teachings concerning the Sacred Heart devotion's value, timeliness and necessity. Those who make this assertion have failed to understand one of the basic teachings of the Council—namely, that doctrinal development within the Church is not heterogeneous but homogeneous. The Church will never contradict today what she has taught yesterday. This erroneous position is most certainly not derived from the teaching of the Council itself nor from the subsequent efforts of the Popes to implement the conciliar teaching into the fabric of Catholic life. In fact, quite the opposite appears to be true. But because this position is all too frequently heard, it is important that we closely examine its basis.

The Council Fathers, in their document on the Sacred Liturgy, *Sacrosanctum Concilium*, wrote:

---

[2]John XXIII, *Journal of a Soul*, trans., Dorothy White (Garden City, N.Y.: Image Books, 1980), pp. 157 - 158

[3] Pope John issued an Apostolic Letter *Inde a primis* on June 30, 1960. In this letter he expressed his great desire that devotion to the Sacred Heart along with devotion to the Holy Name and the Precious Blood should be more widely practised by the Christian people. He spoke of the numerous spiritual benefits which the Sovereign Pontiffs had bestowed upon the devotion to the Sacred Heart. He also acknowledged the consistency of the Papal teaching concerning the devotion's nature, its ability to foster growth in holiness, and its strong doctrinal foundation. In his General Audience of Oct. 17, 1962 in St. Peter's Basilica, he stated

"...there is an altar in this very church...over which there is depicted the great apparition of the Sacred Heart to this privileged Visitationist nun....

"Devotion to the Sacred Heart has brought incalculable benefits to the Church and to mankind. Our days can rightly claim to have the advantage of deeper understanding and greater breadth of vision over those in which the Saint lived."

> Popular devotions of the Christian people, provided they conform to
> the laws and norms of the Church are to be *highly recommended,*
> *especially where they are ordered by the Apostolic See.*[4] [Emphasis
> added.]

There can be no doubt that this teaching of the Council was meant to refer
in a special way to the devotion to the Sacred Heart. This devotion, above all
others in the 20th century, had been ordered by the Holy See. The Popes
themselves, as we have seen, had repeatedly demonstrated its complete
conformity with the laws and norms of the Church. The Council Fathers make
extensive use of the symbolism of the human heart as the center of man's
interior personality and moral conscience (e.g., *Gaudium et Spes* pars. #14 &
16). The heart of Christ is mentioned explicitly in the Pastoral Constitution
on the Church in the Modern World. Here the Fathers, in professing the
Church's faith in the Incarnation, refer to the truth that our Lord loved us
"with a human heart." Here we cite the passage within the context of the
document itself:

> In reality it is only in the mystery of the Word made Flesh that the
> mystery of man truly becomes clear... He who is the "image of the
> invisible God" (Col. 1:15) is Himself the perfect man who has restored
> in the children of Adam that likeness to God which had been dis-
> figured ever since the first sin. Human nature, by the very fact that it
> was assumed, not absorbed, in Him, has been raised in us also to a
> dignity beyond compare. For, by His incarnation, He, the Son of God,
> has in a certain way united Himself with each man. He worked with
> human hands, He thought with a human mind, He acted with a human
> will and with a human heart He loved. [5] (*Gaudium et Spes*, n. 22)

Although the Council did not set out to develop a systematic Christology,
it must be admitted that the mystery of our Lord's Heart or at least that which
is symbolized by His Heart (i.e., His love for His Father and sinful men) was
the living center of its considerations. Because the Fathers took up the broad
and general outlines of all the previous great Christological Councils, it may
be said in a certain sense that Vatican II is the most complete and most lucid
of these councils in the history of the Church. It is *as man* that the Word made
flesh makes reparation to the Father "restoring" the divine order disfigured

---

[4] Austin Flannery, *Vatican Council II: The Conciliar and Post Conciliar Documents*
(Northport, N.Y.: Costello Pub. Co., 1975), p. 7; cf., *Sacrosanctum Oecumenicum Concilium*
Vaticanum II (Typis Polyglottis Vaticanis, 1966), p. 13

[5] *Ibid.*, pp. 922 - 923; cf., *Sacrosanctum Oecumenicum Concilium Vaticanum II, op. cit.,*
pp. 709 - 710

by sin. It is in and through his human body that the Word Incarnate became the nexus in a physical way for the entire universe. This restoration is achieved above all else by Christ's hypostatic assumption of human affectivity and a human heart so that men may be loved by God in a human way. This theological anthropology of Christ as "the innocent Lamb" (GS 22.3) who "loved us with a human heart" is central to the Conciliar teaching on Christ.

The documents of the Council contain and develop many of the themes which the devotion to the Sacred Heart had already propagated and practiced. This is to be expected of course, as quite natural since the devotion, as we have seen, is the summary of our Christian faith.

Although the Council does not use the words "Sacred Heart", the Fathers did speak on at least two occasions of the wound in Christ's side. Here we must remember the clear teaching of Pius XII that what is written of the pierced side of our Lord must also be said of his Heart. Using the rich theological language of the Church's patristic heritage, the Council speaks of the relationship between the Church and the Sacred Liturgy, both of which take their origin from the side (Heart) of Christ. At the very beginning of the constitution on the Sacred Liturgy we find:

> The wonderful works of God among the people of the Old Testament were but a prelude to the work of Christ Our Lord in redeeming mankind and giving perfect glory to God. He achieved His task principally by the paschal mystery of His blessed passion, resurrection from the dead, and glorious ascension, whereby "dying He destroyed our death, and rising He restored our life." *For it was from the side of Christ as He slept the sleep of death upon the cross that there came forth "the wondrous sacrament of the whole Church."* [6] [emphasis added]

Again, at the very beginning of the Dogmatic Constitution on the Church we read:

> The Son, accordingly, came sent by the Father, Who, before the foundation of the world, chose us and predestined us in Him for adoptive sonship. For it is in him that it pleased the Father to restore all things (cf. Eph. 1:4-5, 10). To carry out the will of the Father Christ inaugurated the kingdom of heaven on earth and revealed to us His mystery; by His obedience He brought about our redemption. The Church—that is, the kingdom of Christ—already present in mystery, grows visibly through the power of God in the world. The origin and growth of the Church are symbolized by the blood and water which flowed from the open side of the crucified Jesus (cf. Jn. 19:34), and

---

[6] *Ibid.*, p. 3; cf., *Ibid.*, p. 7

are foretold in the words of the Lord referring to his death on the cross: "And I, if I be lifted up from the earth, will draw all men to myself" (Jn. 12:32 Gk).[7] (*Lumen Gentium*, n. 3)

These references speak precisely to the mystery of the Church—the concept which dominates the entire teaching of the Council. The Fathers of Vatican II, in speaking of the Church as the gift of Christ which springs from His open side (i.e., His Heart) on the cross, also set forth *many other things* which arise from the mystery of the Heart of Jesus and are specially treated in the devotion. Among these themes we may mention the divine and human love of Christ, His presence in the life of the Church, His gift of the Holy Spirit, and the faithful's union with Christ in offering their prayers, actions and sacrifices.

Some have felt that the Church has de-emphasized the devotion because of her efforts to renew the liturgy. The Church most certainly has emphasized the renewal of the liturgy but this does not imply that she has in some way devalued the devotion to the Heart of the Divine Redeemer. This opinion sets up a false dichotomy for the two are not opposed but intimately joined together. The document on the liturgy itself does not allow such a view, nor does Pope Paul VI, in his authoritative interpretation of the document.

The Council Fathers stated in the Constitution on the Liturgy that although "the sacred liturgy does not exhaust the entire activity of the Church... Nevertheless the liturgy is the summit toward which the activity of the Church is directed; it is also the fount from which all her power flows"[8] (*Sacrosanctum Concilium* 9, 10).

This contains the pith of the Church's official teaching concerning the primacy of the Holy Sacrifice of the Mass in the Christian life. The document continues with a reminder to the faithful that "in order that the liturgy may be able to produce its full effects it is necessary that the faithful come to it with proper dispositions," [9] (*Sacrosanctum Concilium* 11) and again that the spiritual life "is not limited solely to participation in the liturgy"[10] (*Sacrosanctum Concilium* 12).

As a logical development of the point, the Fathers, in the next paragraph, "highly recommended" popular devotions of the Christian people "especial-

[7]*Ibid.*, p. 351; cf., *Ibid.*, p. 95
[8]*Ibid.*, p. 142; cf. *Ibid.*, pp. 10 - 11
[9]*Ibid.*, p. 6; cf. *Ibid.*, p. 12
[10]*Ibid.*, p. 7; cf. *Ibid.*, p. 12

ly when they are ordered by the Apostolic See"[11] (*Sancrosanctum Concilium* 13).

The Council further states that in seminaries and religious houses clerics are to be given a liturgical formation in their spiritual life in order that they may celebrate the sacred mysteries "and popular devotions which are imbued with the spirit of the sacred liturgy"[12] (*Sancrosanctum Concilium* 17).

The devotion to the Heart of Jesus is most certainly imbued with the spirit of the liturgy. The Holy See has repeatedly stressed the inseparable bond which exists between the Eucharist and the Heart of Christ. The Holy Eucharist is itself a gift of the Heart of Christ wounded with love for us.[13] This connection, as we have seen in the historical section, was commented upon by the earliest Christian writers who saw the sacramental symbolism of the blood and water which flowed from the opened side of our Lord. It is important to remember that all of the revelations granted by our Lord to St. Margaret Mary took place in a eucharistic setting as the saint prayed before the Blessed Sacrament. Our Lord's very complaint to Margaret Mary concerning the coldness and indifference of men was in regard to the sacrament of His love—the Holy Eucharist. From its very inception, and particularly after the revelations given at Paray-le-Monial, the devotion has focused upon a deeper love, veneration and participation in the august sacrament of love. The external manifestations of this devotion, i.e., the Holy Hour, Benediction, First Fridays, etc. all give evidence to this truth. These practices promote a sound eucharistic spirituality and are of tremendous importance in helping men to live a fully Christian life. This is one of the main reasons why the Holy See has commanded that this greatest of devotions be practiced by all Christians.

The great reform of the Liturgy carried out on February 14, 1969, established that the Feast of "The Most Sacred Heart of Jesus" was to be celebrated on the Friday following the second Sunday after Pentecost. It was given the rank of a "solemnity," which is the highest grade of feast possible and is indicative of the devotion's compatibility with the liturgical renewal

---

[11]*Ibid.*, p. 7; cf. *Ibid.*, p. 12.

[12]*Ibid.*, p. 8; cf. *Ibid.*, p. 12.

[13]It is interesting to note here that in the famous eucharistic miracle of Lanciano (c750AD) the results of the recent scientific investigations of the relics authorized by Pope Paul VI and carried out under the direction of Professor Linoli in 1970 revealed among other things that the host which had turned to flesh was: 1) real flesh; 2) flesh belonging to the human species; and 3) flesh consisting of the *muscular tissue of the heart*. A complete treatment of this famous eucharistic miracle and the scientific investigation of Professors Linoli and Bertelli can be found in Bruno Sammaciccia, *The Eucharistic Miracle of Lanciano*, tr. Rev. Anthony E. Burakowski (Brookings, South Dakota: Our Blessed Lady of Victory) 1976.

sought by the Council.

Pope Paul VI (1963-1978)

These observations and interpretations which we have made concerning the teaching of the Second Vatican Council and the devotion to the Sacred Heart of Jesus are witnessed by the authoritative interpretation given to the Conciliar documents by Pope Paul VI (who was elected Pope on the Feast of the Sacred Heart).

This Pope, who suffered so greatly for the sake of Christ's Body, the Church, explicitly affirmed and explained the teaching of the Council concerning the devotion to the Heart of Christ.

The two primary documents which we shall examine in some detail here were both published at the time of the Council.

The First is the Apostolic Letter, *Investigabiles Divitias Christi*, which was published on February 6, 1965. Pope Paul VI addressed the letter to all Patriarchs, Primates, Archbishops and Bishops of the Catholic world on the occasion of the second centenary of the institution of the liturgical Feast in honor of the Sacred Heart of Jesus by Pope Clement XIII on February 6, 1765. The Pope bases his teaching concerning the devotion to the Sacred Heart contained in this letter, upon the teaching of the Second Vatican Council. He proclaims the devotion an excellent form of piety which focuses upon the person of Christ. He further states that devotion to the Sacred Heart of Jesus imposes itself in a special way because of its intimate connection with the Holy Eucharist.

The mystery of Christ which was expounded so lucidly by the Council is the Holy Father's point of departure.

> "The unfathomable riches of Christ" (Eph. 3:8) which flowed from the pierced side of the Redeemer dying on the Cross, when He reconciled to the Father the entire human race, have been so clearly manifested in recent times by the growing cult to the Sacred Heart of Jesus, that from this devotion the most pleasing fruits have been produced for the benefit of the Church.[14]

The Pope next speaks of the great revelation given to St. Margaret Mary and of our Lord's requests that all men honor His Heart.

> Our most merciful Savior, as it is said, appeared to the devout religious, St. Margaret Mary Alacoque, in the town of Paray-le-

---

[14]Paul VI, Apostolic Letter *Investigabiles Divitias Christi* AAS LVII (1965), P. 298

Monial. Showing Himself to her, He insistently requested that all men
honor His Heart wounded for love of us, by the public recitation of
prayers, and compensate in every way possible for all the injuries
inflicted upon Him. Later as a result of the work of St. John Eudes and
because of other incentives given here and there, it is astonishing how
much the devotion to the Sacred Heart flourished among both the
clergy and the Christian people, and penetrated to almost all parts of
the world.[15]

The Holy Father recalls Clement XIII's approval of the "pious request"
of the Polish Bishops and the Roman Archconfraternity of the Sacred Heart
for the establishment of the liturgical feast. He warmly commends those
preparations taking place around the world for the celebration of the second
centenary of this great event. The Pontiff then speaks of his own desires
concerning these celebrations which are to occur throughout the entire
Church:

> We desire and wish that on this occasion all of you, venerable
> Brothers, Bishops of the Church of God, and the people entrusted to
> your care, celebrate in a fitting manner the institution of the Feast of
> the Sacred Heart.
> We desire that the deep and intrinsic doctrinal foundations which
> throw light upon *the infinite treasures of love* of the Sacred Heart be
> explained to all the faithful in an adapted and complete manner, and
> that special ceremonies be organized for the purpose of developing
> ever more the devotion to the cult which deserves the highest con-
> sideration *[maximi aestimandum]* to the end that all the faithful *[ut
> christifideles universi]* moved by a new spirit, pay due honor to the
> Divine Heart, expiate all kinds of sin with more and more ardent acts
> of submission and conform their whole way of life to genuine love
> which is the fulfillment of the law (cf. Rom. 13,10).[16]

Pope Paul then speaks of the beauty of the symbolism of our Lord's Heart
and the devotion's ability to effect a true *metanoia*, or change of heart:

> For the Sacred Heart of Jesus, the burning furnace of love, is the
> symbol and the expressed image of the eternal love by which "God so
> loved the world, that He gave His only begotten Son" (Jn. 3:16).
> Hence we are certain that these religious celebrations will add much
> to the deep penetration and understanding of Divine Love. We are
> equally confident that all the faithful will derive from them ever

[15]*Ibid.*, p. 298
[16]*Ibid.*, p. 299

greater strength to conform their lives readily to the Gospel, to amend their morals zealously, and to carry out the precepts of Divine Law.[17]

The Holy Father continues, expressing his ardent desire that the faithful participate in the Sacred Liturgy with greater fervor. This is to be accomplished through the practice of the devotion to the Sacred Heart. Pope Paul speaks of the intimate connection which exists between the Heart of Jesus and the sacrament of love. He teaches that the Holy Eucharist is the "outstanding gift" of the Heart of the Savior which was pierced and opened to us to reveal His love:

> We especially desire, however, that through a more intense participation in the august Sacrament of the altar, a greater devotion be given to the Sacred Heart of Jesus, whose outstanding gift is the Eucharist *(praeclarissimum donum est Eucharistia)*. For it is in the sacrifice of the Eucharist that our Savior Himself—"always living to make intercession for us" (Heb. 7:25)—is immolated and received, whose Heart was opened by the lance of the soldier and from which was poured out on the human race a stream of precious blood and water. Also, it is in this excellent crown, the center as it were of all the sacraments, that "spiritual sweetness is tasted at its source, and the memory of the excelling love is recalled which Christ showed in His passion" (St. Thomas Aq., *"Opusculum"* 57). Hence, it is completely fitting that, in the words of St. John Damascene, "we approach it [the Eucharist] with burning desire...so that the fire of our desire, having been enkindled from the coals, burn away our sins, and enlighten our hearts, and in the communication of the Divine fire we be equally set on fire and deified." *(De fide Orthod.* 4,13; P.G. 94, 1150)[18]

Concerning the timeliness of the devotion, the Pontiff writes:

> This, therefore, seems to us to be the most suitable ideal: that devotion to the Sacred Heart—which, we are grieved to say, has suffered somewhat in the estimation of some persons—now reflourish daily more and more. Let it be esteemed by all as an excellent and acceptable form of true piety, which in our times, especially because of the norms laid down in the Second Vatican Council, must be rendered to Christ Jesus the King and center of all hearts, who is the Head of His Body, the Church...the beginning, the first from the dead, "that in all things He may have the first place." (Col. 1:18)[19]

---

[17]*Ibid.*, pp. 299 - 300
[18]*Ibid.*, p. 300
[19]*Ibid.*, p. 300

Here Pope Paul is calling attention to the excellence of the devotion because of its concentration upon the great mystery of the God-man. It focuses upon what is deepest in Him in His innermost being—the mystery of His love, which is the mystery of His Heart. It is timely because it also is in complete accord with the norms of the Second Vatican Council.

The Holy Father, quoting directly from the Council, singles out the devotion to the Heart of Jesus as a special and unique devotion in the life of the Church owing to its intimate connection to the Eucharist:

> Since the venerable Ecumenical Council highly recommends "popular devotions of the Christian people...above all when they are ordered by the Apostolic See" (*Constitution on the Sac. Lit.*, art. 13), this form of devotion seems to impose itself in a particular way. For as mentioned above, it consists essentially in worthily adoring Jesus Christ and offering Him reparation; it is based above all on the sacred mystery of the Eucharist from which, as from all other liturgical actions, flow "the sanctification of men in Christ and the glorification of God, to which all other activities of the Church are directed as to their end, are achieved." (*Ibid.*, art. 10)[20]

Paul VI here gives a twofold reason why all the faithful should practice the devotion: 1) the authority of the Vatican Council; and, 2) the truth of the devotion's Eucharistic foundation.

The Holy Father concludes the letter with a prayer that the upcoming celebrations lead to permanent and authentic growth in holiness for all Christian people:

> Greatly desiring, therefore, that the celebrations which are to be proclaimed be as conducive as possible to permanent progress of the Christian life, we beg for you the abundant gifts of the divine Redeemer. And, in witness of our benevolence, we most willingly impart to you, venerable brethren, and to all priests, religious families and faithful entrusted to your vigilance, our apostolic blessing.[21]

The second document which we shall study is a letter sent to the heads of various religious orders[22] dedicated to the propagation of the devotion of the Sacred Heart of Jesus. This letter was written in response to a letter which the religious superiors of these orders had sent to the Pontiff. *Diserti Inter-*

---

[20]*Ibid.*, pp. 300-301

[21]*Ibid.*, p. 301

[22]*Dilectis Filiis*, Henrico Systerman, SS.CC., Leonardo Carrieri, M.SS.CC., Josepho Van Kerckhoven, M.S.C., Josepho De Palma, S.C.J., Armando Le Bourgeois, C.I.M., Pedro Arrupe, S.J.

oretes was dated May 25, 1965 and is a complement to the apostolic letter *Investigabiles Divitias Christi*.

This letter draws out with even greater clarity the teaching of the Holy Father concerning the devotion. The Pope recalls the deep reflections which the Council made concerning the mystery of the Church. He writes that this mystery cannot be properly understood apart from the eternal love of the Incarnate Word, symbolized by His wounded Heart. The Holy Father begins by thanking the superiors for their letter and for demonstrating their love for the devotion which is the center and special charism of their orders:

> We have also read very carefully the words which came from the bottom of your hearts for they have shown Us with what brilliant charity, you, and your religious confreres hold yourselves toward the Sacred Heart of the divine Savior, toward the mystery of His eternal love, with what fidelity you want to belong to this August Name, in which your Societies find their whole reason for existing, their drive for virtue, the cause and source of their missionary zeal.[23]

The Pope recalls his previous letter in which he expressed his desire that 1) the devotion to the Sacred Heart flourish and grow daily, and 2) that it be assumed by all as an excellent and acceptable form of true piety. He praises those humble groups of religious who give example and "eminent witness" to modern men as to why "they should cultivate this excellent form of piety in order to draw from it 'ever greater strength to conform their lives readily to the Gospel, to amend their conduct zealously, and to carry out the precepts of divine law'."[24]

In keeping with the spirit of renewal called for by Vatican II, the Holy Father exhorts the religious to spread the devotion to the Heart of Christ.

> Therefore We think it your duty, your very life, to fulfill heartily the great vocation you have freely embraced, to spread always more and more love for the Heart of Jesus; that you show everyone by word and example, both the awaited renewal of spirit and conduct, as well as the greater efficiency and vigor in the Institutes which are in the Church— as has been called for by the Ecumenical Council, Vatican II—and that therein they must discover their inspiration and a more dynamic spirit.[25]

---

[23]Paul VI, *Diserti Interpretes*, May 25, 1965, Acta Romana Societatis Jesu, Vol. XIV, p. 585

[24]*Ibid.*, p. 586

[25]*Ibid.*, p. 586

The value of the devotion for the renewal of the Church is stressed by the Pontiff. It is only in the mystery of the Heart of Christ that the mystery of the Church takes on light, since it is from the opened Heart of Christ that the Church is born and nourished:

> For, as everyone knows, the Sacred Council aims especially at bringing about this restoration of discipline, public as well as private, in every corner and field of the Christian life. For this reason it has brought to light the brilliant mystery of the Holy Church. But this mystery can never be properly understood if the attention of the people is not drawn to that eternal love of the Incarnate Word, of which the wounded Heart of Jesus is the outstanding symbol: for, as we read in the dogmatic Constitution which bears its name, "The Church, or, in other words, the kingdom of Christ now present in mystery, grows visibly through the power of God in the world. This inauguration and this growth are both symbolized by the blood and water which flowed from the open side of a crucified Jesus." (*On the Church* #3) For the Church was born from the pierced Heart of the Redeemer, and is nourished there, for "Christ loved the Church and delivered Himself up for her, that He might sanctify her, cleansing her in the bath of water by means of the word." (Eph. 5:25-26)[26]

Using the strongest possible language, the Pope proclaims the importance of the devotion and its timeliness for our modern age:

> Thus it is absolutely necessary *[prorsus necesse est]* that the faithful venerate and honor this Heart, in the expression of their private piety as well as in the services of public cult, for of His fullness we have all received; and they must learn perfectly from Him how they are to live in order to answer the demands of our time.[27]

Again Pope Paul points out the intimate link between the devotion and the Holy Eucharist, for the liturgy finds its source and life in the Heart of Jesus:

> We say the origin and principle of the Sacred Liturgy is found there, for the Heart of Jesus is the sacred temple of God and from there ascends to the Eternal Father the expiatory sacrifice "by which He is able at all times to save those who come to God through Him." (Heb.7:25)[28]

---

[26]*Ibid.*, p. 586
[27]*Ibid.*, p. 586
[28]*Ibid.*, p. 586

The Pontiff next speaks of the ecumenical value of the devotion, for it is from the Heart of Christ that the Church receives the impetus to seek all those means which will bring the separated brethren to full unity with the Holy See:

> It is moreover this Heart that moves the Church to look for all those means and helps which will return the separated brethren to full unity around the See of Peter. [29]

This harks back to the teaching of Pius XII, who said that the Heart of Christ is the symbol of Christian unity. In addition the Church receives the strength of her missionary effort from the unfathomable riches of his Heart:

> She finds there in this Heart the drive to bring it about that those who as yet cannot claim the name of Christian, may know with us "the only true God, and Him Whom He sent, Jesus Christ" (Jn. 17:3); for pastoral zeal and the fire of the missionary are particularly ardent when priests and faithful, for the sake of God's glory, study the example of fraternal charity which Christ has shown to us and direct their efforts to tell everyone about the unfathomable riches of Christ.[30]

The Holy Father proclaims the practice of this devotion "in the hearts of the faithful" to be a fervent desire of the Second Vatican Council:

> Everyone sees that it is the most ardent wish *[flagrantissima optata]* of the Ecumenical Synod, by wise design and under the impulse of the Holy Spirit, to develop this in the hearts of the faithful. In the efforts we must take to bring these good hopes we now are allowed to have to a happy fulfillment, it is necessary to beg again and again for the light and strength of the Divine Savior, Whose wounded Heart offers a very efficacious assistance in their realization.[31]

Pope Paul, throughout the remainder of his pontificate, spoke frequently of the devotion, always with that sense of urgency so characteristic of the writings of his predecessors. The following year, on June 14, 1966, the Pope

---

[29]*Ibid.*, p. 586. "Ut omnes sint unum." This was the prayer of the Heart of Jesus at the Last Supper. Our separated brethren do have many beautiful expressions of devotion to the Heart of Christ. This can be clearly seen in the German of Bach's magnificent *Passion according to St. John* (1723) and *Passion according to St. Matthew* (1729) which speak so beautifully of the suffering Heart of Christ.

Msgr. George Mejía gives an excellent essay on the ecumenical commitment which springs from an understanding of the ecclesiology which is found in the birth of the Church from the wounded Heart of Christ. See *Toward a Civilization of Love* (San Francisco: Ignatius Press, 1981) pp. 101-143.

[30]*Ibid.*, p. 586

[31]*Ibid.*, p. 586-587

again emphasized the timeliness and importance of the devotion. The occasion was his receiving in audience 54 delegates of the general Chapter of the Priests of the Sacred Heart. He quoted at length from his previous letters and spoke of

> ...the noble and worthy form of piety which, especially in the light of the Ecumenical Council should be offered to Christ by centering everyone's attention upon His love, so clearly symbolized by His wounded Heart....
>
> Your spirituality is centered upon the Person of the Redeemer, and more particularly upon His Heart, to offer Him love and reparation. These two characteristics have existed at all times. They are today, We do not fear to say, more actual than ever. Twice since Our election to the Sovereign Pontificate—which took place, We are pleased to recall in your presence, on the liturgical feast of the Sacred Heart—We thought it our duty to recall the timeliness and urgency of this devotion in the Church, the necessity of not allowing it to weaken among the faithful. Walk unhesitatingly along the paths of love and reparation....The special devotion to the Sacred Heart to which you are called by your vocation, needless to say, does not lie solely in the realm of affectivity. You should aspire towards an effective devotion which produces concrete works suited to spread the reign of Christ's love upon earth.[32]

Several months later Pope Paul again spoke in a most powerful way of the timeliness and value of the devotion to the Thirty-First General Congregation of the Jesuits:

> The cult rendered to the Sacred Heart is the most efficacious means to contribute to that spiritual and moral renewal of the world called for by the Second Vatican Council and to accomplish fruitfully the mission entrusted to you to confront atheism.[33]

---

[32]Allocution of Pope Paul VI, June 14, 1966, *L'Osservatore Romano*, June 15, 1966, p. 1

[33]Address of Pope Paul VI to the 31st General Congregation of the Society of Jesus, Nov. 17, 1966

The Pope also spoke of the great value of the symbolism of the Sacred Heart for modern man:

> Mystical understanding came to contemplate Him in the Heart; it has made devotion to the Sacred Heart the fiery furnace and symbol of Christian devotion and activity for us moderns, who value feelings and psychology, and are always oriented toward the metaphysics of love.[34]

Pope John Paul II (1978-   )

Our present Holy Father, Pope John Paul II is most certainly a "man of the heart." In his rich and timely magisterium he has frequently spoken of the heart as the fundamental center of man from which springs everything that he is and does. The Holy Father's emphasis upon the heart of man can be seen in every facet of his work. One so taken with the heart of man could not help but be drawn to the Divine Heart which is so in love with men. The Pope has publicly acknowledged the fact that he has been deeply imbued with the spirit of the devotion which has spoken to him from his youth.[35]

This is certainly most fitting, since this Pope comes from a land which Divine Providence chose to play a key role in the establishment of the liturgical feast of the Sacred Heart, thus fulfilling our Lord's request to St. Margaret Mary.

In his first encyclical *Redemptor Hominis*, Pope John Paul II directs our gaze to the Person of Jesus Christ. Although explicit references to the Heart

---

[34]Paul VI, General Audience, Jan. 27, 1971, *L'Osservatore Romano*, February 4, 1971, p. 1. It was this insight into the power of the symbol of our Lord's Heart and its doctrinal richness which led Pope Paul to speak of the Heart of Christ in the promulgation of the new Divine Office on the Feast of All Saints, 1970:

"Christian prayer is foremost the prayer of the entire community of men which Christ joins to Himself.... But that prayer receives its unity from the Heart of Christ." (Apostolic Constitution promulgating the new Divine Office in *Liturgia Horarum*, Vol. I, p. 15).

The *General Instruction* on the Divine Office also states: "It is the Heart of Christ that God's praise resounds in human words of adoration, propitiation and intercession" (*Liturgia Horarum*, Vol. I, p. 20).

[35]Pope John Paul II, General Audience, June 20, 1979, *L'Osservatore Romano*, June 25, 1979. The Pope's former secretary, Msgr. Magee, who was later made a bishop, said in an interview: "The Pope, after the death of his mother, used to visit the local church with his father and pray there before the image of the Sacred Heart. He always went to confession on the First Friday of each month and today says the votive Mass of the Sacred Heart whenever possible. He also has a deep love of the Litany of the Sacred Heart which he sings every day during the month of June."

of Christ are few,[36] because of its emphasis upon Christ it can greatly deepen our appreciation of the devotion to the Sacred Heart. The encyclical presents many of the great truths which are contained in the devotion.

Early in the encyclical the Holy Father speaks of the importance of the word "heart" as the center of man. It is to this center that Christ addresses himself and there seeks to enter. To demonstrate this truth he calls upon the teaching of the Second Vatican Council, which speaks of Christ, the God man, who loved with a human heart. In his revelation of the mystery of the Father's love, Christ also reveals the whole truth about man:

> In its penetrating analysis of the "modern world," the Second Vatican Council reached that most important point of the visible world that is man, by penetrating like Christ the depth of the human consciousness and by making contact with the inward mystery of man, which in Biblical and non-Biblical language is expressed by the word "heart." Christ, the Redeemer of the world, is the one who penetrated in a unique and unrepeatable way into the mystery of man and entered his "heart."
>
> Rightly therefore does the Second Vatican Council teach: "The truth is that only in the mystery of the Incarnate Word does the mystery of men take on light. For Adam, the first man, was a type of him who was to come (Rom. 5:14), Christ the Lord. Christ the new Adam, in the very revelation of the mystery of the Father and of his love, *fully reveals man to himself* and brings to light his most high calling." And the Council continues: "He who is the 'image of the invisible God' (Col. 1:15), is himself the perfect man who has restored in the children of Adam that likeness to God which had been disfigured ever since the first sin. Human nature, by the very fact that it was assumed, not absorbed, in him, has been raised in us also to a dignity beyond compare. For, by his Incarnation, he, the son of God, *in a certain way united himself with each man*. He worked with human hands, he thought with a human mind. He acted with a human will, and with a human heart he loved."[37]

The Pope continues, reflecting upon this conciliar teaching: that it is only in Jesus Christ, in the mystery of the love of His Heart, that mankind is reconciled to the Father:

---

[36]The Holy Father refers explicitly to the Heart of Christ in section (9); on two occasions he cites St. Matthew's Gospel 11:29, which speaks of our Lord's meekness and humility of heart; in paragraph 8 he quotes from *Gaudium et Spes* with its reference to the fact that our Lord loved with a human heart; in section 4, n. 14, the Apostolic Letter of Pope Paul VI on devotion to the Sacred Heart *Investigabiles Divitias* is cited; and lastly, in section 7, n. 36, the Litany of the Sacred Heart is cited.

[37]John Paul II, *Redemptor Hominis*, no. 8 AAS 71 (1979)p. 273-274

As we reflect again on this stupendous text from the Council's teaching, we do not forget even for a moment that Jesus Christ, Son of the living God, became our reconciliation with the Father. He it was, and he alone, who satisfied the Father's eternal love, that fatherhood that from the beginning found expression in creating the world, giving man all the riches of creation, and making him "little less than God," in that he was created "in the image and after the likeness of God."

He and He alone also satisfied that fatherhood of God and that love which man in a way rejected by breaking the first Covenant and the later covenants that God "again and again offered to man." The redemption of the world—this tremendous mystery of love in which creation is renewed—is, at its deepest root, the fullness of justice in a human Heart—the Heart of the First-born Son—in order that it may become justice in the hearts of many human beings, predestined from eternity in the First-born Son to be children of God and called to grace, called to love.[38]

The encyclical focuses attention upon the great mystery of man's redemption in Jesus Christ. Although it does not deal specifically with devotion to the Heart of Christ, it does eloquently speak of the devotion's timeliness since it touches upon so many basic elements of the devotion. It proclaims the absolute centrality of Christ as the Redeemer of man. It is in "the Heart of the First-born Son" that the mystery of love lies; from this Heart the new creation springs forth. The merciful love of Christ "constantly making intercession for us" restores man and elevates him to his supernatural destiny as an adopted son of his heavenly Father. The encyclical also stressed the revelation of the Father, the gift of the Holy Spirit and the gift of the Church which participates in our Lord's redemptive mission especially in the eucharistic sacrifice. The encyclical exhorts all the faithful to a deeper commitment in love to Christ and our fellow man.

The Pope also speaks of the maternal heart of the Blessed Virgin Mary:

We can say that the mystery of the Redemption took shape beneath the heart of the Virgin of Nazareth when she pronounced her "fiat." From then on, under the special influence of the Holy Spirit, this heart, the heart of both a virgin and a mother, has always followed the work of her Son and has gone out to all those whom Christ has embraced and continues to embrace with inexhaustible love. For that reason her heart must also have the inexhaustibility of a mother. The special characteristic of the motherly love that the Mother of God inserts in

---

[38]*Ibid.*, n. 9 AAS 71 (1979), p. 272-273

the mystery of the Redemption and the life of the Church finds expression in its exceptional closeness to man and all that happens to him. It is in this that the mystery of the Mother consists. The Church, which looks to her with altogether special love and hope, wishes to make this mystery her own in an ever deeper manner. For in this the Church also recognizes the way for her daily life, which is each person.[39]

Devotion to the Immaculate Heart of Mary has always accompanied the devotion to the Divine Heart of her Son. These two are joined by the closest bonds since

> ... by God's will, in carrying out the work of human Redemption, the Blessed Virgin Mary was inseparably linked with Christ in such a manner that our salvation sprang from the love and sufferings of Jesus Christ to which love and sorrows of His mother were intimately united.[40]

The Holy Father's frequent use of the word "heart" as representative of the inner mystery of man has created a climate most favorable to the spread of the devotion. For it is in the Heart of Jesus that his innermost mystery of merciful love is revealed to man. All these elements within the encyclical speak of the validity and great value which the devotion possesses for our modern age.

This great truth was re-echoed again by John Paul II in his message to the young people of France during his meeting with them at Parc des Princes on June 1, 1980. The Holy Father urged the young to overcome the manifold evils which confront them by raising their eyes to Jesus Christ and contemplating his immense love for us symbolized by his open Heart:

> You are also worth what your heart is worth. The whole history of mankind is the history of the need of loving and being loved.... Whatever use humans make of it, the heart—the symbol of friendship and love—has also its norms, its ethics. To make room for the heart in the harmonious construction of your personality has nothing to do with mawkishness or even sentimentality. The heart is the opening of the whole being to the existence of others, the capacity of divining them, of understanding them. Such a sensitiveness, true and deep, makes one vulnerable. That is why some people are tempted to get

---

[39] *Ibid.*, n. 22 AAS 71 (1979), p. 332-333
[40] Pius XII, *Haurietis Aquas, op. cit.*, p. 352

rid of it by hardening one's heart.

Young people of France, raise your eyes more often toward Jesus Christ! He is the man who loved most and most consciously, most voluntarily and most graciously. Meditate on Christ's testament: "There is no greater proof of love than to give one's life for those one loves." Contemplate the Man-God, the man with the pierced heart![41]

In his General Audience of June 20, 1979 the Holy Father called upon all Christians to contemplate with particular adoration and love the mystery of the Heart of Jesus. He spoke of the great importance of the Feast of the Sacred Heart of Jesus in relation to the liturgical cycle of the Church.

> Thus at the end of this fundamental liturgical cycle of the Church—which began with the first Sunday of Advent and passed through the time of Christmas, then of Lent and of the Resurrection up to Pentecost, the Sunday of the Holy Trinity, and Corpus Christi—the feast of the Divine Heart, of the Sacred Heart of Jesus presents itself discreetly. *All this cycle is enclosed definitively in it: in the heart of the Man-God. From it, too, the whole life of the Church irradiates every year.*[42] [emphasis added]

In his Angelus message of June 24, 1979, the Pope again spoke of the spiritual riches contained in the devotion to the Heart of Christ. It is the Heart of Christ which gives life to the Church, awakens apostolic zeal, sensitizes man's moral sense and gives the Christian a spirit of loving reparation:

> The Heart of the Redeemer vivifies the whole Church and draws men who have opened their hearts to the "unfathomable riches" of this one Heart.
>
> This spiritual bond always leads to a great awakening of apostolic zeal.
>
> Adorers of the Divine Heart become men with a sensitive conscience: and when it is granted to them to have relations with the Heart of Our Lord and Master, in them there also springs up the need of atonement for the sins of the world, for the indifference of so many hearts and their negligences.[43]

The Pope continues speaking of the *necessity* of offering loving reparation

---

[41]John Paul II, Message to the Youth of France, June 1, 1980, *L'Osservatore Romano*, June 16, 1980, p. 14

[42]John Paul II, General Audience, June 20, 1979, *L'Osservatore Romano*, June 25, 1979, p. 12

[43]John Paul II, Angelus Message of June 24, 1979, *L'Osservatore Romano*, July 2, 1979, p. 2

to the Heart of Christ:

> How necessary this host of watchful hearts is in the Church in order
> that the love of the divine Heart may not remain isolated and unre-
> quited! Among this host special mention deserves to go to all those
> who offer their sufferings as living victims in union with the Heart of
> Christ, pierced on the crosss. Thus transformed with love, human
> suffering becomes a particular leaven of Christ's work of salvation in
> the Church.[44]

Loving reparation to Jesus in the Most Holy Eucharist is a central theme
in the devotion to the Sacred Heart. Some have felt the idea of reparation to
be dated and have associated it with a "pre-Vatican II mentality." Not so
according to Pope John Paul II. In his Apostolic Letter to all Bishops of the
Church *On the Mystery and Worship of the Holy Eucharist*, the Holy Father
returns to this theme. In speaking of the worship proper to the Eucharistic
mystery which is directed towards God the Father through Christ in the Holy
Spirit, the Pope continues:

> And this adoration of ours contains yet another special characteristic.
> It is compenetrated by the greatness of that human death, in which the
> world, that is to say each one of us, has been loved "to the end." Thus
> it is also a response that tries to repay that love immolated even to the
> death on the Cross: it is our " Eucharist," that is to say our giving him
> thanks, our praise of him for having redeemed us by his death and
> made us sharers in Immortal life through his Resurrection. [45]

The worship which we direct to the Triune God, which "above all accom-
panies and permeates" the Sacred Liturgy, "must fill our churches also
outside the timetable of Masses."[46]

The Eucharist which is the gift of the loving Heart of Jesus should always
receive special honor and veneration and *must* find expression in various
forms of Eucharistic devotion:

> Indeed, since the Eucharistic mystery was instituted out of love, and
> makes Christ's sacramentally present, it is worthy of thanksgiving and
> worship. And this worship must be prominent in all our encounters
> with the Blessed Sacrament, both when we visit our churches and when
> the sacred species are taken to the sick and administered to them.

---

[44]*Ibid.* p. 2

[45]John Paul II, Apostolic Letter on the Mystery and Worship of the Holy Eucharist,
February 24, 1980, n. 3 AAS 72 (1980) pp. 117-118

[46]*Ibid.* n. 3, p. 118

Adoration of Christ in this Sacrament of love must also find expression *in various forms of Eucharistic devotion*: personal prayer before the Blessed Sacrament, hours of adoration, periods of exposition—short, prolonged and annual (Forty Hours)—Eucharistic benediction, Eucharistic processions, Eucharistic Congresses. A particular mention should be made at this point of the Solemnity of the Body and Blood of Christ as an act of public worship rendered to Christ present in the Eucharist, a feast instituted by my predecessor Urban IV in memory of the institution of this great Mystery. All this therefore corresponds to the general principles and particular norms already long in existence but newly formulated during or after the Second Vatican Council.[47]

The Pope continues, referring to the spirit of Eucharistic reparation as a *proof of that authentic renewal which was sought by the Second Vatican Council*:

The encouragement and the deepening of the Eucharistic worship are *proofs of that authentic renewal* which the Council set itself as an aim and of which they are *the central point*. And this, venerable and dear Brothers, deserves separate reflection. The Church and the world have a great need of Eucharistic worship. Jesus waits for us in this Sacrament of love. Let us be generous with our time in going to meet him in adoration and in contemplation that is full of faith and ready to make reparation for the great faults and crimes of the world. May our adoration never cease.[48]

According to the teaching of John Paul II, loving reparation to the Heart of Jesus in the Blessed Sacrament is of tremendous importance today. It is an integral part of that renewal of the Church and world envisioned by the Council. The Fathers of Vatican II frequently spoke in the Conciliar documents of the Christian duty to offer ourselves and our entire lives in union with the sacrifice of Christ.

The Holy Father again turned his attention to the Devotion to the Sacred Heart of Jesus and the idea of Eucharistic worship and veneration in his visit to the Basilica of the Sacred Heart at Montmartre on June 1, 1980. The Holy Father spoke of the intimate link between the Heart of Jesus and the sacrament of love which is so beautifully manifested at the Basilica of the Sacred Heart in Paris.

We are at Montmartre, in the Basilica of the Sacred Heart, *consecrated to the contemplation of Christ's love present in the Blessed*

---

[47]*Ibid.*, n. 3, pp. 118-119
[48]*Ibid.*, n. 3, p. 119

Sacrament.

We are in the evening of the first of June, the first day of the month particularly dedicated to meditation, to contemplation of Christ's love manifested by His Sacred Heart.

Here, day and night, Christians gather in succession to seek "the unsearchable riches of Christ" (cf. Eph. 3:8).

We are called not only to meditate on, and contemplate, this mystery of Christ's love; we are called to take part in it. *It is the mystery of the Holy Eucharist, the center of our faith, the center of our worship of Christ's merciful love manifested in his Sacred Heart*, a mystery which is adored here night and day, in this basilica, which thereby becomes one of those centers from which the Lord's love and grace radiate in a mysterious but real way on your city, on your country and on the redeemed world. [49] [emphasis added]

The Holy Father speaks of the Heart of Christ as the source of salvation and as the origin of the Church:

We come here to meet the Heart pierced for us, from which water and blood gush. It is the redeeming love which is at the origin of salvation, of our salvation which is at the origin of the Church.[50]

It is of interest to note that the Holy Father speaks of the flow of the blood and water from the Heart of Christ in the present tense. This is because the Heart of Christ is continually the source of that heavenly font of grace which effects "our salvation" today. The Pope develops this point in speaking of the timeliness of the devotion:

Now still, today the living Christ *loves us and presents his heart to us as the source of our redemption*: "Semper vivens ad interpelandum pro nobis" (Heb. 7:25). At every moment, we are enveloped, in the love of this heart "which loves men so much and which is so little loved by them." [51] [emphasis added]

The Holy Father also directed attention to the spiritual value of this devotion which focuses upon the love of Christ. By focusing upon the love manifested by Christ in his earthly life as contained in the Gospels, the devout soul will be led by the "mystical ladder" of the Lord's Heart into the bosom of the Most Holy Trinity:

---

[49] John Paul II, Meditation at the Basilica of the Sacred Heart in Montmartre, June 1, 1980, *L'Osservatore Romano*, June 16, 1980, p. 15
[50] *Ibid.*, p. 15
[51] *Ibid.*, p. 15

Figure 26:

Statue of the

Sacred Heart,

Montmartre,

Paris.

> We come here to contemplate the love of the Lord Jesus: his compassionate kindness to everyone during his earthly life; his predilection for children, the sick, the afflicted. Let us contemplate his heart burning with love for his Father, in the fullness of the Holy Spirit. Let us contemplate his infinite love, that of the eternal Son, who leads us to the very mystery of God.[52]

The Holy Father took several other subsequent occasions to recall his visit to Montmartre in order to urge the faithful to once again raise their eyes to contemplate the love of Christ revealed in his heart and celebrate the solemnity "which has a centuries-old tradition and an ever living topicality in the Church."[53]

The contemporary and perennial value of the devotion was manifested most dramatically by John Paul II in his encyclical *Dives in Misericordia*. In order to come to a proper understanding of the centrality of the devotion of the Heart of Christ we must examine the overall plan of the encyclical.

As in *Redemptor Hominis*, the Pope again stresses that it is only in the mystery of Christ that the mystery of man is revealed in the totality of truth. So also it is only in Christ that the wondrous mystery of the Father's merciful love is revealed to man. As our Lord said to St. Philip, "He who has seen me has seen the Father" (Jn. 14:9). The God who dwells in unapproachable light is made known to man in "the Incarnation of Mercy." With Christ, in Christ and through Christ, God becomes particularly visible in his mercy.

The Holy Father speaks of this revelation of merciful love in Jesus as the very center of his messianic message:

> Christ, then, reveals God who is Father, who is "love," as St. John will express it in his first letter; Christ reveals God as "rich in mercy," as we read in St. Paul. This is not just the subject of a teaching; it is a reality made present to us by Christ. Making the Father present as love and mercy is, in Christ's own consciousness, the fundamental touchstone on his Mission as the Messiah; ...Christ, in revealing the love-mercy of God, at the same time demanded from people that they also should be guided in their lives by love and mercy. This requirement forms part of the very essence of the messianic message, and constitutes the heart of the Gospel ethos.[54]

---

[52] *Ibid.*, p. 15

[53] John Paul II, Angelus Message of June 15, 1980, *L'Osservatore Romano*, June 23, 1980, p. 2; see also Angelus Message of June 8, 1980 *L'Osservatore Romano*, June 16, 1980, p. 2

[54] John Paul II, *Dives in Misericordia*, n. 3 AAS 72 (1980), pp. 1184 - 1185

The Pope next addresses himself to the concept of mercy as found in the Old Testament and in our Lord's parable of the Prodigal Son. This quite naturally leads to a discussion of the "*mysterium paschale*." The passion, death and resurrection of Christ reveals God's justice which "springs completely from love: from the love of the Father and of the Son and completely bears fruit in love."[55] It is in the paschal mystery that the revelation of merciful love finds its culmination. Closely connected to this mystery is the "maternal heart"[56] of Mary which was united intimately to the heart of her Son:

> It was precisely this "merciful" love, which is manifested above all in contact with moral and physical evil, that the heart of her who was the Mother of the Crucified and Risen One shared in singularly and exceptionally—that Mary shared in. In her and through her this love continued to be revealed in the history of the Church and of humanity. This revelation is especially fruitful because in the mother of God it is based upon the unique fact of her maternal heart, on her particular sensitivity, on her particular fitness to reach all those who most easily accept the merciful love of a mother. This is one of the great life-giving mysteries of Christianity, a mystery intimately connected with the mystery of the incarnation. [57]

The Pope next recalls that the mystery of God continues from generation to generation down to our present time. The generation of the present age is a privileged one since progress has opened so many possibilities for the future. He speaks of the great wonders and goods which have been brought about through man's creative activity and intelligence. Despite this advancement there are ominous signs of world-wide uneasiness. This is because of the deep dichotomy which lies within man himself (*Gaudium et Spes* #10). The Pope speaks of the fundamental values which are being eroded within modern society. The list is strikingly similar to the evils enumerated by Leo XIII, Pius XI and Pius XII in their Sacred Heart encyclicals:

> One cannot fail to be worried by the decline of many fundamental values, which constitute an unquestionable good not only for Christian morality but simply for human morality, for moral culture: these values include respect for human life from the moment of conception, respect for marriage in its indissoluble unity, and respect for the

---

[55]*Ibid.*, n. 7

[56]Along with the references to the hearts of Jesus and Mary, the Holy Father again speaks of "heart as the fundamental center of man" on at least 20 different occasions. These many references to the heart of man in the encyclical greatly contribute to an atmosphere conducive to the spread of the devotion.

[57]John Paul II, *Dives in Misericordia*, n. 9; p. 1209

stability of the family. Moral permissiveness strikes especially at this most sensitive sphere of life and society. Hand in hand with this go the crisis of truth in human relationships, lack of responsibility for what one says, the purely utilitarian relationship between individual and individual, the loss of a sense of the authentic common good and the ease with which this good is alienated. Finally, there is the "desacralization" that often turns into "dehumanization": the individual and the society for whom nothing is "sacred" suffer moral decay, in spite of appearances.[58]

Another reason for grave concern is that the very concept of justice has all too frequently suffered from distortion in our modern world. Because of this, it must always be accompanied with a deep spirit of fraternal love:

> And yet it would be difficult not to notice that very often programs which start from the idea of justice and which ought to assist its fulfillment among individuals, groups and human societies, in practice suffer from distortions. Although they continue to appeal to the idea of justice, nevertheless experience shows that other negative forces have gained the upper hand over justice, such as spite, hatred and even cruelty. In such cases, the desire to annihilate the enemy, limit his freedom or even force him into total dependence, becomes the fundamental motive for action; and this contrasts with the essence of justice, which by its nature tends to establish equality and harmony between the parties in conflict.
>
> The experience of the past and of our own time demonstrates that justice alone is not enough, that it can lead to the negation and destruction of itself, if that deeper power, which is love, is not allowed to shape human life in its various dimensions.[59]

The Holy Father next directs his attention to the role which the mercy of God must play in the mission of the Church. He speaks of the communication of God's merciful love as a *vital necessity* for the Church of our day:

> The Church of our time, constantly pondering the eloquence of these inspired words and applying them to the sufferings of the great human family, must become more particularly and profoundly conscious of the need to bear witness in her whole mission to God's mercy, following the footsteps of the tradition of the Old and the New Covenant, and above all of Jesus Christ himself and his apostles. The Church must bear witness to the mercy of God revealed in Christ, in the whole

[58]*Ibid.*, n. 12; pp. 1216 - 1217
[59]*Ibid.*, n. 12; pp. 1215 - 1216

of his mission as Messiah, professing it in the first place as a salvific truth of faith and as necessary for a life in harmony with faith, and then seeking to introduce it and to make it incarnate in the lives of both her faithful and as far as possible in the lives of all people of goodwill.[60]

The profession of the mercy of God must be the way for the Church if she is to implement the renewal sought by the Vatican Council:

> The Church lives an authentic life when she professes and proclaims mercy—the most stupendous attribute of the Creator and of the Redeemer—and when she brings people close to the sources of the Savior's mercy of which she is the trustee and dispenser.... The contemporary Church is profoundly conscious that *only on the basis of the mercy of God* will she be able to carry out the tasks that derive from the teaching of the Second Vatican Council, and, in the first place, the ecumenical task which aims at uniting all those who confess Christ.[61]

How is the Church to implement this teaching which is so central and necessary in her contemporary life? The Holy Father unequivocally states that this is accomplished by turning to the mystery of the Heart of Christ. The Heart of Christ is seen as the focal point which is central to the great revelation of merciful love:

> "He who has seen me has seen the Father." The Church professes the mercy of God, the Church lives by it in her wide experience of faith and also in her teaching, constantly contemplating Christ, concentrating on him, on his life and on his Gospel, on his cross and resurrection, on his whole mystery. Everything that forms the "vision" of Christ in the Church's living faith and teaching brings us nearer to the "vision of the Father" in the holiness of his mercy. *The Church seems in a particular way to profess the mercy of God and to venerate it when she directs herself to the heart of Christ. In fact, it is precisely this drawing close to Christ in the mystery of his heart which enables us to dwell on this point—a point in a sense central and also most accessible on the human level—of the revelation which constituted the central content of the messianic mission of the Son of Man.*[62] [Emphasis added.]

In drawing people close to the Heart of Jesus the Pope exhorts the faithful to a constant meditation upon the Word of God and a "conscious and mature" participation in the Eucharist and in the sacrament of reconciliation. The

---

[60]*Ibid.*, n. 13; p. 1217
[61]*Ibid.*, n. 13; pp. 1219 - 1221
[62]Ibid., n. 13; pp. 1218 - 1219

Pope harks back to a familiar theme of so many encyclicals of the 20th century—the growing evil of secularization:

> The more the human conscience succumbs to secularization, loses its sense of the very meaning of the word "mercy," moves away from God and distances itself from the mystery of mercy, the more the Church has the right and the duty to appeal to the God of mercy, "with loud cries." These "loud cries" should be the mark of the Church of our times, cries uttered to God to implore His mercy, the certain manifestation of which she professes and proclaims as having already come to Jesus crucified and risen, that is, in the Paschal Mystery. It is this mystery which bears within itself the most complete revelation of mercy, that is, of that love which is more powerful than death, more powerful than sin and every evil, the love which lifts man up when he falls into the abyss and frees him from the greatest threats.[63]

Mercy is an indispensable element in the establishment of the "civilization of love." The Church will succeed in her mission by "drawing from the wells of the Savior" as Pope John Paul writes:

> The basis of the Church's mission, in all the spheres of the numerous pronouncements of the most recent Council and in the centuries-old experience of the apostolate, is none other than "drawing from the wells of the Savior." This is what provides many guidelines for the mission of the Church in the lives of individual Christians, of individual communities, and also of the whole people of God. This "drawing from the wells of the Savior" can be done only in the spirit of that poverty to which we are called by the words and example of the Lord: "You received without pay, give without pay."[64]

Authentic devotion to the Sacred Heart with its emphasis upon the

---

[63]*Ibid.*, n. 15; p. 1228
[64]*Ibid.*, n. 14; p. 1227

Eucharist and the fraternal apostolate is presented by Pope John Paul II in *Dives in Misericordia* as the most fitting way in which modern man may profess the divine mercy of God which is the "outstanding" and "necessary" mission of the Church today. By entering into the mystery of the Heart of Christ, accessible to all men, we may come to know the riches of the merciful love of Christ which reveals in turn the merciful love of our heavenly Father.

Here we should mention that a new impetus[65] has been given to the devotion by the revelations of Divine Mercy given to Sister Faustina, a Sister of Mercy in Poland. Pope John Paul II is known to have great enthusiasm along with the rest of the Church in Poland for these revelations which were given between 1930 and 1938.

The year 1983 was proclaimed a Jubilee Year by Pope John Paul II in order to celebrate the 1900th anniversary of the Redemption. It was a year which the Pope wished to be fulfilled with the mystery of the Heart of Christ. This can be seen in the Pope's personal selection of "Iam Portas Redemptori" as the official hymn of the year. [66] The Pope has continued to speak out with even greater frequency concerning the Heart of Christ.[67]

On February 11, 1984, the Feast of Our Lady of Lourdes, the Apostolic Letter *Salvifici Doloris* (On the Christian Meaning of Human Suffering) was released. The Holy Father spoke of human suffering as "the deepest need of

---

[65] Sister Faustina has described a mystical experience which occurred on February 22, 1931: "I saw Jesus dressed in a white garment. He held out one hand raised in blessing and with the other, He was touching the garment at the breast. From under the garment came two rays of light, one red, the other pale. Then Our Lord spoke, 'Paint a picture according to the vision you see and with the inscription, "Jesus, I trust in Thee." I desire that this picture be venerated first in your chapel and then throughout the whole world'." This apparition was repeated several times and she was told of the significance of the symbolism by our Lord Himself. "The rays on the picture represent the blood and water which gushed forth from the depths of My Mercy when My agonizing Heart was opened on the Cross. The pale rays symbolize the water, which justifies the soul; the red rays represent the blood which is the life of the soul. These rays shield the soul before the wrath of My Father. Fortunate is he who lives in their shelter, for the just hand of God will never reach Him." Then He gave her a short prayer and told her to recite it often: "O Blood and Water, which has gushed forth from the Heart of Jesus as a font of Mercy for us, I trust in Thee."

[66] This hymn by Pierre Paul, OMV sings beautifully of the renewal of our hearts which spring from the Heart of Jesus: "Open the portals of our hearts / to Jesus Christ Redeemer! / 'Tis Christ who knows the hearts of men. / What need is there to tremble? / To Whom shall we go, Master? / There is no life apart from you. / Attract your people to your Heart, / O Jesus, crucified Love. / The whole life of your Church, Lord, / breathes forth your sweet Redemption; / t'was born upon the Holy Cross / from the pierced Heart of Jesus. / O wounded Heart of Jesus, / the sparkling font, redemption's source, / draw near to Jesus all in need / who seek the living waters."

[67] See the papal homily on the Solemnity of the Sacred Heart, June 28, 1984 at Gemelli Hospital (*L'Osservatore Romano*, July 16, 1984); the Angelus Message of July 1, 1984 (*L'O.R.*, July 9, 1984). The Sacred Heart became a major theme during John Paul's pastoral visit to Canada in September, 1984. Two outstanding homilies were preached by the Pope which centered upon the theology of the devotion in Toronto and Vancouver.

the heart." The Pope, in this beautiful document, drew out how Jesus Christ conquered suffering through love:

> "For God so loved the world that he gave his only Son, that whoever believes in Him should not perish but have eternal life." These words, spoken by Christ in His conversation with Nicodemus, introduce us into the very heart of *God's salvific work*. And in this, love is manifested, in the infinite love both of that only-begotten Son and of the Father who for this reason "gives" His Son. This is love for man, love for the "world": it is salvific love.[68]

The Holy Father recalls the Fourth Song of the Suffering Servant in the Book of Isaiah. Christ as the Man of Sorrows is a theme which has always found a central role in devotion.

> He had no form or comeliness that we should look at him,
> and no beauty that we should desire him.
> He was despised and rejected by men;
> *a man of sorrows*, and acquainted with grief;
> and as one from whom men hide their faces
> he was despised, and we esteemed him not.
> Surely he has borne our griefs
> and carried our sorrows;
> yet we esteemed him stricken,
> smitten by God, and afflicted.
> But he was wounded for our transgressions,
> he was bruised for our iniquities;
> upon him was the chastisement that made us whole,
> and with his stripes we are healed.
> All we like sheep have gone astray;
> we have turned every one to his own way;
> and *the Lord has laid on him the iniquity of us all.*[69]

This "Man of Sorrows" is the "Lamb of God" who takes away the sins of the world through the salvific love of his heart which alone is capable of reconciling man to God.

> In His suffering, sins are cancelled out precisely because He alone as the only-begotten Son could take them upon Himself, accept them

---

[68]John Paul II, *Salvifici Doloris*, #14; the Latin text of *Salvifici Doloris* may be found in AAS Vol. N. 3, 1 Mar 1984
[69]*Ibid.*, #17

with that love for the Father which overcomes the evil of every sin; in a certain sense He annihilates this evil in the spiritual space of the relationship between God and humanity, and fills this space with good.[70]

John Paul focuses upon the mysteries of Gethsemane and Golgotha where Christ takes onto Himself "with full awareness of the mission that he has to fulfill" the suffering of all humanity prophesied by Isaiah. Because of the love in his heart for his Father and sinful mankind, though innocent, he suffers voluntarily.

> He was oppressed, and he was afflicted,
> yet he opened not his mouth;
> like a lamb that is led to the slaughter
> and like a sheep that before its shearers is dumb,
> so he opened not his mouth.
> By oppression and judgement he was taken away;
> and as for his generation, who considered that
> he was cut off out of the land of the living,
> stricken for the transgression of my people?
> And they made his grave with the wicked
> and with a rich man in his death,
> although he had done no violence,
> and there was no deceit in his mouth.[71]

After referring to Psalm 22, the great messianic psalm spoken by Christ on the cross, the Holy Father states (in reference to Jn. 7:37), "The cross of Christ has become a source from which flow rivers of living water."

The Pope then develops the Pauline theology of the Christian's obligation to share in the sufferings of Christ for the sake of his body which is the Church. By uniting our individual sufferings to the cross of Christ, our sufferings become meritorious and reveal the creative dimension of suffering.

Here in the mystery of Christ's suffering the meaning of human suffering is revealed. As the Christian takes up his own cross and unites it to the cross of Christ, the salvific meaning of his own suffering is manifested by the crucified God-Man who speaks from the cross.

> He asks for the meaning of his suffering and an answer to this question
> on the human level. Certainly he often puts this question to God, and
> to Christ. Furthermore, he cannot help noticing that the One to whom

---

[70]*Ibid.,* #17
[71]*Ibid.,* #18

he puts the question is Himself suffering and wishes *to answer him* from the cross, *from the heart of His own suffering.* Nevertheless, it often takes time, even a long time, for this answer to begin to be interiorly perceived. For Christ does not answer directly and He does not answer in the abstract this human questioning about the meaning of suffering. Man hears Christ's saving answer as he himself gradually becomes a sharer in the sufferings of Christ.[72]

The year 1985 produced a record number of papal talks on the Sacred Heart.[73] In February of 1986, the Pope undertook his pastoral visit to India. On numerous occasions he spoke of the Heart of Christ. The devotion to the Sacred Heart has always been strong in the Church in India. This is yet another sign of the power and universality of the heart as a religious symbol. The Pope sought to strengthen and give new impetus to the devotion. The highlight of this was the consecration of Delhi to the Sacred Heart in the presence of India's 124 bishops who had assembled in the Cathedral of the Sacred Heart at the beginning of the pastoral visit.[74]

On May 18, 1986, the Solemnity of Pentecost, the Pope issued his encyclical *Dominum et Vivificantem* (On the Holy Spirit in the Life of the Church and the World). This encyclical is a profound reflection upon the theology of the Holy Spirit. The Paraclete, from the outset, is presented by the Holy

---

[72]*Ibid.,* #26

[73]In a major address to the Church in Italy which had assembled in Loreto the Pope delivered on April 11th what has been characterized as a "constitution" for the post-conciliar Italian Church. He set before the Church assembly Reconciliation as their major task and again presented our Lord's Heart as the source of strength for the Church.

"Reconciliation, this immense stream of grace and forgiveness which flows upon us from Christ's Heart *passes though* the Church. With words which remain emblematic, the Second Vatican Council said about it: 'The Church, in Christ, is in the nature of a sacrament—a sign and instrument, that is, of communion with God and of unity among men.'" (Address at Loreto, April 11, 1985)

The Pope also throughout the summer months at Castel Gandolfo devoted his Angelus Message to a series of meditations on the Litany of the Most Sacred Heart of Jesus.

[74]Here, in his address and consecration, we can see the value given by Pope John Paul II to the efficacy and timeliness of public consecration to the Heart of our Lord as King of Kings and Prince of Peace:

"Dear Brothers and Sisters in Christ,

"In the solemn joy of this moment, as I begin my pastoral visit to India and as I consecrate the Archdiocese of Delhi to the Sacred Heart of Jesus, let our first action be to praise and bless our God. Let us glorify him for his love for the world which is shown to us in the heart of his Son. In the human heart of the Son of Mary the eternal love of God came to abide; and through Christ's human life, and especially through his death on the Cross, the tender mercy of God was revealed.

" 'For God so loved the world that he gave his only Son, that whoever believes in him should not perish but have eternal life' (Jn. 3:16). This is the Good News of our Redemption. This is the saving message of the Sacred Heart of Jesus. This is the Gospel which I have come here today to proclaim to you. During these days I wish also with you to

Father as being the gift of the heart of Christ.

> In fact, according to the Gospel of John, the Holy Spirit is given to us with the new life, as Jesus foretells and promises of the great day of the Feast of Tabernacles: "If any one thirst, let him come to me and drink. He who believes in me, as scripture has said, 'Out of his heart shall flow rivers of living water'." And the Evangelist explains: "*This he said about the Spirit*, which those who believed in him were to receive." It is the same simile of water which Jesus uses in his conversation with the Samaritan woman, when he speaks of a "spring of water welling up to eternal life"... [75]

This Johannine and Patristic theme remains central throughout the encyclical.[76] The flow of water, as we have seen in the scriptural section, is for St. John a gift of the Holy Spirit. The promise of Christ in Jn. 7:37 is fulfilled with the piercing of our Lord's Heart on Calvary. This is implied in a number of passages in the encyclical where the gift of the Spirit is linked to the cross and

---

show my respect and esteem—beyond the limits of the Church—to every person in India. In this too we are impelled by the love of Christ.

" 'O Sacred Heart of Jesus, Burning Fire of Love, have mercy on us and make our heart like your own.'

"Lord Jesus Christ, Redeemer of the human race, to your most Sacred Heart we turn with humility and trust, with reverence and hope, with a deep desire to give to you glory and honour and praise.

"Lord Jesus Christ, Savior of the world, we thank you for all that you are and all that you do for the little flock and all the twelve million people living in this Archdiocese of Delhi, which includes those entrusted to the stewardship of this nation.

"Lord Jesus Christ, Son of the Living God, we praise you for the love that you have revealed through your Sacred Heart, which was pierced for us and which has become the fountain of our joy, the source of our eternal life.

"Gathered together in your Name, which is above all other names, we consecrate ourselves to your most Sacred Heart, in which dwells the fullness of truth and charity.

"In consecrating themselves to you, the faithful of the Archdiocese of Delhi renew their desire to respond in love to the rich outpouring of your merciful love.

"Lord Jesus Christ, King of Love and Prince of Peace, reign in our hearts and bring us to share in the victory of your Sacred Heart. May all we say and do give glory and praise to you and to the Father and the Holy Spirit, one God living and reigning for ever and ever. Amen."

[75] John Paul II, *Dominum et Vivificantem*, #1; the Latin text may be found in AAS Vol. LXXVIII N.9, Sept. 2, 1986

[76] See #3, #4, #5, #6, #8, #10, #11, #13, #14, #21, #23, #25, #39, #40, and #41.

Redemption.[77]

When speaking of the great theophany at our Lord's baptism, the Pontiff again speaks explicitly of our Lord's heart which alone can give the Spirit, for it alone possesses the fullness of the Spirit.

> That which during the theophany at the Jordan came to speak "from outside", from on high, here comes "from within", that is to say *from the depths of who Jesus is*. It is another revelation of the Father and the Son, united in the Holy Spirit. Jesus speaks only of the fatherhood of God and of his own sonship—he does not speak directly of the Spirit who is Love and thereby the union of the Father and the Son. Nonetheless *what he says of the Father and of himself the Son flows* from that *fullness of the Spirit* which is in him, which fills his heart, pervades his own "I", inspires and enlivens his action from the depths. Hence that "rejoicing in the Holy Spirit". The union of Christ with the Holy Spirit, a union of which he is perfectly aware, is expressed in that "rejoicing", which in a certain way renders "perceptible" its hidden source. Thus there is a particular manifestation and rejoicing which is proper to the Son of Man, the Christ-Messiah, whose humanity belongs to the Person of the Son of God, substantially one with the Holy Spirit in divinity. [78]

It is through this gift of love, this gift of the Heart pierced on Calvary, that sin is overcome through the power of the Spirit.

> In a word, this inscrutable and indescribable *fatherly "pain" will bring about* above all the wonderful *economy of redemptive love* in Jesus Christ, so that through the *mysterium pietatis* love can reveal itself in the history of man as stronger than sin. So that the "gift" may prevail!
>
> According to the *Letter to the Hebrews*, on the way to his "departure" through Gethsemane and Golgotha, the same *Jesus Christ* in his own humanity *opened himself totally* to this *action of the Spirit-*

---

[77]"The Holy Spirit will come insofar as Christ will depart through the Cross: he will come not only *afterwards*, but *because of* the Redemption accomplished by Christ, through the will and action of the Father."

"'If I do not go away, the Counsellor will not come to you; but if I go, I will send him to you.' Describing his 'departure' *as a condition* for the 'coming' of the Counsellor, Christ links the new beginning of God's salvific self-communication in the Holy Spirit to the mystery of the Redemption."

"The *Paschal events*—the Passion, Death and Resurrection of Christ—are also the *time of the new coming* of the Holy Spirit, as the Paraclete and the spirit of truth." "He brings him at the price of his own 'departure': he gives them his Spirit as it were through the wounds of his crucifixion: 'He showed them his hands and his side. It is in the power of this crucifixion that he says to them: 'Receive the Holy Spirit'.'"

[78]John Paul II, *Dominum et Vivificantem*, #21; see also #39 and #40.

Paraclete, who from suffering enables eternal salvific love to spring forth.[79]

The supreme motive for this gift is the fire of Charity, which involves the love of all Three Divine Persons.

> The Holy Spirit as Love and Gift *comes down, in a certain sense, into the very heart of the sacrifice* which is offered on the Cross. Referring here to the biblical tradition we can say: *He consumes this sacrifice with the fire of the love* which unites the Son with the Father in the Trinitarian communion. And since the sacrifice of the Cross is an act proper to Christ, also in this sacrifice he *"receives" the Holy Spirit*. He receives the Holy Spirit in such a way that afterwards—and he alone with God the Father—can *"give him" to the Apostles, to the Church, to humanity.*[80]

It is through the loving sacrificial death of Christ that the Spirit may cleanse and sanctify mankind in "the depths of the human heart."

On October 4, 1986, Pope John Paul II left Rome for his 31st pastoral visit outside Italy. The Pope flew to Lyons to begin his second visit as Pontiff to France. This trip is of particular importance to our study because the Pope made Paray-le-Monial one of the major stops on his itinerary (which also included Taizé, Ars and Annecy). The Pope used the visit to again focus attention on the timeliness of the devotion to the Sacred Heart.

The papal activities at Paray included a Pontifical Mass on Sunday, October 5th, an Angelus Address, a visit to the Basilica of the Sacred Heart, a visit to the Visitation Monastery, a Radio Message to prisoners in Lyons and a visit to the Chapel of Blessed Claude de la Columbière. During the visit to the Chapel of the great Jesuit, the Holy Father personally delivered a message in the form of a papal letter to Fr. Kolvenbach, the Superior General of the Society of Jesus.

The Pope spoke out forcefully and with a sense of urgency concerning the timeliness and perennial value of the devotion. In his homily at the Pontifical Mass he took as his theme the words of the prophet Ezechiel, "I will give to you a new heart..." (Ez. 36:26) which speaks of that conversion which is a true *metanoia*:

> We are in a place where these words of the prophet Ezechiel resound powerfully. They were confirmed here by a poor and hidden servant of the Sacred Heart of our Lord, St. Margaret Mary. The truth of this

---

[79]*Ibid.*, #39, #40
[80]*Ibid.*, #41

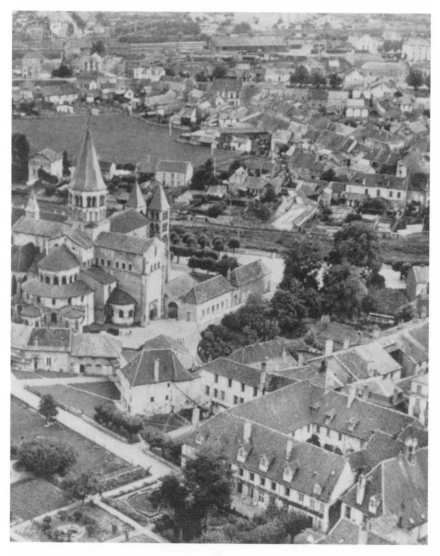

Figure 27: Aerial view of Paray-le-Monial.

promise has very often been confirmed by Revelation throughout the course of history, in the Church, through *the experience of the saints*, of the mystics, of souls consecrated to God. All of *the history of Christian spirituality* bears witness that the life of the person who believes in God, looking towards the future in hope, and called to the communion of love, is the life of the heart, the *"interior" life of man*. It is enlightened by the marvellous truth of the Heart of Jesus who offers himself for the world.[81]

The Pope next speaks of the Divine Providence which revealed this message of the Heart of Christ at such a crucial time in the history of the Church.

> Why was *the truth about the Heart of Jesus* confirmed for us in a special manner here, in the seventeenth century, so to speak, *on the threshold of modern times*?[82]

Here the Holy Father is calling attention to the timeliness of the devotion by placing the revelation "on the threshold of modern times." The Pope then draws attention to the link between the Heart of Christ and his encyclical *Dives in Misericordia* by stating that he was "happy to repeat the message of the God who is *rich in mercy*."

John Paul then spoke of the heart of man as having been created to be the "home of love" but all too often has become the "center of rejection of God."

> The heart is also *the central core of the conversion* which God desires on the part of man and for man, so as to enter into his intimacy, into his love. God did not create man to be indifferent or cold, but to be *open to God*. How lovely the Prophet's words are: "I will remove your heart of stone, and I will give you a heart of flesh" (Ez. 36:26)! *The heart of flesh*, a heart *that has a human sensitivity* and *a heart capable of letting itself be moved by the breath of the Holy Spirit*.[83]

This human heart must be purified by the Spirit which flows to us from the pierced Heart of Christ. After quoting from Jn. 19:32-34, he speaks of the open heart of the God-Man as his final revelation and "his ultimate testimony." The Holy Father here grounds the devotion in Scripture and speaks of its development through the ages, culminating in the revelations of Paray and again reiterates that the message of Paray is for the entire Church in our

---

[81]*L'Osservatore Romano*, 27 Oct. 1986, p. 3
[82]*Ibid.*
[83]*Ibid.*

modern era.

> John, the Apostle who stood at the foot of the Cross, understood this;
> in the course of the centuries, the disciples of Christ and the masters
> of the faith have understood it. In the seventeenth century, a nun of
> the Visitation received this testimony anew at Paray-le-Monial; Mar-
> garet Mary transmits it to the whole Church on the threshold of
> modern times.[84]

The Pontiff next recalls the teaching of his encyclical *Dominum et
Vivificantem* by stating explicitly that the Holy Spirit promised by Christ
sprang from the open Heart.

> Through the Heart of His Son, pierced on the Cross, *the Father has
> freely given us everything. The Church and the world receive the Consoler,*
> the Holy Spirit. Jesus has said, "If I go away, I will send him to you"
> (Jn. 16:7). His pierced heart bears witness that he "has gone away."
> Now he sends the Spirit of truth. The water that flows from his pierced
> side is the sign of the Holy Spirit: Jesus had announced to Nicodemus
> the new birth "of water and the Spirit" (cf. Jn. 3:5). The words of the
> Prophet are accomplished: "I will give you a new heart, I will put a new
> spirit in you."[85]

The Pontiff next turns his attention to St. Margaret Mary and speaks movingly
of the glory of this chosen soul.

> *St. Margaret Mary knew* this wonderful mystery, *the overwhelming
> mystery of divine Love.* She had experienced the depth of the words of
> Ezechiel: "I shall give you a heart."
>   Throughout her *life* that was hidden in Christ, she was marked by
> the gift of this Heart that offers itself without limit to all human hearts.
> She was totally absorbed by this divine mystery,...
>   All her life, St. Margaret Mary *burned with the living flame of that
> love* which Christ came to kindle in the history of man.
>   Here at Paray-le-Monial, this humble servant of God *seemed to
> cry out to all the world*, like the Apostle Paul before her, "who will be
> able to separate us from the love of Christ?" (Rom. 8:35)[86]

The Pope, like a constant refrain, as if speaking out to all who would call
the devotion dated or unsuitable to modern times, speaks of the message as
not limited to the 17th century but of vital importance today particularly in

---

[84]*Ibid.*
[85]*Ibid.*
[86]*Ibid.*

reference to the family.

> In the seventeenth century, the same question rang out, posed by Margaret Mary to the Christians of that period, at Paray-le-Monial.
> In our day, the same question re-echoes, addressed to each of us. To each one in particular, in the light of the experiences of family life.[87]

The Pope speaks of the great evils which are destroying families today: poor preparation for the sacraments; misunderstanding of love and fidelity by reducing it to individual desire and egoistic self-seeking; divorce, which deprives children of the balanced support they should find in the mother and father; contraception and abortion. These are all sins which offend the Creator, who is the source of all goodness and love, and "Christ the Savior, who gave his wounded heart", to enable his brothers to freely love as God intended. The love of the Heart of Christ beckons man and is *still* the answer to these eternal questions.

> Yes, the *essential question is always the same*. The danger is always the same: *that man is separated from love!*
> Man is uprooted from the deepest terrain of his spiritual experience. Man is *condemned to have* once again a *"heart of stone"*, is deprived of the "heart of flesh" that would be capable of responding correctly to good and evil. The heart that is sensitive to the truth of man and to the truth of God, the heart capable of welcoming the breath of the Holy Spirit, the heart made strong by the strength of God.
> The essential problems of man—yesterday, today and tomorrow—are found on this level. The one who says, "I will give you a new heart", wishes to include in this word everything that makes man "become more."[88]

The devotion to the heart of Christ is presented here as an effective means of supporting the moral teaching of the Church in "today's confused and contradictory situation."

Recalling the teaching of the Apostolic Constitution *Familiaris Consortio* and of Vatican II's *Gaudium et Spes* concerning conjugal love and family life, the Pope calls upon families to open themselves to the saving and healing love offered to them by the Heart of Christ:

> Yes, thanks to the sacrament of marriage, in the Covenant with

---

[87]*Ibid.*
[88]*Ibid.*, p. 4

divine wisdom, in the Covenant with the infinite love of the Heart of Christ, you families are given the means to develop in each of your members the riches of the human person and of his call to the love of God and men.

Welcome the presence of the Heart of Christ, entrusting your home to him. May he inspire your generosity and your fidelity to the sacrament in which your covenant was sealed before God! May the charity of Christ help you to welcome and aid your brothers and sisters who are wounded by separation and are left alone; your fraternal witness will help them to discover more easily that the Lord does not cease to love those who suffer.[89]

The Pontiff ends this magnificent homily by stressing the harmony which exists between the message of Sacred Scripture and the revelation given to Margaret Mary. This should be a source of confidence to all Christian families in their unique role of building the civilization of love.

With Paul of Tarsus, with Margaret Mary, we proclaim the same certainty: neither death nor life, neither the present nor the future, neither the powers nor any other creature, *nothing will be able to separate us from the love of God*, which is in Jesus Christ.

I am certain of this...nothing will ever be able...!

Today, we are in Paray-le-Monial to renew this certainty in ourselves: "I will give you a heart...."

Before the open Heart of Jesus, we seek to draw from him the true love that our families need.

The family unit has a fundamental role in the construction of the civilization of love.[90]

Before the final blessing in the Mass at Paray-le-Monial the Pope led the

---

[89]*Ibid.*, p. 4
[90]*Ibid.*

large crowd in the Angelus in which he linked the role of Mary's "motherly heart" to the revelation of the heart of her Son. [91]

The Holy Father next journeyed to the Visitation Monastery where he addressed the nuns. Here the Pope gave an eloquent thanksgiving for the benefits that have flowed to the Church and world through the devotion. He began by quoting from the words which our Lord spoke to St. Margaret Mary and prayed for the saint's continued intercession.

> "See this heart which loved men so much that it spared itself nothing, to the point of being exhausted and consumed to bear witness to them of its Love."
>
> I am moved as I give thanks for this message which was received and transmitted here by St. Margaret Mary Alacoque. Beside her tomb, I ask her to help men unceasingly so that they may discover the love of the Saviour and let themselves be penetrated by it.[92]

What follows is a veritable litany of thanksgivings offered by the Vicar of Christ for all those blessings which have shone forth from the Monastery at Paray-le-Monial. First of all for the extraordinary graces given to the Visionary of Paray:

> Let us give thanks for the mystical experience of St. Margaret Mary. In her hidden existence, she received the knowledge of the power and the beauty of the love of Christ in a particularly powerful way. In eucharistic adoration, she contemplated the Heart that was pierced for the salvation of the world, wounded by men's sin, but also the "living spring", as is testified by the light that streams from the scars of his risen body.

Next, the Pope speaks of the saint's mystical union with Christ:

---

[91] The Pope's Angelus address at Paray-le-Monial: "At the close of this celebration, the moment for the Angelus has now come. Let us now invoke the Blessed Virgin Mary, who replied to the Angel's message in the full availability of her faith. Mary, daughter of Israel, you have proclaimed the mercy that is offered to men from generation to generation by the good will of the loving Father. Mary, Holy Virgin, servant of the Lord, you bore in your womb the precious fruit of the divine mercy. Mary, who kept in your heart the Words of salvation, bear witness to the world of God's absolute fidelity to his love. Mary, you followed your Son Jesus to the foot of the Cross, in the 'fiat' of your motherly heart, you were one, without reserve, with the redemptive sacrifice. Mary, Mother of mercy, show your children the Heart of Jesus, which you saw opened, so that it might be for ever the source of life. Mary, present in the midst of the disciples, you bring near to us the life-giving love of your risen Son. Mary, Mother attentive to the dangers and trials of the brothers of your Son, do not cease to lead them on the path of salvation. Mary, you who showed the Heart of your Son to Margaret Mary in this place, grant that we may follow your example of humble fidelity to his love." (*L'Osserv. Romano*, 27 Oct 1986, p.4)

[92] *L'Osservatore Romano*, 27 Oct 1986, p.4

252 Heart of the Redeemer

Let us give thanks for the intimacy of the humble nun with the Savior. She generously offered the suffering which came to her in many forms, in union with the Passion of Christ in reparation for the sin of the world. She knew herself to be both a witness of the salvation wrought by the Son of God, and also called to associate herself with the work of mercy by offering herself.

The Holy Father then spoke of the vital role played by Bl. Claude:

Let us give thanks for the privileged meeting of the holy nun and Blessed Claude de la Colombière. The support of this faithful disciple of St. Ignatius permitted Margaret Mary to overcome her doubts and to discern the authentic inspiration of her extraordinary experience. This relationship is a model of balance in spiritual counselling. In great trials, Father de la Colombière himself received enlightened counsels from the one whom he was counselling.

He then mentions the great increase in devotion to the Blessed Sacrament:

Let us give thanks for the vast development of adoration and of eucharistic communion which took on a new impetus here. Thanks to the cult of the Sacred Heart which was promoted especially by the Visitation nuns and by the Jesuit Fathers, and was finally approved by the Popes. The particular devotion of First Fridays of the month has produced much fruit, following the urgent messages received by Margaret Mary. And I cannot forget that the bishops of Poland obtained the office of the Mass of the Sacred Heart from Clement XIII in 1765, almost a century before the feast was extended to the universal Church in 1856.

Finally, the Pope recalls both the religious inspiration found in this sacred spot and the great act of Leo XIII in his encyclical *Annum Sacrum*.[93]

During his visit to the chapel of Bl. Claude, the Pope used the opportunity to remind the Society of Jesus of the importance of the devotion and the special role which our Lord entrusted to the Society. The Pope set forth the example of Bl. Claude as an "exemplary son" of the Society of Jesus to whom, according to the witness of St. Margaret Mary, Christ himself had entrusted the task of spreading devotion to His Heart. Recalling Jesuit successes in the past, he exhorted the members of the Society to greater effort in their position as official propagators of the devotion.

I know with what generosity the Society of Jesus accepted this marvel-

---

[93]*Ibid.*, p. 5

lous mission, and with what ardor it sought to fulfill it as well as possible in the course of these three centuries: but I desire, on this solemn occasion, to exhort all members of the Society to be even more zealous in promoting this devotion, which corresponds more than ever to the expectations of our time.[94]

It is interesting to note once again the Holy Father's *insistence* here on the timeliness of the devotion. He further stresses this point and adds that the devotion's essential elements have a *perennial* value!

> In fact, if the Lord in his providence wished that a powerful drive in favour of the devotion to the Heart of Christ, under the forms indicated in the revelations received by St. Margaret Mary, should go forth from Paray-le-Monial in the seventeenth century, at the threshold of modern times, the essential elements of this devotion belong in a permanent fashion to the spirituality of the Church throughout her history; for since the beginning, the Church has looked to the Heart of Christ pierced on the Cross, from which blood and water flowed forth as symbols of the sacraments that constitute the Church; and, in the Heart of the Incarnate Word, the Fathers of the Christian East and West saw the beginning of all the work of our salvation, fruit of the love of the divine Redeemer. This pierced Heart is a particularly expressive symbol of that love.[95]

The Pope reminded the Jesuits that the devotion fits in beautifully with Ignatian spirituality which seeks "to know Christ intimately" and to speak to him: *cor ad cor loquitur* ("heart speaks to heart").

The Pontiff then spoke of the teaching of the Second Vatican Council and how only the Heart of Christ reveals to man the true meaning of life. It is the only way to build the civilization of love.

> When the Second Vatican Council recalls that Christ, the Incarnate Word, "loved us with the heart of a man," it assures us that "his message, far from diminishing man, helps his progress by shedding light and giving life and freedom; apart from him, nothing can fill the human heart" (cf. *Gaudium et Spes*, n. 22, 21). In the Heart of Christ, man's heart learns to know the genuine and unique meaning of his life and of his destiny, to understand the value of an authentically Christian life, to keep himself from certain perversions of the human heart, and to unite the filial love for God and the love of neighbor. The true reparation asked by the Heart of the Savior will come when the

---

[94] *Ibid.*, p. 5
[95] *Ibid.*, p. 5 & 7

civilization of the Heart of Christ can be built upon the ruins heaped up by hatred and violence.[96]

The Pope clearly and forcefully manifests his will in this matter to the Society by exhorting them to greater effort, using very strong language and reminding the Jesuits again that the spread of the devotion was a mission entrusted to them by Christ himself:

> For these reasons, I desire that you pursue with persevering action the spread of the genuine cult of the Heart of Christ, and that you may always be ready to lend effective help to my brothers in the episcopate in order to promote this cult everywhere, taking care to find the means most appropriate to present it and to put it into practise, so that the people of today, with their mentality and sensitivity, may find it in the true response to their questions and expectations.
>
> Just as I entrusted to you in a particular way the Apostolate Prayer last year, on the occasion of its congress—and this Work is closely linked to the devotion to the Sacred Heart—I ask you today in a similar way, in the course of my pilgrimage to Paray-le-Monial, to do everything that is possible to accomplish ever better this mission that Christ himself has entrusted to you, the spread of devotion to his divine Heart.[97]

The Pope concluded by recalling the innumerable spiritual benefits of the devotion which speak again of the devotion's timeliness, especially as they touch the Eucharist and the Sacrament of Reconciliation:

> The abundant spiritual fruits produced by the devotion to the Heart of Jesus are widely acknowledged. This devotion, finding expression especially in the practice of the holy hour and confession and communion of the first Friday of the month, has contributed to stimulate generations of Christians to pray more and to participate more frequently in the Sacraments of Penance and Eucharist. These are the paths that we should propose to the faithful of today also.[98]

On March 25, 1987, the Solemnity of the Annunciation, the Pope issued

---

[96]*Ibid.*, p. 7
[97]*Ibid.*
[98]*Ibid..*

his encyclical *Redemptoris Mater*, which dealt with the Blessed Virgin Mary in the life of the pilgrim Church. This beautiful reflection speaks on a number of occasions of the *heart* of Mary.[99] This again helps create a climate most favorable for a theology of the heart. The union of the heart of Mary and her Son is brought into relief by the Holy Father.

> Indeed, "the deepest truth about God and the salvation of man is made clear to us in Christ, who is at the same time the mediator and the fullness of all revelation." In her exultation Mary confesses that she finds herself *in the very heart of this fullness* of Christ. [100]

And again:

> ...the new motherhood of the Mother of the Redeemer: a spiritual motherhood, born from the heart of the Paschal Mystery of the Redeemer of the world. It is a motherhood in the order of grace, for it implores the gift of the Spirit, who raises up the new children of God, redeemed through the sacrifice of Christ: that Spirit whom Mary too, together with the Church, received on the day of Pentecost.[101]

From this brief examination of the magisterial teaching of our modern conciliar era we find a solemn affirmation of all previous Papal teaching concerning the devotion to the Sacred Heart of Jesus. There is no rupture in the continuity or power of this teaching. The Church has clearly shown her thinking concerning the great value of this devotion. The spirit of the devotion is not only in complete harmony with the teachings of the Second Vatican Council but is one of the most effective means by which the great reform and renewal of Christian life may be accomplished.

---

[99]The following are some instances in which the Pope speaks of Our Lady's heart: #36, Mary's personal experience, the ecstasy of her heart shows forth; and #37, drawing from Mary's heart, from the depth of her faith, expressed in the words of the Magnificat, the Church renews herself. The Holy Father has also spoken of his love for the title of "Our Lady and the Sacred Heart" as "beautiful" and "so full of meaning and inspiration" (*L'Osservatore Romano*, 5 Oct 1987).

[100]John Paul II *Redemptoris Mater*, #36; the Latin may be found in AAS, Vol. LXXIX, N. 4, 2 Ap 1987

[101]*Ibid.*, #44

Figure 28: *"The Sacred Heart," oil on canvas, by the French artist Odilon Redon (1840-1916). The Louvre.*

VI.

Devotion to the Sacred Heart of Jesus: A Grace for the Modern Era and All Times

"On different occasions I have expressed my conviction that devotion to the Sacred Heart corresponds more than ever to the expectations of our times. I have stressed that the essential elements of this devotion 'belong in a permanent fashion to the spirituality of the Church throughout her history'."
John Paul II, to Missionaries of the
Sacred Heart, *L'O. R.*, Oct. 5, 1987

At this point in our study we have examined the doctrinal foundations of the devotion, its lengthy history and the teaching of the magisterium. We have demonstrated the devotion's solid doctrinal base and have found the objections in this area to be groundless. We likewise found a rich scriptural basis for the devotion, particularly regarding the biblical expression of "heart" as the center of man's being. The objection that the devotion to the Sacred Heart of Jesus is not "scriptural" was shown to be both superficial and untenable. In our examination of the history of the devotion through the patristic, medieval and modern eras we found that the devotion most certainly did not originate from the revelations given to St. Margaret Mary, but gradually emerged, with the aid of the Holy Spirit from the veneration of the humanity of Christ and his sacred Passion. In our examination of the teaching of the magisterium we have seen the unique position which this devotion has been given in the life of the Church. Far from being a devotion whose time has come and gone, the magisterium speaks of the devotion to the Sacred Heart of Jesus as the extraordinary remedy for the extraordinary needs of our time.[1]

This being the case, what are we to say of the criticism still being leveled at the devotion? It would appear that most of this criticism springs from a deep ignorance of the true nature of the devotion.

A study of the status of the Sacred Heart devotion in the United States which was made by the Center of Applied Research in the Apostolate seems to support our position.[2] The study, which centered upon the response of Catholic educators, revealed a tremendous need for education about the devotion's true nature and its doctrinal foundation. A surprisingly large number of these Catholic educators had not read either *Haurietis Aquas* or any of the other magisterial documents dealing with the devotion.

As we have already seen, the CARA study further acknowledges that

> ...those religious who were best acquainted with the papal documents were also the ones that were most alert, most interested, and most motivated regarding the devotion and also the most objective in their views.[3]

If individuals were more familiar with the official teaching of the Church concerning the devotion (as presented in our magisterial section) much of

---

[1] The Church has approved the many forms of the devotion and has integrated these into her life: these forms include the Feast of the Sacred Heart, the Office of the Sacred Heart, the Litany of the Sacred Heart, special votive masses, Mass and communion of reparation, Holy Hours, the Act of Consecration on the Feast of Christ the King, the Act of Reparation on the Feast of the Sacred Heart and the Enthronement of the Sacred Heart in the home or institution.

[2] CARA, *The Sacred Heart Devotion: A Christocentric Spirituality for Our Times* (Milwaukee/Rome: International Institute of the Heart of Jesus, 1977)

[3] *Ibid.*,pp. 217, 209

this ignorance could be eliminated. I have come across many instances of this tragic ignorance in the course of my teaching. For example, I met a priest of the Sacred Heart of Jesus who told me that the devotion held little meaning for him although he was *interested* in it. As we continued our conversation he related that he really knew very little about the devotion. It had never been formally taught or presented to him during his formation. This, unfortunately, is not an isolated example.

Because of this widespread ignorance, the devotion is seen as merely the outward manifestations of popular piety. Some of these forms of personal piety have become stumbling blocks which hinder the acceptance and authentic practice of the devotion. At other times, the manner in which the devotion has been presented by some spiritual writers and preachers has had the same effect.

Prayers in many devotional books are overly sentimental and frequently make use of exaggerated expressions (e.g., I annihilate myself a million times in reparation for my sins... Alas, I do not have torrents of tears to lament day and night to offer some consolation!) which are not in keeping with our modern idiom.[4] This sentimentalism has produced an excessively lachrymose form of spirituality which tends towards pessimism. Many spiritual authors of the 19th century cultivated this type of sentimental piety in their portrayal of St. Margaret Mary's spirituality. It was as if all this great saint ever did was spend her life weeping constantly over the suffering of Jesus. This morose emphasis does not do justice to the true glory of St. Margaret Mary's spirituality.

The Heart of Jesus, which was pierced for our transgression, is now the triumphant Heart of the glorified Lord who reigns in heavenly splendor. Some spiritual authors and preachers wrote and spoke as if Christ was still actually suffering physical torments. Frequent references were made to the

---

[4]Unfortunately, there has been a great deal of desacralization which has gone on in the name of updating the language. Much of this stems from a loss of the profound sense of the Divine Majesty and the accompanying horror of sin which offends that Majesty. The ICEL translation of the Mass is a classic example of what not to do. This loss can be seen in a comparison between the ICEL text and the literal Latin.

Latin: "As suppliants, therefore, most merciful Father, we beg and beseech You, through Jesus Christ, Your Son, our Lord that You will regard as accepted and bless these gifts, these offerings, these holy, unspotted sacrifices, which we offer You first of all for Your holy catholic Church: that You may deign to give her peace and protection, to unite and guide her the whole world over."

ICEL: "We come to you, Father, with praise and thanksgiving, through Jesus Christ your Son. Through him we ask you to accept and bless these gifts we offer you in sacrifice. We offer them for your holy catholic Church; watch over it, Lord, and guide it."

Updating the language of prayers should not mean the destruction of beauty or the failure to elevate one's thoughts to the glory of God.

"poor prisoner of the tabernacle." Some of these expressions bordered upon being doctrinally unsound. At times, the artistic representations of the Sacred Heart have been insipid and all too frequently self-pitying and effeminate.

Another problem is that some who have promoted the devotion in the past placed too great an emphasis upon the promises which our Lord made to St. Margaret Mary. This is particularly true concerning the great promise of final perseverance for those who receive communion on nine consecutive First Fridays. This promise was made to the person who completely surrenders himself in a deep and unconditional act of faith. It is a beautiful expression of the Lord's desire to share Himself with us in His sacrament of love. This is essentially the same promise which our Lord made in the Gospel to those who would eat His flesh and drink His blood (Jn. 6:65). It was unfortunate that this was at times presented as a simplistic guarantee of salvation in return for a merely external observance.

It must be stressed, however, that *none of these problems touch the essence of the devotion as it is taught and practiced by the Church*. Sometimes the reaction to these excesses and the criticism of the devotion seem to spring from a spiritual pride that may in turn lead to a willful ignorance. All Christians must guard against such a tendency. Many criticisms also reveal a rationalistic spirit which is incapable of understanding any genuine religious experience. Still other criticisms reveal the dearth of any deeply genuine affectivity in our present age. True misunderstandings can and must be cleared away by making an effort to judiciously improve the language, art and most importantly, the overall presentation of the devotion. Emphasis must be given to the Church's teaching concerning the devotion's doctrinal and scriptural foundations. Such a balanced presentation will clearly demonstrate those aspects of the devotion which possess perennial validity. This was the great appeal which was made by Pius XII, who called repeatedly for deeper study and meditation upon the foundations of the devotion.

Obligation to Practice the Devotion

The deepening of our understanding is very important because this devotion, if properly understood, "imposes itself in a special way" since Divine Love is the proper object of the devotion.[5] We maintain that all Catholics are obliged to practice the devotion to the Sacred Heart of Jesus, and we shall now examine the nature of this obligation.

To begin with, the liturgical cult of the devotion is not presented as

---

[5]Paul VI, *Investigabiles Divitias Christi, op. cit.*, p. 301

optional. In the liturgy for the Solemnity of the Feast we are given a form of the devotion which is binding for the prayer of the Church. On that particular day all priests in the Latin rite who wish to say Mass and all the faithful who desire to participate in the sacred liturgy must honor the Divine Heart of Jesus.

As so many popes have taught, devotion to the Heart of Jesus is not just one devotion among other devotions. Karl Rahner stressed this very point in commenting upon Pius XI's reference to the devotion as *totius religionis summa:*

> This heart does in truth hold a central position, as the point through which everything passes to the ultimate center, the Father. To this extent, devotion to the Sacred Heart is not simply a special devotion among other such, limited to certain clearly defined prayers and practices, which one might set aside at will or replace by some other "devotion".[6]

Pius XII later referred to this special primacy and its obligatory character in *Haurietis Aquas*:

> There are those who, confusing and confounding the primary nature of this devotion with various individual forms of piety which the Church approves and encourages but does not commend, regard this as a kind of additional practice which each may take up or not according to his own inclination.[7]

Pope Pius XI spoke with great clarity of the obligation incumbent upon all Christians to make reparation to the Sacred Heart of Jesus. Pius XII, as we saw in the magisterial section, wrote that those who treat the devotion as if it were of little consequence or simply view it as an ordinary form of piety are doing something "rash, harmful, and deserving of God's displeasure."[8]

A Christian is not obliged to practice all the devotions which are approved by the Church but he may not reject one which has received the Church's blessing. Some forms of piety are not meant for all people and some may not suit the taste or mentality of certain individuals. Nevertheless we must admit that there are elements of spirituality and exercises of piety in the devotion to the Sacred Heart which can and must be accepted by all because they are either an essential part of the Christian life or intimately connected with it.

---

[6]Karl Rahner, "Some Theses on the Theology of the Devotion," in J. Stierli, ed. *Heart of the Savior, op. cit.,* p. 144

[7]Pius XII, *Haurietis Aquas, op. cit.,* p. 312

[8]*Ibid.,* p. 346

Such elements cannot be accepted or rejected according to the whim of the believer. Christians have a holy duty to study and learn of this devotion because of the valuable or even vital help which it offers. Although one individual may not impose one form of spirituality upon another, the Church may declare to the faithful the duty of practicing a particular devotion. It is the magisterium that teaches which devotional practices are necessary for all believers. It is the function of the magisterium to pass judgment upon the importance of various devotions and to teach which are obligatory. The Church has clearly revealed her thinking concerning devotion to the Heart of the Incarnate Word—it is to be accepted and practiced by all.

> Is it possible that there is any service of God more obligatory and necessary, and at the same time more excellent and attractive than the one which is dedicated to love?[9]

The Christian is called upon to form his judgment in the light of this teaching. The Jesuit theologian, Schwendimann, wrote concerning this point:

> If then some form of piety is proposed, we ought first to hear what the Church says about its nature, importance, and suitability. When it appears from this that it is a good form of piety, we must see how the Church recommends it, and whether and to what degree she urges the faithful to practice it. If the recommendation is strong and constant, then each one according to his ability is obliged to respond to the exhortation, and if he is a pastor of souls, he ought to provide sufficient instruction for his people and give them the opportunity to put it into practice.[10]

With its approval of popular devotions "especially where they are *ordered* by the Apostolic See" (*Sacrosanctum Concilium*, p. 13), the Vatican Council gave its full authority to urge the acceptance of the devotion to the Heart of Jesus. This, as we have seen, was made manifest by the authentic interpretation given by Pope Paul VI in *Investigabiles Divitias Christi*. Hence, the devotion has been ordered by the Apostolic See and since the Church also demands that a "...loyal submission of the will and intellect must be given, in a special way, to the authentic teaching authority of the Roman Pontiff"[11]

---

[9] *Ibid.*, p. 346

[10] Friedrich Schwendiman, *Devotion to the Sacred Heart and the Society of Jesus Today* trans. Alban J. Dachauer (Rome: Apostleship of Prayer, 1970), p. 37

[11] Flannery, *op. cit.*, p. 379: cf., *Sacrosanctum Oecumenicum Concilium Vaticanum II, op. cit.*, p. 138

(*Lumen Gentium*, 25), the constant teaching of the Popes must be seen as making the devotion obligatory.

Of course, the existence of an obligation does not in any way prevent its free and joyful accomplishment! There are many forms which the devotion to the Heart of Jesus may take. As Rahner observed: "Devotion to the Sacred Heart can appear in the most various shapes and degrees of intensity."[12] Let us recall here the magnificent teaching of Trent, which reminds us:

> God does not command the impossible; but when He commands, He cautions you to do what you can, and also to pray for what you cannot do, and He helps you so you can do it.[13]

In his book entitled *The Devotion to the Sacred Heart of Our Lord Jesus Christ*, Fr. Jean Croiset speaks with great spiritual insight of the dispositions necessary for practicing devotion to the Sacred Heart.[14] The four dispositions are: 1) a great horror of sin; 2) a lively faith; 3) a great desire to love Jesus Christ ardently; and 4) interior recollection. He also presents four obstacles which would hinder the practice of the devotion: 1) tepidity; 2) self-love; 3) secret pride; and 4) some unmortified passion. It is important that every Christian examine his conscience in order to remove anything that would hinder his acceptance and fruitful practice of this "priceless gift" which our Lord has given to his Church. In revealing His Most Sacred Heart, Christ "willed in an extraordinary and special way"[15] to draw men to the contemplation and adoration of the mystery of God's most merciful love for humanity. Christ himself chose to use His Heart as the most fitting symbol of this love. This has been recognized by the Church:

> In this special manifestation Christ pointed to His Heart, with definite and repeated words, as the symbol by which men should be attracted to a knowledge and recognition of His love; and at the same time He established it as a sign or pledge of mercy and grace for the needs of the Church of our times.[16]

The revelation of our Lord's Heart springs from the abundance of God's special grace. But, in setting forth the obligation to practice the devotion, the Church does not force men to obey. However, the obligation to practice the

---

[12]Rahner, *op. cit.*, p. 146

[13]Denzinger-Schönmetzer, *op. cit.*, #1536, p. 373

[14]Fr. Jean Croiset, *The Devotion to the Sacred Heart of Our Lord Jesus Christ* tr. Patrick O'Connell (Milwaukee: International Institute of the Heart of Jesus, 1976), pp. 81 - 108

[15]Pius XII, *op. cit.*, p. 340

[16]*Ibid.*, p. 340

Figure 29: Ibarran's "Sacred Heart"

devotion can be ignored only to one's spiritual loss.

A deeper catechesis of the devotion to the Heart of Christ must be developed. United to this catechesis it is also necessary for us to deepen our prayer and meditation that we may fulfill the will of Christ and his Church so powerfully revealed in the words of Pope Paul VI:

> Thus it is absolutely necessary that the faithful venerate and honor this Heart, in the expression of their private piety as well as in the services of public cult, for of His fullness we have all received; and they must learn perfectly from Him how they are to live in order to answer the demands of the time.[17]

The Perennial Validity of the Devotion

The special timeliness and the urgent need of the devotion which has been so frequently stressed by the magisterium does not allow us to view the devotion as being dated. Far from being dated, Karl Rahner writes that the message of Paray-le-Monial is directed precisely to our modern age which is characterized by the secularization of life as initiated by the French Revolution:

> What was the situation into which the massage of Paray-le-Monial was addressed as a compelling imperative? It cannot be described exclusively nor even principally in terms of Jansenism. Not only was Jansenism and its range of ideas too ephemeral a phenomenon to provoke such an answer, but the message only became effective in a period no longer swayed by Jansenism. In view of the way the message did actually take effect and of the guidance of the Church by the Holy Ghost, that explanation is untenable.
>
> The message must therefore be intended for the modern situation in general, which properly began only with the French Revolution. This period is characterized, and that in ever increasing measure, by the secularization of life (of the state, society, economy, science, art). The religious values of Christianity are being progressively eliminated from modern life, and the burden of belief is resting more and more exclusively on the personal decision of the individual. The Christian world, which could once carry a man almost independently of his own decision, is subject to unceasing attenuation. Every man must live, irrespective of whether he decides for or against Christianity, in a situation marked by the outward, and therefore also inward, "absence of God", a situation which corresponds to Golgotha and Gethsemane

---

[17]Paul VI, *Diserti Interpretes, op. cit.*, p. 586

in the life of Jesus (Mk. 14, 32ff.; 14, 32ff.), where life is to be found in death, where abandonment implies the deepest proximity to God, and where the power of God parades itself in weakness.[18]

Those who claim that the devotion is not acceptable to modern man are making an unwarranted claim and spreading a falsehood. Is it possible that our Lord would give to his Church in this most trying hour a special grace which is incomprehensible, distasteful and of little spiritual benefit?

In a society increasingly characterized by unbridled hedonism and militant atheism it is most certain that a devotion which emphasizes penance, sacrifice and reparation will not be popular with some people. This difficulty was observed by Pius XI in his encyclical *Caritate Christi Compulsi*:

> The notion of the need of penance and expiation is lost in proportion as belief in God is weakened, and the idea of an original sin and of a first rebellion of man against God becomes confused and disappears.[19]

Christians are not immune to this miasma. The modern world's denial of God and the reality of sin has created, even within the Church, a disdain for the fundamentals of the Christian spiritual life. Pope Paul VI himself had made reference to the "smoke which has entered the house of God." It does not take a great deal of acumen to see the deleterious effect which this "crisis of faith" has had upon the devotion to the Sacred Heart. This does not mean however that the devotion is dated. On the contrary, there has never been a greater need for its practice. Karl Rahner, commenting upon Pius XI's encyclical *Miserentissimus Redemptor*, states his belief that our Lord's request to St. Margaret Mary for reparation to be made to his Sacred Heart is of even greater importance today:

> The devotion in the strict sense, as it issued "new" from Paray-le-Monial and was appropriated by the Church, especially by the encyclical *Miserentissimus Redemptor* of Pius XI, is in a very positive sense the product of circumstances. But since, as was indicated above, these circumstances are still with us and show no sign of changing, indeed are only now revealing all their breadth and gravity, the cult of the Sacred Heart can only become more and more seasonable. If the devotion, understood in its proper and most profound sense, has suffered a reverse in very recent times, this is not because it is ill

---

[18]Karl Rahner, *op. cit.*, p. 141
[19]Pius XI, *Caritate Christi Compulsi, op. cit.,* p. 189

adapted to our age. Such a reverse is rather itself a sign that "charity has grown cold".[20]

The objection that the Church no longer needs the devotion is ludicrous. It is not our position to judge whether we need this special grace or not. That judgment belongs to God. Since He has offered this grace precisely for our age, is it not utter foolishness to reject it or treat it as useless?

The Holy See has taught that the devotion to the Sacred Heart of Jesus offers a complete summary of the whole mystery of redemption. This complete synthesis of faith reveals such an intimate union with the basic truths of the Christian faith and also so much theological richness that it truly possesses a validity for today and all times.

The devotion's perennial value, according to the teaching of Pius XII, is due to its deep union and perfect conformity with Christian dogma. The Pope made many references to this truth in *Haurietis Aquas*. He spoke of scripture, tradition and the sacred liturgy as "the deep untainted source" for the devotion. It is in the Sacred Scripture that we find the word "heart" used so frequently as the fundamental center of man. The devotion to our Lord's Heart as the fundamental center of his divine Person is intimately tied into the language of scripture itself in which it finds its richest expression. It is in the Word of God as it is cherished and expounded by the living Church that we are to find the fundamental elements of the devotion which are perennially valid and therefore constantly burgeoning forth within the Church. Even though the words of the Bible have been fixed for thousands of years, the God who speaks to us today already had us in mind when He inspired them of old. God is always present to speak to us through them as though it was at this very instant that they were uttered for the first time. This is one of the reasons why Pope John Paul II spoke of the devotion as having an "ever living topicality" in the Church.[21] The language of Sacred Scripture shall keep the devotion to the Heart of Jesus perennially fresh since it shall always live and develop within the tradition of the Church as she prays and meditates upon God's Word. In addition to the Scripture's frequent use of the word "heart"

---

[20]Rahner, *op. cit.*, p. 1434; This is the position which was taken by Pope John Paul II in his Address at Paray-le-Monial Oct. 5, 1985. see *L'Osservatore Romano*, Oct. 27, 1985, p. 3

[21]This teaching was again recalled by John Paul II in his address at Castel Gandolfo to the General Chapter delegates of the Missionaries of the Sacred Heart. "On different occasions I have expressed my conviction that devotion to the Sacred Heart corresponds more than ever to the expectations of our times. I have stressed that the essential elements of this devotion "belong in a permanent fashion to the spirituality of the Church throughout her history'." *L'Osservatore Romano* Oct. 5, 1987, p. 16

and its great revelation of God's infinite love, it must be remembered (as we demonstrated in our scriptural study of the devotion) that the revelation of the pierced Heart of the Messiah *belongs to the original message and meaning of Sacred Scripture.* [22]

The perennial value of the devotion is further evidenced by the fact that it rests upon an article of faith. Let us recall here the teaching of Pius XII:

> ...His Heart, the noblest part of human nature, is hypostatically united to the Person of the divine Word. Consequently, there must be paid to it that worship of adoration with which the Church honors the Person, the Incarnate Son of God Himself. We are dealing here with an article of faith, for it has been solemnly defined in the general Council of Ephesus and the second Council of Constantinople.[23]

The veneration of our Lord's Heart is an outgrowth of devotion to Christ's sacred humanity. So intimate is the devotion's identification with the truths of the Incarnation and the love due to Christ in His sacred humanity that Pope Pius XII taught that it had *always existed* within the Church.

> We are convinced, then, that the devotion which we are fostering to the love of God and Jesus Christ for the human race by means of the revered symbol of the pierced Heart of the crucified Redeemer has never been altogether unknown to the piety of the faithful.... [24]

The devotion has always existed within the Church because it belongs to the very essence of Christianity.

> It is therefore essential, at this point, in a doctrine of such importance and requiring such prudence, that each one constantly hold that the truth of the natural symbol by which the physical Heart of Jesus is related to the Person of the Word, entirely depends upon the fundamental truth of the hypostatic union. Should anyone declare this to be untrue he would be reviving false opinions, more than once condemned by the Church, for they are opposed to the oneness of the Person of Christ even though the two natures are each complete and distinct.[25]

Karl Rahner, in his study of the timeliness of the devotion also defends

---

[22] Hugo Rahner, "On the Biblical Basis of the Devotion" in J. Stierli, ed., *Heart of the Savior, op. cit.*, pp. 22 - 29

[23] Pius XII, *Haurietis Aquas, op. cit.*, p. 316

[24] *Ibid.*, p. 339; This teaching was echoed by John Paul II in his letter to Fr. Kolvenbach. See *L'Osservatore Romano* Oct. 27, 1986, p. 7.

[25] *Ibid.*, p. 344

this concept of the perennial validity which the devotion has because of its unique relationship to Christian truth:

> All the ingredients of devotion to the Sacred Heart are borrowed from dogma, and in this sense the devotion is valid for all ages of Christianity. These elements are themselves so important and suggestive, and they fit so naturally under the concept of the heart, that one can truly say: Just as there always has been a certain devotion to the Heart of Jesus, since the earliest days of the Church, so will there always be one.[26]

Arguing in a similar vein, the French Jesuit theologian Bertrand de Margerie writes that the devotion to the Sacred Heart of Jesus belongs to the enduring essence of Christianity:

> The devotion to the Heart of Jesus has always been present, is now present, and will continue to be present in the Church. This devotion implicitly belongs to the permanent essence of Christianity; it was already germinally contained in the worship of the wounds of the glorified Christ rendered by Mary, the Apostles, and many Christians. Even if it is not explicitly recognized, this devotion abides wherever true Christianity abides.[27]

The pierced Heart of the Incarnate Word is the clearest image of the all embracing fullness of God and the chief sign and symbol of the threefold love with which our Lord unceasingly loves His eternal Father and all mankind. It will never lose its value to communicate the great truths of our salvation.

> Hence the wound of the most Sacred Heart of Jesus, now that He has completed His mortal life, remains through the course of the ages a striking image of that spontaneous charity by which God gave His only begotten Son for the redemption of men.... His most Sacred Heart never ceased and never will cease to beat with calm and imperturbable pulsations. Likewise, *it will never cease to symbolize the threefold love with which He is bound to His heavenly father and the entire human race.*[28] [emphasis added]

When we examine the theological richness of the devotion, we can clearly see why Pope Pius XI referred to this devotion as the *summa totius religionis.*

---

[26]K. Rahner, *op. cit.*, p. 143

[27]Bertrand de Margerie, "A Theological Evaluation of the CARA Study on the Sacred Heart Devotion," in CARA, *The Sacred Heart Devotion, A Christocentric Spirituality for our Times, op. cit.*, p. 41

[28]Pius XII, *op. cit.*, pp. 334 - 328

The theological depth of the devotion is of tremendous value for our present age. The primacy and importance of the devotion is determined chiefly by the nature of its object—God's merciful love.

Catholic spirituality cannot be formed simply upon the basis of religious experience. It must be firmly grounded in the objective truth of dogma. The spiritual life must blossom from a lively faith and the great truths of God's revelation as they are taught by the Church. A spirituality which is deeply rooted in the central truths of the Faith will lead to a richer and more fully developed spiritual life. It should also provide greater insight into the wondrous unity of Catholic Truth. The devotion to the Sacred Heart of Jesus leads us to the very center of Christian dogma.[29]

The Sacred Heart and the Trinity

To begin with, the devotion to the Heart of Jesus draws us into the bosom of the Holy Trinity. His heart is the mystical ladder which reveals Christ as the Mediator of divine graces. It is Christ who sits at the right hand of the Father continually making intercession for us. This Trinitarian theocentrism is of particular importance today when Christians live in an atmosphere of secularism and atheism. The devotion leads us to contemplate the great Christian revelation of God who is love: "Beloved, let us love one another, for love is from God. And everyone who loves is born of God, and knows God. He who does not love does not know God; for God is love" (I Jn. 4:7-8). Christ loves us with the same divine love which he shares in common with the Father and Holy Spirit. He revealed this love to us in a most striking and moving way by allowing his Heart to be pierced by the lance of a soldier. This open Heart reveals in all its depth the grandeur of the Father's merciful love who "so loved the world that he gave his only-begotten Son, that those who believe in him may not perish but have eternal life" (Jn. 3:16).

Likewise, the love of the Holy Spirit is revealed in the Incarnation as the fruit of the personal love between the Father and Son. The fruitful love of the Holy Spirit is further revealed in the gush of the waters of salvation which sprang from the Heart of Christ as he hung upon the Cross. In the center of the mystery of the cross we see the mystery of the heart of the God-man, which opened to us, reveals the great mystery of triune love.[30]

---

[29] This dogmatic richness was beautifully set forth in Pope John Paul II's homily in Vancouver, B.C., Sept. 18, 1984.

[30] An excellent treatment of this theme may be found in Card. Luigi Mario Ciappi, OP, *The Heart of Christ, the Center of the Mystery of Salvation* (Rome: CdC. Publishers, 1981) p. 121-167

The Sacred Heart and Christ's Humanity

The devotion which, as we have seen, is deeply theocentric, is also at the same time anthropocentric. Christ reveals the whole truth about man. It is only in the mystery of Christ that we can fully understand man. Pope John Paul II spoke of this great paradox:

> The more the Church's mission is centered upon man—the more it is, so to speak anthropocentric—the more it must be confirmed and actualized theocentrically, that is to say, be directed in Jesus Christ to the Father. While the various currents of human thought both in the past and at the present have tended and still tend to separate theocentrism and anthropocentrism, and even to set them in opposition to each other, the Church, following Christ, seeks to link them up in human history in a deep and organic way. And this is also one of the basic principles, perhaps the most important one, of the teaching of the last council. Since, therefore, in the present phase of the Church's history we put before ourselves as our primary task the implementation of the doctrine of the great Council, we must act upon this principle with faith, with an open mind and with all our heart. In the encyclical already referred to I have tried to show that the deepening and the many-faceted enrichment of the Church's consciousness, resulting from the Council, must open our minds and our hearts more widely to Christ. Today I wish to say that openness to Christ, who as the Redeemer of the world fully "reveals man to himself," can only be achieved through an ever more mature reference to the Father and His love. [31]

What better way to communicate this great paradoxical truth and implement the teaching of the Council than to deeply contemplate the Heart of the Man-God?

The Sacred Heart and Christocentric Spirituality

This leads us quite naturally to the devotion's value as a Christocentric spirituality. One of the devotion's greatest gifts for our age is its ability to reveal and guard the central truth of the Incarnation. Here we see that the devotion draws the mind to a meditation upon the mysteries of our salvation. The reality of the Incarnation is manifested, for we are lucidly taught that God truly became man. Jesus had a truly human body like our own with a real physical heart. His human appearance was no illusion. The Church's insistence upon the adoration of the physical heart of Christ in virtue of the

---

[31] John Paul II, *Dives in Misericordia, op. cit.*, n. 1, p. 1179

hypostatic union is a continuation of the teaching of Chalcedon and a defense against any return to a Docetic Christology. This truth protects the faithful from a gnostic separation of the transcendent in the Mystery of Christ. The pierced Heart of Jesus also reminds us of the Redemption and speaks of our Lord's self-sacrifice for our salvation. This wounded Heart reveals in a manner more profound and compelling than any other image or mystery the authentic nature of our redemption. The truly sorrowful, bloody character of the work of our Savior is impressed upon the mind. It is the most fitting symbol for that "emptying of self" *(kenosis)* which St. Paul speaks of in his epistle to the Philippians as being so communicative of Christ's spirit:

> Have this mind in you which was also in Christ Jesus, who though he was by nature God, did not consider being equal to God a thing to be clung to, but emptied himself, taking the nature of a slave and being made like unto men. And appearing in the form of man, He humbled Himself, becoming obedient to death, even to death on a cross. (Phil. 2:5-8)

The devotion to the Heart of Jesus, with the doctrinal emphasis it places upon His sacred humanity, is a wonderful aid for so many people in the world today who are seeking a personal relationship with Christ. It is a spirituality which stresses *familiaritas cum Christo* and, with the aid of grace, enables the believer to penetrate into the innermost center of Christ and find the mystery of his Heart—the mystery of his infinite love.

In so doing, the devotion also protects against any Nestorian tendency since Christ's human and divine love spring from the center of the same divine Person. It is certainly a most profoundly beautiful truth and one well worth contemplating: namely, that now in the depths of Divinity there beats a heart just like our own.

The Sacred Heart and Devotion to Mary

Of course, one cannot speak of the Incarnation without reference to the Mother of the Lord. Devotion to the Heart of Jesus and devotion to the Immaculate Heart of Mary have always been inseparably linked. The teaching of the Holy See has always demonstrated this truth:

> In order that favors in greater abundance may flow on all Christians, nay, on the whole human race, from the devotion to the most Sacred Heart of Jesus, let the faithful see to it that to this devotion the Immaculate Heart of the mother of God is closely joined. For, by God's will, in carrying out the work of human Redemption the Blessed

Virgin Mary was inseparably linked with Christ in such a manner that our salvation sprang from the love and the sufferings of Jesus Christ to which the love and sorrows of His Mother were intimately united. It is, then, entirely fitting that the Christian people—who received the divine life from Christ through Mary—after they have paid their debt of honor to the Sacred Heart of Jesus should also offer to the most loving Heart of their heavenly Mother the corresponding acts of piety, affection, gratitude and expiation. [32]

Pope John Paul II has again called attention to the importance of the maternal heart of Mary in the plan of Redemption:

We can say that the mystery of the Redemption took shape beneath the heart of the Virgin of Nazareth when she pronounced her "fiat". From then on, under the special influence of the Holy Spirit, this heart, the heart of both a virgin and a mother, has always followed the work of her Son and has gone out to all those whom Christ has embraced and continues to embrace with inexhaustible love. For that reason her heart must also have the inexhaustibility of a mother. The special characteristic of the motherly love that the Mother of God inserts in the mystery of the redemption and the life of the Church finds expression in its exceptional closeness to man and all that happens to him. It is in this that the mystery of the Mother consists.[33]

The devotion to the Heart of Jesus, by communicating the great truths of the Incarnation and Redemption, establishes a firm foundation for authentic devotion to Mary, revealing her true glory as *Theotokos*.

The Sacred Heart and the Mystical Body

The devotion can also deepen our understanding of the mystery of the Church. This was a topic of central importance in the teaching of the Second Vatican Council. The birth of the Church from the wounded side of Christ is a central doctrine of Patristic teaching and is restated, as we have seen, in the documents of Vatican II. As Eve was formed from the side of Adam as he slept, so also was the Church formed from the side of Christ as he slept in death on the cross. The moment of her birth is also the day of her espousals. It was at that moment that Christ gave freely his Heart to his spotless Bride.

This rich patristic and conciliar teaching manifests and proclaims the Church to be the loving gift of the Heart of Jesus to mankind. Meditation

---

[32] Pius XII, *Haurietis Aquas, op. cit.*, p. 352
[33] John Paul II, *Redemptor Hominis, op. cit.*, n. 22; see also *Mater Recemptoris* nos. 7-24

upon the mystery of the Church (as the gift of the Heart of Jesus) can cultivate a deeper love for the Church as the Bride of Christ. This is most important today when Mother Church is attacked from the outside by the forces of paganism and from within by her own children. Such a meditation may strengthen the supernatural vision of the Church. This vision is all too frequently obscured today by a shallow and truncated understanding which views the Church in primarily political or legalistic terms.

The Sacred Heart and the Eucharist

This understanding of the Church naturally leads us to the sacramental value of the devotion since the blood and water which flow from the Heart of Christ are signs of the seven sacraments, and particularly the two chief sacraments of the Church, Baptism and Eucharist. Catholic theology views the seven sacraments as an extension in time of the Incarnation. Here the Church, as dispenser of these heavenly graces, shows forth her maternal fecundity and solicitude: in the sacrament of baptism, whereby she begets children; and in the sacrament of the Eucharist, whereby she feeds them. The understanding of the sacraments as gifts to the Church from the Heart of Jesus may help us to view them not so much as mechanical vehicles for dispensing grace but rather as the primary channels of Christ's boundless love.

The mystical Body of Christ is nourished, strengthened and vivified by the fountain of living waters which flow from the Heart of Christ. Of course the Eucharist is, in the words of Pope Paul VI, "the outstanding gift of the Heart of Jesus."[34] As the sacrament of love *par excellence*, the Eucharist possesses a primacy as the noblest of the sacraments. The devotion to the Sacred Heart of Jesus consists essentially in concentrating the Christian life upon the Holy Eucharist.

> The devotion to the Blessed Eucharist and the devotion to the Sacred Heart are two sister devotions. They are so intimately united, they complete each other so perfectly, that the one calls for the other, as if necessarily. Not only can the first of these devotions not prejudice the second; but they augment each other reciprocally, because they complete each other and perfect each other.
>
> The Sacred Heart, the Blessed Eucharist, love are one and the same thing! In the Tabernacle we find the Host; in the heart, Love, Infinite Love, divine Charity, God the Principle of life, living and vivifying. But more still: the ineffable miracle of the Eucharist can be

---

[34] Paul VI, *Investigabiles Divitias Christi, op. cit.*, p. 300

explained only by love; by the love of God, yes, but by the love of Jesus, God and Man. Now the love of Jesus is the love of His Heart: it is His Heart, to sum up all in one word. Thus, the Blessed Eucharist is explained only by the Sacred Heart.[35]

This is truly one of the greatest values of the devotion for our age, especially in view of the teachings of the Second Vatican Council concerning the liturgy. The Holy See has constantly stressed this important truth. Let it suffice for us to recall here the teaching of Paul VI: "The origin and principle of the Sacred Liturgy is found there [in the Sacred Heart], for the Heart of Jesus is the sacred temple of God from which there ascends to the eternal Father the expiatory sacrifice...."[36]

Countless souls have found devotion to the Sacred Heart a practical spirituality which has assisted them in their effort to live the Gospel between Masses and to help prepare for the next Mass.[37]

The Sacred Heart and the Apostolate

This devotion which reveals so clearly and beautifully the love of Christ for men cannot be simply "passive," but must find fulfillment in the fraternal apostolate. A truth if correctly understood will always have practical consequences. Accordingly, the dogmatic richness of the devotion to the Heart "which is so in love with men" cannot help but manifest concern for our brothers in need.[38] The devotion, in a certain sense carries within itself powerful torrents of heavenly graces which fill the true practitioner—the true lover, with an apostolic zeal for souls. Who could contemplate the pierced Heart of Jesus immolated for the love of men and not feel compelled to serve his brother?

It is often heard today that devotion to the Sacred Heart was fine for the

---

[35]Mother Louise Margaret Claret de la Touche, *The Sacred Heart and the Priesthood*, tr. Patrick O'Connell (Rockford, Ill.: Tan Books & Pub., 1979), pp. 184 - 185

[36]Paul VI, *Diserti Interpretes, op. cit.*, p. 586

[37]For an excellent treatment of the Eucharistic Heart of Jesus see Bertrand de Margerie, *Christ for the World: The Heart of the Lamb*, tr. Malachy Carroll, (Milwaukee: The International Institute of the Heart of Jesus, 1973), pp. 1 - 10; see also an excellent article by Cardinal Luigi Ciappi, "The Worship of the Sacred Heart", *L'Osservatore Romano*, July 6, 1981, p. 2

[38]This is the core of the great message of merciful love communicated so powerfully to Sr. Josefa Menendez in *The Way of Divine Love* (Rockford, Ill.: Tan Books & Pub., 1973).

19th century, with its emphasis on individualism and one's personal relationship with God, but not for the 20th century. Modern man must "seek Christ in his fellowman." This is undoubtedly true to a certain extent but we are not likely to find him there unless we have already fostered, in our own lives, a personal relationship with Christ. If we set aside personal prayer and contemplation, and concentrate exclusively on activity, we shall be discarding the Christian inspiration. If we are to find Christ in others, it is absolutely vital that we have a supernatural outlook which is impossible without personal prayer.

This is the understanding which makes Mother Teresa of Calcutta the world leader in the service apostolate to the poor. She insists that her nuns begin each day with Mass and meditation before the Blessed Sacrament.[39] She knows that the more one can come to recognize Christ behind the bread in the tabernacle, the better able he will be to see Him in the faces of the suffering, the sick and the destitute. We have only succeeded in deceiving ourselves if we think we can dismiss prayer and meditation for mere activity. The wounded Heart of Christ tells us that it was his love for all men that made Him face death. Modern man's concern for an apostolate of activity to improve the world can draw much strength from this devotion. So many idealists become disillusioned if their work does not meet with instant success. The devotion here serves as a reminder of the cross which can be a source of grace for suffering perseverance in imitation of the Lord. It will also help these individuals to restructure their values in a more proper order—to avoid the efforts to replace the worship belonging to God by the worship of man.

The Sacred Heart and the Interior Life

The devotion also helps to develop a spirit of interiority. As we seek to view all of life from the interior of Christ, we in turn are led into the depths of our own being.[40] In the constant rush of modern life with consumerist advertising and many other pressures, we are unceasingly being called out of ourselves. We may become desensitized to the indwelling of the Holy Spirit

---

[39]David Porter, a biographer of Mother Teresa's early years in Skopje, Serbia, said that she would often visit the Church of the Sacred Heart. Here she attended Mass joyfully and would frequently, in silence, take her place in the empty church. She enjoyed praying on her own and was often found kneeling before the statue of the Heart of Jesus.

[40]This particular value of the devotion is beautifully illustrated in Han Urs von Balthasar, *Heart of the World*, tr. Erasmo S. Leiva (San Francisco: Ignatius Press, 1978)

in our souls. The Heart of Jesus overcomes this danger and beckons us to internal peace, recollection and sensitivity to the supernatural life of grace within.[41]

The Sacred Heart and Universal Brotherhood

The devotion's emphasis upon loving reparation which seeks to make up for unrequited love strengthens the sense of community and universal brotherhood. It is a practice which unites us to Christ and to one another. The offering of loving reparation is an application of the doctrine of the Communion of Saints and may in turn heighten the Christian's awareness of his responsibility to care for his brothers and sisters in the Mystical Body. It may also cultivate a sense of the value of sacrifice and self-denial which is so necessary for a world filled with hedonistic selfishness. In addition, reparation impresses upon the mind the terrible reality of sin which is so frequently ignored or denied today. This in turn will sensitize the conscience, arouse true contrition and lead to a more fruitful reception of the sacrament of reconciliation. Who could contemplate our Lord's Heart overwhelmed with reproaches, bruised for our offenses and victimized for our sins and not deepen his awareness of the great evil of sin?

The Sacred Heart and Reparation

The desire to console our Lord, who has suffered so terribly for our sins, is another central theme of the devotion which finds its origin in the very nature of reparation itself. This practice which has been warmly approved and encouraged by the Church[42] is not simply a pious gesture but a beautiful way in which the soul may unite itself to the beloved.[43]

From this we may see that the devotion to the wounded Heart of Jesus also speaks most eloquently to those who are sick and suffering. By uniting their suffering to the passion of Christ, their acts of suffering and love fulfill a vital role in the co-redemptive mission of the Church. Their union with Christ crucified enables their works to take on satisfactory merit in order that they make up in their bodies what is lacking in the sufferings of Christ (Col.

---

[41]See Leo Joseph Cardinal Suenens' beautiful meditation "Loving Through the Power of the Holy Spirit" in *Towards a Civilization of Love, op. cit.*, pp. 87-100. Also Card. Ratzinger's meditations in *Behold the Pierced One* (San Francisco: Ignatius Press, 1984)

[42]Pius XI, *Miserentissimus Redemptor*, AAS XX, 1928

[43]Cf., for an excellent treatment of the value of consolation see Angelico A. Koller, *Reparation to the Sacred Heart: Theology of Consolation* (Hales Corner, Wis.: The Priests of the Sacred Heart, 1971)

1:24). Redemption in God's wondrous plan was to be accomplished not only by substitution (i.e., Christ suffering for us) but through loving union and solidarity with the members of His Body, the Church, down through the ages. This is most certainly a great mystery which calls for deep reflection.

All these forms of loving reparation are participations in the redemptive love of Christ which is received with coldness and indifference. Reparation speaks powerfully of man's freedom, his great dignity and the importance of his actions in the life of the Mystical Body.

We could speak here of many other theological values which the devotion possesses, such as its ability to deepen our understanding of the priesthood[44] or its ability to demonstrate the psychological values of the use of religious symbols (a point often overlooked by modern iconoclasts), but this brief examination should suffice as an intimation of the great values of the devotion. Although many of these values are to be found in other devotions, it is only in the devotion to the Sacred Heart of Jesus, the "summary of the whole mystery of Redemption,"[45] that we find such an abundance and harmonious unity.

In the devotion, all the great truths of revelation and our redemption converge. They spring from the Heart of the Savior and lead back to it. Here the mystery of the love of the most Holy Trinity breaks through to regenerate the world as we in turn are led into the very mystery of the Triune love. Here we find a most perfect and intimate union between piety and doctrine.

It is only in the Heart of the Lord that we find a heart of perfect love. This perfect love forms the very center of His Person. At the very core of our faith is the beautiful and powerful truth communicated by the Spirit to St. John that "God is love." In the devotion to the Heart of Jesus we experience the wondrous reality of His infinite love for us. This is why the Popes have spoken of the Heart of Christ as the great sign and symbol of the victory of faith, hope

---

[44]Mother Louise Margaret Claret de la Touche, *The Sacred Heart and the Priesthood*, *op. cit.*; cf., Cardinal Humberto Medeiros, "The Heart of Jesus and Priestly Holiness", an address given to The National Congress of the Sacred Heart of Jesus on Sept. 14, 1978 (Milwaukee, Wis.: International Institute of the Heart of Jesus).

[45]Piux XII, *Haurietis Aquas, op. cit.*, p. 336. A fine example of the richness of the devotion can be seen in the variety of theological topics and themes addressed by the participants at the Sacred Heart Symposium April 8-11, 1980. See Leo Scheffczyk ed. *Faith in Christ and the Worship of Christ* (San Francisco: Ignatius Press, 1986).

and charity over the evils of the present age.[46]

Today when we so acutely feel the limitations of our human condition and know all too well that our shallow efforts to live and love are becoming parched and dry, we must turn to that divine source of the living waters of salvation which flow unceasingly from the open Heart of Christ.

The devotion to the Sacred Heart of Jesus is a devotion whose time has just arrived. We are only just beginning to realize the depth contained in this priceless gift which our Lord has given to His Church. It shall help us to appreciate, in this age in which charity has grown cold, the powerfully effective role which emotion and affectivity can play in the spiritual life.[47]

Everywhere throughout the world today we find a widespread renewal of interest in and enthusiasm for the devotion. The decline of the devotion in the period immediately preceding and following the Council now appears to be a temporary one. With a deeper reflection and study of the Conciliar documents, we shall realize the devotion to be of even greater importance today. This is why Pope John Paul II singled out the vital importance of devotion to the Heart of Christ. The devotion in a "particular way" communicates God's merciful love for mankind which must be *the way for the Church* in the post-conciliar era.[48]

The spirituality fostered by the devotion to the Sacred Heart of Jesus, as our Lord Himself requested it and as it is strongly approved and encouraged by the magisterium of the Church, can best meet the spiritual needs of our age. It is a form of spirituality which may be practiced by all, from the simplest of the faithful to the most learned of theologians. Because it emphasizes *familiaritas cum Christo* it is marvelously suited to aid priests, religious and laity alike in their quest for personal holiness. If practiced in the family, devotion to the Heart of Jesus may greatly assist the Christian home to effectively counter those pagan elements of culture which can work their way into the sanctuary of the domestic church.[49]

This is the devotion which will enable us as Christians to effect the

---

[46]For an interesting insight into the value of the symbol of the Sacred Heart for modern man see Cardinal Wright's address to the Heart of Jesus, Catholic Congress of August 23, 1975 entitled "The Sacred Heart of Jesus, a Symbol for Our Time," published in *The Laity*, Vol. III, no. 6, June 1975, pp. 221 - 217

[47]See Dietrich von Hildebrand, *The Sacred Heart: An Analysis of Human and Divine Affectivity* (Dublin: Helicon Press Inc, 1965).

[48]John Paul II, *Dives in Misericordia, n. 13 & n. 14*

[49]For an excellent presentation of the values of the devotion to the Sacred Heart for the Christian family see Francis Larkin, *Enthronement of the Sacred Heart* (Boston: The Daughters of St. Paul, 1978).

"trans-secularization" of the world.[50]

Only love can set the world aflame. Today since the forces of secularism and atheism constantly work with such diabolical intensity, the Christian world must respond to our Lord's appeal with a crusade to establish the love of Christ who "came to cast fire upon the earth" (Lk. 13:49). Let all the People of God again turn their gaze to the Heart of Jesus, the *fornax ardens caritatis*. This shall certainly guide us as we continue our pilgrimage which shall end in the house of our Father:

> This surely, will bring an intensification of bliss which there are no words to describe. We cannot imagine what it will mean to us, how we shall feel, as we gaze through the wound in His pierced side at the vision of our Master's Heart—the Heart that calls for love and adoration; the Heart on fire with love for us; the Heart in which we shall read our names—inscribed, all of them in letters of love. My name in His Heart!—the love of Jesus will leave us wondering; but there will be no doubt about it. The prophet was speaking in our Lord's name, when he said: "What, can a woman forget her child that is still unweaned, pity no longer the son she bore in her womb? Let her forget; I will not be forgetful of thee. Why, I have cut thy image on the palm of My hands." These words will grow in the telling as Jesus repeats them to us in heaven: " What, can a woman forget her child? Let her forget; I will not be forgetful of thee. Why, I have cut thy name deep in My Heart." There it is, the ultimate consolation: our Lord loves us so dearly, we have an indelible place in His Heart....
>
> Let us make our way, then, cheerfully and happily through the difficulties of this fleeting life. Let us welcome with open arms all the mortifications and trials that we shall meet along the road. They will not last, we can be sure of that; death will put an end to them eventually, and we shall go to a new life which knows only joys unfailing, perfect satisfaction and eternal peace.[51]

---

[50]See de Margerie, *Christ for the World: The Heart of the Lamb, op. cit.*

[51]St. Francis de Sales, "Sermon on the second Sunday in Lent" February 20, 1622 *Oeuvres*, Vol. X, sermon lvii pp. 243 - 247, tr. Vincent Kerns in *St. Margaret Mary: Her Autobiography* (London: Darton, Longman & Todd Lt., 1976) pp. XV - XVI. For the complete set of St. Francis' Lenten sermons see Lewis S. Fiorelli, ed., *The Sermons of St. Francis de Sales for Lent* (Rockford, Illinois: Tan Books and Publishers Inc. 1987).

Appendix:
Living the Heart of Christ

Having explored the theological richness of the Sacred Heart, the question naturally arises as to how one can practice the devotion. I would like to offer here a number of concrete suggestions which I have found helpful for fostering individual and parish devotion.

1. Invoke our Lord under the aspect of his Heart in prayer. As the Epistle to the Hebrews tells us, Christ is our great high priest who continues to make intercession for us to the Heavenly Father. This natural symbol of the merciful love of Christ can readily become part of our vocal and mental prayer.

2. Make a daily offering in the morning of all your "prayers, works, joys and sufferings of the day" to the Heart of Christ. This offering of one's self to the Heart of Christ can be renewed during the course of the day with short prayers, such as, "All for you most Sacred Heart of Jesus"; or "Heart of Jesus help me to love you more and more." In this way, we become aware of our Lord's presence, and speak to Him as a loving companion.

3. Our daily offering should be "in union with the Holy Sacrifice of the Mass throughout the world." Attendance at daily Mass, or whenever possible, in which we recognize the Eucharist as the gift of his Heart, is an excellent way to practice the devotion. Visits to the Blessed Sacrament, in which one becomes aware of the loving Heart which beats behind the eucharistic veil, can further deepen our appreciation of Christ's *loving* gift in this wonderful sacrament.

4. Make a formal act of consecration to the Heart of Jesus in which you surrender and re-dedicate yourself to the Heart of the Divine King. This formal act should not be made only once. It should be renewed frequently, at least once a month.

5. Family consecration and home enthronement, which is a social acknow-ledgement of the sovereignty of the Heart of Christ over a Christian family, can greatly deepen the devotion. In this ritual, which may include Mass and parental blessing of the children, an image of the Sacred Heart is placed in a prominent place in the home as a reminder that Christ reigns in the domestic church. It is important to remember that our Lord promised that where the image of his Heart is honored he would bring peace to the home, unite the families, bless them in all their undertakings, bestow the graces necessary for their state in life and be a secure place of refuge in life and death.

6. Seek to cultivate a spirit of reparation to the Heart of Christ in prayer and good works. A spirit of reparation shows a concern for unfaithful love and seeks to make up for our own sins and the sins of others (e.g., abortion, sacrilege to the Eucharist, etc.).

7. Attend Mass on the First Fridays of each month as our Lord requested and make a communion of reparation in which you thank the Lord for the loving sacrifices of his life.

8. Make a Holy Hour on the Thursday night before First Friday at church or at home. During this hour we can read, pray the litany or do whatever helps us to give consolation to Christ in his agony. We can also offer our love to Christ who continues to suffer in his members on earth and unite our own personal sufferings to his.

9. One should become an apostle of the Heart of Christ. This can be done through: a) personal prayer; b) prayer with others; c) having in hand extra badges, pictures, prayer cards, books, etc. for distribution to others. On the parish level, the devotion can be fostered through a) homilies which unveil the theological richness of the devotion; b) prayers of the faithful at Mass which include petitions to the Heart of Christ and the intentions of the Apostleship of Prayer; c) stocking devotional leaflets in the vestibule and parish resource center; d) celebrating the votive Mass of the Sacred Heart whenever possible, especially on First Fridays; e) celebrating in a special way liturgical days of significance for the devotion, i.e., the Solemnity in June, the Feast of Christ the King, Corpus Christi, St. Margaret Mary, Bl. Claude de la Colombière, St. John the Evangelist, St. John Eudes, etc.; f) conducting a parish Holy Hour each month.

The following organizations may be contacted for literature and devotional materials:

Apostleship of Prayer
Auriesville, NY 12012

International Institute of the Heart of Jesus
7700 W. Blue Mound Road
Milwaukee, WI 53213
        or
14 Borgo Angelico
00193 Rome Italy

National Enthronement Center
3 Adams Street
Fairhaven, MA 02719

Sacred Heart League
Walls, MS

Families for Christ
        or
Men of the Sacred Heart
6026 W. Harwood Avenue
Orlando, FL 32811

Soul Assurance Prayer Plan
P.O. Box 1632
Chicago, IL 60690

Bibliography

Dogmatic Foundations

Aland, K., ed. *The New Testament in Greek and English.* New York: American Bible Society, 1966.

Aquinas, Thomas, St. *Summa Theologica.* 5 vols. Matriti: Biblioteca De Autores Cristianos, 1961. English translation by the Fathers of the English Dominican Province. New York: Benziger Brothers, 1947.

Athanasius, St. *The Orations of St. Athanasius Against the Arians.* Translated by W. C. L. London: Griffith, Farran, Ikeden & Welsh, n.d.

Barth, Karl. *Church Dogmatics.* Vol I, Edinburgh: T. & T. Clark, 1970.

Bea, A., Rahner, H., Rondet, H., Schwendimann, R. *Cor Jesu.* Rome: Herder, 1959.

Becker, Joachim. "The Heart in the Language of the Bible." *Faith in Christ and the Worship of Christ.* San Francisco: Ignatius Press, 1986.

Boros, Ladislaus. *God is With Us.* New York: Herder, 1967.

Brown, Raymond E. *The Gospel of St. John.* Vol XIII of *New Testament Reading Guide.* edited by Ahern, B., Sullivan, K., Heidt, W. 14 vols. Collegeville, Minnesota: The Liturgical Press, 1968.

Brown, Raymond E., Fitzmyer, Murphy, ed. *The Jerome Biblical Commentary.* Englewood Cliffs, NJ: Prentice Hall, 1968.

Buttrick, George A., ed. *The Interpreter's Dictionary of the Bible.* Vol II. New York/Nashville: Abingdon Press, 1965.

Centro di Documentazione Instituto per le Scienze Religiose. *Conciliorum Ecumenicorum Decreta.* Bologna: Herder, 1962.

Chalcedon, Council of. *Sybolum Chalcedonese. Enchiridion Symbolorum.* Ed. Denzinger Schonmetzer. Rome: Herder, 1976.

Ciappi, Luigi. "The Worship of the Sacred Heart." *L'Osservatore Romano.* July 6, 1981.

Clarkson, J. F., Edwards, E. H., Kelly, W. J., Welch, J. J. ed. & trans. *The Church Teaches.* St. Louis: Herder, 1965.

Colunga, A., Turrado, L. ed. *Biblia Vulgata.* Matriti: Biblioteca de Autores Cristianos, 1965.

Cozens, M. L. *A Handbook of Heresies.* London: Sheed & Ward, 1974.

Cyril of Alexandria, St. *Anathematismi Cyrilli Alex. Enchiridion Symbolorum.* Ed. by Denzinger-Schönmetzer. Rome: Herder, 1976.

Damasus I, Pope, St. *Tomus Damasi. Enchiridion Symbolorum.* Ed. by Denzinger-Schönmetzer. Rome: Herder, 1976.

Denzinger-Schönmetzer. *Enchiridion Symbolorum.* ed XXXVI. Rome: Herder, 1976.

Ephesus, Council of. *Actio I Cyrillianorum. Enchiridion Symbolorum.* Ed. by Denzinger-Schönmetzer. Rome: Herder, 1976.

Fuller, Reginald C. *A New Catholic Commentary on Holy Scripture.* London: Thomas Nelson and Sons Ltd., 1975.

Galot, Jean. "Revelation of Salvation, the Testimony of His Love." *L'Osservatore Romano.* September 7, 1981.

Garrigou-Lagrange, Reginald. "E tealogicamente esatta l'esspressione: Consolare il Cuore di Gesu?" *Vita Christiana.* 16, 1947.

____. *Our Savior and His Love for Us.* Trans. by Bouchard. St. Louis: Herder, 1951.

____. *The Savior.* Trans. by Bede Rose. St. Louis: Herder, 1950.

Hardon, John. *The Catholic Catechism.* Garden City, New York: Doubleday and Co., 1975.

Hefele, Charles. *A History of the Christian Councils.* Vols. I, II, III. Edinburgh: T. & T. Clark, 1894.

Henchey, Joseph CSS. "Old Testament Background to Devotion to the Sacred Heart of Jesus." Unpublished Lecture, Pontifical University of St. Thomas Aquinas, 1981.

Hoffman, Norbert. "Atonement and the Ontological Coherence Between the Trinity and the Cross." *Towards A Civilization of Love.* San Francisco: Ignatius Press, 1985.

Leo I, Pope, St. *Tomus Leonis. Enchiridion Symbolorum.* Edited by Denzinger-Schönmetzer. Rome: Herder, 1976.

Malatesta, Edward, Solano, Jesus. *The Heart of Christ and the Heart of Man.* Rome: Pontifical Gregorian University, 1978.

Margerie, Bertrand de. *The Human Knowledge of Christ.* Boston: The Daughters of St. Paul, 1980.

McKenzie, John. *Dictionary of the Bible.* Milwaukee: The Bruce Publishing Co., 1965.

MacKenzie, Roderick A. F. *The Book of Psalms.* Vol XXIII of *New Testament Reading Guide.* Edited by Ahern, B., Sullivan, K., Heidt, W., 31 vols. Collegeville, Minn: The Liturgical Press, 1967.

Newman, J. H. *Essay on the Development of Christian Doctrine.* Westminster, Md: Christian Classics Inc., 1968.

Nicea, Council of. *Symbolum Nicaenum. Enchiridion Symbolorum.* Edited by Denzinger-Schonmetzer. Rome: Herder, 1976.

Pius VI, Pope. *Auctorem Fidei. Enchiridion Symbolorum.* Edited by Denziger-Schonmetzer. ed. XXXVI. Rome: Herder, 1976.

Pius XII, Pope. *Sempiternus Rex. Acta Apostolicae Sedis.* 43, 1951.

Potterie, Ignace de la. "The Biblical Basis of the Theology of the Heart of Christ: Jesus' Sovereignty, His Obedience to His Father, His Filial Consciousness." *Towards A Civilization of Love.* San Francisco: Ignatius Press, 1985.

Rahner, Hugo, "On the Biblical Basis of the Devotion." *Heart of the Savior.* Edited by J. Stierli. New York: Herder, 1958.

Sacred Congregation for Divine Worship. *General Instruction of the Liturgy of the Hours.* 1967.

Schroeder, H.J. *Disciplinary Decrees of the General Councils.* New York: Vail Ballau Press, 1937.

Schwendimann, Frederich. *Devotion to the Sacred Heart and the Society of Jesus Today.*

Translated by Alban J. Dachauer. Rome: Apostleship of Prayer, 1970.

Stierli, Josef. "The Dogmatic and Religious Value of the Devotion to the Sacred Heart." *Heart of the Savior*. Edited by J. Stierli. New York: Herder, 1958.

The Catholic Biblical Association. *A Commentary on the New Testament*. The Catholic Biblical Association, 1942.

The National Apostleship of Prayer. *In the Bible the Mystery of the Sacred Heart of Jesus*. Tamil Nadu, India: The National Office Apostleship of Prayer, n.d.

The National Office Apostleship of Prayer and Eucharistic Crusade. *Liturgy of the Mystery of the Heart of Christ*. Orlando, Florida: Sacred Heart Publication Center, 1976.

The History of the Devotion

à Kempis, Thomas. *Prayers and Meditations on the Life of Christ. Opera Omnia* Edited by Michael J. Pohl. Vol. V Friburg, Brisigavorum: Herder, 1922.

Albert the Great, St. *In Joannem. Opera Omnia*. Edited by August Borgnet. Vol. 24. Paris: Ludovicum Vives, 1899.

Albert the Great, St. *In IV Sententiarum. Opera Omnia*. Vol. 29. (Ibidem).

_____. *De Eucharistia. Opera Omnia*. Vol. 38. (Ibidem).

_____. *Sermon 27 de Eucharistica. Opera Omnia*. Vol. 13. (Ibidem).

Ambrose, St. *Enarrationes in 12 Psalmos. Patrologia cursus completus Latina*. Edited by J. P. Migne. Vol. 14. Paris: Garnier Fratres, 1878.

Anselm, St. *Liber Meditationum et Oratium. Patrologia cursus completus Latina*. Edited by J. P. Migne. Vol. 158. Paris: Garnier Fratres, 1878.

Augustine, St. *De Sancta Virginitate. Patrologia cursus completus Latina*. Edited by J. P. Migne. Vol. 140. Paris: Garnier Fratres, 1878.

_____. *In Psalmo LVI. Patrologia Latina..* Vol. 36. (Ibidem).

_____. *Tractus in Joannem. Patrologia Latina*. Vol. 35. (Ibidem).

Aumann, Jordan. "The Contribution of the French School and St. Francis de Sales to the Devotion to the Sacred Heart." Unpublished lecture, Pontifical University of St. Thomas Aquinas.

Baier, Walter. "Key Issues in Medieval Sacred Heart Piety." *Faith in Christ and the Worship of Christ*. San Francisco: Ignatius Press, 1986.

Bainvel, Jean V. *Devotion to the Sacred Heart*. London: Burns and Oates, 1924.

_____. "La Devotion au Sacré Coeur." *Dictionnaire de Theologie Catholique*. Vol. III. par. 1, Paris: Librarie Letouzey et Aré, 1938.

Barbet, Pierre. *A Doctor at Calvary*. Garden City, New York: Image Books, 1963.

Bede, St. *Homilia XXXV. Opera Omnia*. Edited by J. A. Giles. Vols. V & VI. Londinii: Veneunt apud Whittaker et Socios, 1834.

_____. *In Cantica Canticorum. Opera Omnia*. Vols. LX & X. (Ibidem).

Bernard, St. *In Cantica Canticorum. Patrologia cursus completus Latina*. Edited by J.P. Migne. Vol. 183. Paris: Garnier Fratres, 1978.

_____. *Vitis Mystica. Patrologia Latina*. Vol. 183. (Ibidem).

Bonaventure, St. *Itinerium Mentis in Deum. Opera Omnia*. Vol. V Quaracci, 1882-91.

_____. "The Mystical Vine." *Opera Omnia*. Vol. VIII. (Ibidem).

Bridget of Sweden, St. *The Magnificent Promises*. South Bend, Indiana: Marian Publication, 1971.

Broderick, J. *St. Peter Canisius*. London: Sheed and Ward, 1938.

Catherine of Siena, St. *The Dialogues of the Seraphic Virgin Catherine of Siena*. Translated by A. Thorold. London: Burns, Oates and Washbourne, 1925.

Charmot, F. *Ignatius Loyola and Francis de Sales*. St. Louis: Herder, 1966.

Cognet, Louis. *Histoire de la Spiritualité Chrétienne*. Vol. III. Paris: Aubier, 1966.

Chrysostom, John St. *Ad Romanos. Patrologia cursus completus Graeca*. Edited by J.P. Migne. Vol. 60. Paris: Garnier Fratres, 1866.

____. *In Joannem Homil. Patrologia Graeca*. Vol. 59. (Ibidem).

Dirksen, A. *Elementary Patrology*. St. Louis: Herder, 1959.

Eudes, John St. *Meditations on Various Subjects*. New York: P. J. Kennedy and Sons, 1947.

____. *The Sacred Heart of Jesus* and *The Kingdom of Jesus*. New York: P.J. Kennedy and Sons, 1946.

Eudes, John. *The Sacred Heart of Jesus*. Translated by Richard Flower, OSB. New York: J. P. Kennedy and Sons, 1946.

Eusebius of Caesarea, *Historia Ecclesiae. Patrologia cursus completus Graeca*. Edited by J.P. Migne. Vol. 20. Paris: Garnier Fratres, 1866.

____. *In Isaiam. Patrologia Graeca*. Vol. 24 (Ibidem).

Gertrude the Great, St. *Prayers*. London: Burns and Lambert, 1861.

____. *The Exercises*. Westminster, Maryland: The Newman Press, 1956.

____. *The Love of the Sacred Heart*. London: Burns, Oates, and Washbourne, 1921.

____. *St. Gertrude the Great: Herald of Divine Love*. Clyde, Missouri: Benedictine Convent of Perpetual Adoration, 1955.

Graffin, R. ed. *Patrologia Syriaca*. Vol. I. Paris: Firmin-Didgt et Socii, 1894.

Gregory the Great, St. *In Cantica Canticorum. Patrologia cursus completus Latina*. Edited by J.P. Migne. Vol. 79. Paris: Garnier Fratres, 1878.

____. *Liber Sacramentorum, In Nativ. S. Joannem. Patrologia Latina*. Vol. 78. (Ibidem).

____. *Moralia in Job. Patrologia Latina*. Vol. 76 (Ibidem).

Habig, M. A. *St. Francis of Assisi: Omnibus of Sources*. Chicago, Illinois: The Franciscan Herald Press, 1976.

Hamon, Auguste. "Dévotion au Sacré Coeur." *Dictionnaire de Spiritualité*. Vol. II. par. 5. Paris: Benuchesnenet Ses Fils, 1948.

____. *Histoire de la Dévotion au Sacré Coeur*. 5 vols. Paris: Benuchesnenet Ses Fils, 1923-39.

Husslein, Joseph C. *Social Wellsprings: Fourteen Epochal Documents by Pope Leo XIII*. Milwaukee: The Bruce Publishing Co., 1940.

Heinzer, Felix. "The Suffering Humanity of Christ as the Source of Salvation in Maximus the Confessor." *Faith in Christ and the Worship of Christ*. San Francisco: Ignatius Press, 1986.

Hesychius. *In Psalmos. Patrologia cursus completus Graeca*. Edited by J.P. Migne. Vol. 93. Paris: Garnier Fratres, 1866.

Hilary, St. *In Psalmos LXIX. Patrologia cursus completus Latina*. Edited by J.P. Migne. Vol. 9. Paris: Garnier Fratres, 1878.

Irenaeus, St. *Adversus Haereses. Patrologia cursus completus Graeca*. Edited by J.P. Migne. Vol. 7. Paris: Garnier Fratres, 1866.

Juliana of Norwich. *Revelations of Divine Love*. Translated by M. L. del Mastro. Garden City, New York: Image Books, 1977.

Justin, St. *Dialogus cum Tryphone Judaeo. Patrologia cursus completus Graeca*. Edited by J.P. Migne. Vol. 6. Paris: Garnier Fratres, 1866.

Kanters, G. *Le Coeur de Jesus dans la litterature chrétienne des douze premiers siedes*. Paris: Avignon, 1930.

Leclercq, Vandenbroucke, Bouyer. *The Spirituality of the Middle Ages*. London: Burns and Oates, 1968.

Loyola, Ignatius St. *The Spiritual Exercises*. Westminster, Maryland: The Newman Press, 1951.

Ludolph of Saxony. *Vita Jesu Christi*. Ventiis: Valerium Bonellum, 1587.

McGratty, Arthur R. *The Sacred Heart Yesterday and Today*. New York: Benzinger Brothers Inc., 1951.

Mechthild of Hackborn. *Prayers*. London: Burns and Lambert, 1861.

Migne, J.P., ed. *Patrologia cursus completus Latina*. 221 vols. Paris: Garnier Fratres, 1878.

____. *Patrologia cursus completus Graeca*. 161 vols. (Ibidem). 1866.

Mulhern, Philip. "The History of the Devotion to the Sacred Heart." Unpublished lecture, Pontifical University of St. Thomas Aquinas, 1978.

Most, William G. *The Consciousness of Christ*. Front Royal, VA: Christendom College Press, 1980.

Newman, J.H. *Essay on the Development of Christian Doctrine*. Westminster, Maryland: Christian Classics Inc., 1968.

Paulinus, *Epistola. Patrologia cursus completus Latina*. Edited by J.P. Migne. Vol. 61. Paris: Garnier Fratres, 1878.

Quodvultdeus. *De Symbolo ad Catechumenos. Patrologia cursus completus Latina*. Edited by J.P. Migne. Vol. 40. Paris: Garnier Fratres, 1878.

Rahner, Hugo. "The Beginnings of the Devotion in Patristic Times." *Heart of the Savior*. Edited by J. Stierli. New York: Herder, 1958.

Richstaetter, Karl. *Illustrious Friends of the Sacred Heart of Jesus*. London: Herder, 1930.

Sales, Francis de. *Introduction to the Devout Life*. Garden City, New York: Image Books, 1972.

____. *Treatise on the Love of God*. 2 vols. Rockford, Illinois: Tan Books and Publishers Inc. 1975.

Sitwell, G. *Spiritual Writers of the Middle Ages*. New York: Hawthorn, 1961.

Stierli, Joseph. "Devotion to the Sacred Heart from the End of Patristic Times Down to St. Margaret Mary. *Heart of the Savior*. Edited by J. Stierli. New York: Herder, 1958.

____. "The Development of the Church's Devotion to the Sacred Heart in Modern Times." *Heart of the Savior*. (Ibidem).

Suso, Henry. *The Life of Henry Suso*. Translated by T.F. Knox. London: Burns, Lambert, and Oates, 1865.

Tauler, J. *Exercita D. Ioannis Thauleri*. Lugduni: S. B. Honorati, 1556.

Tertullian. *De Anima. Patrologia cursus completus Latina*. Edited by J.P. Migne. Vol. 2. Paris: Garnier Fratres, 1878.

Theodoret. *In Cantica Canticorum. Patrologia cursus completus Graeca*. Edited by J.P. Migne. Vol. 81. Paris: Garnier Fratres, 1866.

Walsh, Eugene A. "The French School of Spirituality." *The New Catholic Encyclopedia*. 13, 1966.

Walz, A. *De Veneratione Divini Cordis Iesu*. Pontificium Institutum Angelicum, 1937.

Wuerl, Donald. *Fathers of the Church*. Huntington, Indiana: Our Sunday Visitor Inc., 1975.

St. Margaret Mary Alacoque and Her Divine Mission

Benedict XV, Pope. "Bull of Canonization." *Acta Apostolicae Sedis*. 12, 1920.

Bougaud, Emile. *Life of St. Margaret Mary Alacoque*. New York: Benzinger Brothers, 1920.

Croiset, Jean. *La Dévotion au Sacré Coeur de N.S. Jésus-Christ d' aprés l'édition definitive 3e de Lyon 1694*. Montrevil-sur-Mer: Imprimerie Notre-Dame des Pres, 1895.

____. *The Devotion to the Sacred Heart of Our Lord Jesus Christ*. Translated by Patrick O'Connell. Milwaukee, Wisconsin: International Institute of the Heart of Jesus, 1976.

Galliffet, Joseph Francios de. *De cultu sacrosancti Cordis Dei ac Domini Nostri Iesu Christi*. Rome: Salvioni, 1726.

Guitton, Georges. *Perfect Friend*. St. Louis: B. Herder Co., 1956.

Hamon, Auguste. *Vie de la Bienheureuse Marguérite-Marie*. Paris: Gabriel Beauchesne et Cie, 1908.

____. *Histoire de la Dévotion au Sacré Coeur*. 5 vols. Paris: Gabriel Beauchesne et Cie, 1923-39.

Herbst, Clarence A., ed. and tr. *Letters of St. Margaret Mary Alacoque*. Orlando, Florida: Men of the Sacred Heart, 1976.

Kerns, Vincent., ed. and tr. *The Autobiography of St. Margaret Mary*. London: Darton Longman & Todd Ltd., 1976.

La Colombière, Claude de. *The Spiritual Direction of Blessed Claude de la Colombière*. Translated by Mother M. Philip. London: Burns, Oates, and Washbourne, 1934.

____. *Faithful Servant: Spiritual Retreats and Letters*. Translated by W.J. Young. St. Louis: Herder, 1960.

Margaret-Mary, St. *Vie et Ouvres de Sainte Marguérite-Marie Alacoque*. Nouvelle Edition Authentique, Publiée par le Monastère de la Visitation de Paray-le-Monial, Paris: Poussielgue, 1920.

Mattes, Anton; "Devotion to the Sacred Heart of Jesus in Modern Times: The Influence of St. Margaret Mary Alacoque." *Faith in Christ and the Worship of Christ*. San Francisco: Ignatius Press, 1986.

Tickell, George. *The Life of Blessed Margaret Mary*. New York: P. J. Kennedy, 1900.

Wenisch, Paul. *The Promises of Our Lord to Saint Margaret Mary*. India: The National Office, Apostleship of Prayer, n.d.

Yeo, Margaret. *These Three Hearts*. Milwaukee: The Bruce Publishing Co., 1940.

The Devotion and the Magisterium

Abbott, Walter M. *The Documents of Vatican II.* New York: American Press, 1966.

Benedict XV, Pope. "Bull of Canonization." *Acta Apostolicae Sedis.* 12, 1920.

____. "Letter to Fr. Mateo Crawley-Boevey." *Acta Apostolicae Sedis.* 7, 1915.

____. *De scientia animae Christi.* Decr. S. Officii. June 5, 1918 *Acta Apostolicae Sedis.* 10. 1918.

Ciappi, M.L. "From the Encyclical *Haurietis Aquas* to the Encyclical *Dives in Misericordia*: Confirmation and Development of Devotion to the Sacred Heart of Jesus." *Towards A Civilization of Love.* San Francisco: Ignatius Press, 1985.

Courtney, Francis. "Devotion to the Sacred Heart: The Encyclical *Haurietis Aquas.*" *Clergy Review.* 42, June 1957.

Dachaver, Alban. *The Sacred Heart.* Milwaukee: The Bruce Publishing Co., 1954.

Donnelly, Malachi. *"Haurietis Aquas* and Devotion to the Sacred Heart." *Theological Studies.* March 1957.

Flannery, Austin, ed. *Vatican Council II: The Conciliar and Post-Conciliar Documents.* Northport, New York: Costello Publishing Co., 1975.

Flannery, Austin, ed. *Vatican II: More Post-Conciliar Documents.* Northport, NY: Costello Publishing Co., 1985.

Gutzwiller, R. "Notes on Some Official Texts of the Church's Devotion to the Sacred Heart." *Heart of the Savior.* Edited by J. Stierli. New York: Herder, 1958.

____. "On the Biblical Character of the Litany to the Sacred Heart." *Heart of the Savior.* (Ibidem).

Hamell, Patrick J. "Devotion to the Sacred Heart: The encyclical *Haurietis Aquas.*" *The Irish Ecclesiastical Record.* October 1956.

Heer, Joseph. "The Soteriological Significance of the Johannine Image of the Pierced Savior." *Faith in Christ and the Worship of Christ.* San Francisco: Ignatius Press, 1986.

John XXIII, Pope. *Journal of a Soul.* Translated by Dorothy White. Garden City, New York: Image Books, 1980.

John Paul II, Pope *Redemptor Hominis. Acta Apostolicae Sedis.* 71, 1979.

____. *Dives in Misericordia. Acta Apostolicae Sedis.* 72, 1980.

____. *Salvifici Doloris, AAS* Vol. LXXVI N. 3, 1 Mar 1984; *Dominium et Vivicantem, AAS* Vol. LXXVIII N. 9, 2 Sept 1986; *Redemptoris Mater, AAS Vol. LXXIX* N. 4, 2 Ap 1987.

____. "Apostolic Letter on the Mystery and Worship of the Holy Eucharist." February 24, 1980. *Acta Apostolicae Sedis.* 72, 1980.

____. "General Audience June 20, 1979." *L'Osservatore Romano.* June 25, 1979.

____. "Angelus Message, June 24, 1979." *L'Osservatore Romano.* July 2, 1979.

____. "Message to the Youth of France." June 1, 1980. *L'Osservatore Romano.* June 16, 1980.

____. "Meditation at the Basilica of the Sacred Heart at Montmartre." June 1, 1980. *L'Osservatore Romano.* June 16, 1980.

____. "Angelus Message June 8, 1980." *L'Osservatore Romano.* June 16, 1980.

____. "Angelus Message June 15, 1980." *L'Osservatore Romano.* June 23, 1980.

____. "Addresses at Paray-le-Monial". *L'Osservatore Romano.* October 27, 1986.

Kiefer, William J. *Leo XIII: A Light From Heaven.* Milwaukee: The Bruce Publishing Co.,

1961.

Leo XIII, Pope. *Annum Sacrum. Acta Leonis.* 19, 1900.

Men of the Sacred Heart. *Mass of the Sacred Heart of Jesus.* Orlando, Florida: Reconciliation Press, 1979.

Nilles, Nicholas. *De rationibus festorum Beatissimi Cordis Jesu et puerissimi Cordis Mariae.* Oeniponte, 1873.

Paul VI, Pope *Investigabiles Divitias Christi. Acta Apostolicae Sedis.* 57, 1965. English translation published as an appendix to *Haurietis Aquas.* ed. Orlando, Florida: Sacred Heart Publication Center, 1974.

____. *Diserti Intepretes. Acta Romana Societatis Jesu.* Vol. XIV May, 25, 1965. English translation published as an appendix to *Haurietis Aquas.* ed. Orlando, Florida: Sacred Heart Publication Center, 1974.

____. "Allocution to the General Chapter of Priests of the Sacred Heart." June 14, 1966. *L'Osservatore Romano.* June 15, 1966.

____. "Address to the Thirty-first General Congregation of the Society of Jesus." November 17, 1966. *Documents of the Thirty-first General Congregation of 1966.* Private Circulation, 1967.

____. "General Audience, January 27, 1971." *L'Osservatore Romano.* February 4, 1971.

Pius VI, Pope. *Auctorem Fidei. Enchiridion Symbolorum.* Edited by Denzinger-Schönmetzer. ed. XXXVI. Rome: Herder, 1976.

Pius XI, Pope. *Quas Primas. Acta Apostolicae Sedis.* 17, 1925.

____. *Miserentissimus Redemptor. Acta Apostolicae Sedis.* 20, 1928.

____. *Caritate Christi Compulsi. Acta Apostolicae Sedis.* 24, 1932.

Pius XII, Pope. *Summi Pontificatus. Acta Apostolicae Sedis.* 35, 1943.

____. *Mystici Corporis. Acta Apostolicae Sedis.* 35, 1943.

____. *Mediator Dei. Acta Apostolicae Sedis.* 39, 1947.

____. *Sempiternus Rex. Acta Apostolicae Sedis.* 43, 1951.

____. *Haurietis Aquas. Acta Apostolicae Sedis.* 48, 1956.

Secretaria Generalis., ed. *Sacrosanctum Oecumenicum Concilium Vaticanum II: Constitutiones, Decreta, Declarationes.* Typis Polyglottis Vaticani, 1966.

The Apostleship of Prayer. *Norms for Moderating the Eucharistic Crusade of the Apostleship of Prayer.* Rome: The Gregorian University Press, 1958.

Selected Works Dealing with the Theology of the Sacred Heart of Jesus

Aumann, Jordan. *Spiritual Theology.* Huntington, Indiana: Our Sunday Visitor, 1979.

Aumann, Jordan; Mulhern, Philip; and O'Donnell, Timothy. *Devotion to the Heart of Jesus.* Rome: Institute of Spirituality, Pontifical University of St. Thomas Aquinas, 1982.

Aver, Johann. "Devotion to the Sacred Heart and the Theology of Conversion." *Faith in Christ and the Worship of Christ.* San Francisco: Ignatius Press, 1986.

Arnoudt, Peter J. *The Imitation of the Sacred Heart of Jesus.* Rockford, Illinois: Tan Books and Publishers Inc., 1974.

Balthasar, Hans Urs von. *Heart of the World*. Translated by Erasmo S. Leiva. San Francisco: Ignatius Press, 1978.

Bea, A., Rehner, R., Schwedimann, F. *Cor Iesu*. 2 vols. Rome: Herder, 1959.

Biskupek, A. *The Litany of the Sacred Heart* Milwaukee: The Bruce Publishing Co., 1956.

Bouyer, Louis. *Introduction to Spirituality*. Collegeville, Minnesota: Liturgical Press, 1961.

Bruni, J.P. "Devotion to the Sacred Humanity." *New Catholic Encyclopedia*. Vol. 5. 1966.

Center for Applied Research in the Apostolate. *The Sacred Heart Devotion: A Christocentric Spirituality for Our Times*. Milwaukee/Rome: International Institute of the Heart of Jesus Inc., 1977.

Curran, J.W. *The Thomistic Concept of Devotion*. River Forest, Illinois: Dominican House of Studies, 1941.

Elders, Leo. "The Inner Life of Jesus in the Theology and Devotion of St. Thomas Aquinas." *Faith in Christ and the Worship of Christ*. San Francisco: Ignatius Press, 1986.

Gaidon, Maurice. "The Civilization of Love Today." *Towards A Civilization of Love*. San Francisco: Ignatius Press, 1985.

Galot, J. *The Heart of Christ*. Westminster, Maryland: The Newman Press, 1953.

Garrigou-Lagrange, Reginald. *The Three Ages of the Spiritual Life*. 2 vols. St. Louis: Herder, 1960.

Gloutin, E. *Catechetical Value of a Symbolic Sign: The Wounded Heart of Jesus*. Rome: International Institute of the Heart of Jesus, 1979.

Gomes, C.F. "The Love of the Incarnate Word for His Father." *Towards A Civilization of Love*. San Francisco: Ignatius Press, 1985.

Gutzwiller, R. "The Opposition." *Heart of the Savior*. Edited by J. Stierli, New York: Herder, 1958.

Hardon, John and Diehl, Thomas. *Teaching the Devotion to the Sacred Heart*. Chicago: Loyola University Press, 1963.

Hildebrand, Dietrich von. *The Sacred Heart: An Analysis of the Human and Divine Affectivity*. Baltimore: The Helicon Press, 1965.

Hoffman, Norbert. "Atonement and the Spirituality of the Sacred Heart: An Attempt at an Elucidation by Means of the Principle of 'Representation.' " *Faith in Christ and the Worship of Christ*. San Francisco: Ignatius Press, 1986.

Kern, Walter. *The Lover of Mankind and His Sacred Heart: Similarities Between East and West*. Buffalo, New York: Apostleship of Prayer, 1978.

____. *Updated Devotion to the Sacred Heart*. Canfield, Ohio: Alba House Communication, 1975.

Koller, Angelico. *Reparation to the Sacred Heart: A Theology of Consolation*. Hales Corner, Wisconsin: The Priests of the Sacred Heart, 1971.

La Touche, Margaret Claret de. *The Sacred Heart and the Priesthood*. Translated by Patrick O'Connell. Rockford, Illinois: Tan Books and Publishers Inc., 1979.

Larkin, Francis. *Enthronement of the Sacred Heart*. Boston, Massachusetts: The Daughters of St. Paul, 1978.

____. *Understanding the Heart*. Orlando, Florida: Sacred Heart Publications Center, 1975.

Margerie, Bertrand de. *Christ for the World: The Heart of the Lamb*. Translated by Malachy Carroll. Chicago: Franciscan Herald Press, 1973.

____. "A Theological Evaluation of the CARA Study on the Sacred Heart Devotion."

Published as an appendix in *The Sacred Heart Devotion: A Christocentric Spirituality for Our Times*. Center for Applied Research in the Apostolate. Milwaukee/Rome: International Institute of the Heart of Jesus, 1977.

Medeiros, Humberto Cardinal. *The Heart of Jesus and Priestly Holiness*. An address given to the National Congress of the Sacred Heart of Jesus, Sept. 14, 1978. Milwaukee, Wisconsin: International Institute of the Heart of Jesus, 1978.

Mejia, Jorge. "Born From the Side of Christ: An Orientation for One Church." *Towards A Civilization of Love*. San Francisco: Ignatius Press, 1985.

Menendez, Josefa. *The Way of Divine Love*. Rockford, Illinois: Tan Books and Publishers Inc., 1973.

Milward, Peter. "Devotion to the Sacred Heart." *American Ecclesiastical Review*. 142, June 1960.

Moell, C. J. "Sacred Heart Devotion." *New Catholic Encyclopedia*.. Vol. 12.

Newman, J.H. Cardinal. *Meditations and Devotions*. London: Burns and Oates, 1964.

O'Connell, Patrick. *Devotion to the Sacred Heart, The Essence of Christianity and the Center of the Divine Plan of Redemption*. Wexford, Ireland: John English and Co., 1951.

O'Connell, Robert. "Theology of Devotion to the Sacred Heart." *Dominica*. 44 Summer, 1959.

Pesch, C. *Our Best Friend*. Translated by B.A. Housmann. Milwaukee: Bruce Publishing Company., 1953.

Petrovits, Joseph. *Devotion to the Sacred Heart*. St. Louis: Herder, 1918.

Plus, Raoul. *Reparation*. London: Burns, Oates and Washbourne, 1931.

Pozo, Candido. "The Heart of Mary, Heart of the New Eve." *Towards A Civilization of Love*. San Francisco: Ignatius Press, 1985.

Quesnell, Quentin. "Theology of the Sacred Heart: God's Love." *Irish Theological Quarterly*. 25 July, 1959.

Rahner, Karl. "Some Theses on the Theology of the Devotion." *Heart of the Savior*. Edited by J. Stierli. New York: Herder: 1958.

Ratzinger, J. *Behold the Pierced One*. San Francisco: Ignatius Press, 1986.

Ratzinger, Joseph. "The Paschal Mystery as Core and Foundation of the Devotion to the Sacred Heart." *Towards A Civilization of Love*. San Francisco: Ignatius Press, 1985.

Scheffczyk, Leo. "Devotion to Christ as a Way of Experiencing Him." *Faith in Christ and the Worship of Christ*. San Francisco: Ignatius Press, 1986.

Scheffczyk, Leo ed. *Faith in Christ and the Worship of Christ*. San Francisco: Ignatius Press, 1986.

Stierli, Joseph, ed. *Heart of the Savior*. New York: Herder, 1958.

Suenens, L. J. "Loving Through the Power of the Holy Spirit." *Towards A Civilization of Love*. San Francisco: Ignatius Press, 1985.

Sutcliffe, E.F. "The Heart and Love." *The Irish Theological Quarterly*. 19 July, 1952.

Schwendimann, Frederich. *Devotion to the Heart of Christ and the Society of Jesus Today*. Rome: Apostleship of Prayer, 1970.

Tanquerey, A. *The Spiritual Life*. Tournai: Desclée and Co., 1930.

von Balthasar, Hans Urs. "The Work of the Suffering of Jesus: Discontinuity and Continuity." *Faith in Christ and the Worship of Christ*. San Francisco: Ignatius Press, 1986.

The Apostleship of Prayer. "Devotion to the Sacred Heart at the Present Time." *The

Apostleship of Prayer Director's Service. n. 1. January 1971.

____. "The Devotion to the Sacred Heart in Pastoral Work Today." *The Apostleship of Prayer Director's Service.* n. 2. 1971.

Verheylesoon, Louis. *Devotion to the Sacred Heart.* Rockford, Illinois: Tan Books and Publishers Inc., 1978.

Walsh, Michael J. *The Heart of Christ in the Writings of Karl Rahner.* Rome: Gregorian University Press, 1977.

Williams, Margaret. *The Sacred Heart in the Life of the Church.* New York: Sheed and Ward, 1957.

Wright, John Cardinal. "The Sacred Heart of Jesus: A Symbol for Our Time." *The Laity.* Vol. III, No. 6, June 1975.

____. *The Heart of Christ the Center of the Mystery of Salvation.* Rome: CdC Publishers, 1983.

Index

List of Figures